COMPLETE BOOK OF
VEGETARIAN
COOKING

COMPLETE BOOK OF

VEGETARIAN COOKING

JANET SMITH

LONGMEADOW
PRESS

The recipe for *Wild Mushroom Strudel* on page 78 is
reproduced courtesy of Roselyne Masselin of *La Cuisine
Imaginaire Cookery School*.

ISBN 0-681-00731-1

Special Photography: James Murphy
Editor: Helen Southall
Design: Patrick McLeavey
Illustrations: Hilary Downing

Typeset by Textype Typesetters, Cambridge
Printed and bound at Butler & Tanner Ltd, Frome, England

First Longmeadow Press Edition

0 9 8 7 6 5 4 3 2 1

CONTENTS

INTRODUCTION

A meatless diet is no longer regarded as bizarre or cranky. Vegetarian eating has taken on new vitality and dimensions and now attracts a large percentage of the population.

There are as many different types of vegetarian as there are reasons for being one. The term vegetarian covers a wide range of diets but the one thing they all have in common is that they are meat and fish free. Vegans are very strict vegetarians; they won't eat any animal product whatsoever, including gelatin and, in some cases, honey. Look for vegan recipes marked with the V symbol in the index (see page 222). Less strict vegetarians eat eggs, cheese, butter, and milk. Some eat cheese, butter, and milk but will not eat eggs. Others prefer a wholefood diet. This book has something for everyone. All the recipes have been thoroughly tried and tested; they were enjoyed by vegetarians as well as by confirmed meat-eaters.

BALANCING A VEGETARIAN DIET

Many people make the mistake of assuming that a vegetarian diet is automatically healthier than a carnivore's. This isn't always the case – there are good and bad vegetarian diets. It is not enough simply to stop eating meat; the nutrients that would normally be obtained from meat must be replaced. It's quite common for vegetarians to rely too heavily on dairy products like cheese and eggs which are high in saturated fats and calories. Such a limited diet is not only unhealthy but will eventually become boring and tedious.

As with any diet, variety is important. If a wide range of foods is eaten, a vegetarian diet is no more likely to be lacking nutritionally than any other diet. However, it is useful to have a basic understanding of nutrition and the importance of certain foods – even if it's only to convince meat-eaters that a vegetarian diet is healthy! So here's our brief guide, pinpointing the important areas.

PROTEIN
Contrary to popular belief, there are lots of good vegetable sources of protein, such as beans, grains, nuts, tofu, and texturized vegetable protein as well as eggs, cheese, milk, and yogurt.

Protein is made up of smaller units called amino acids. They form about 75 per cent of the body's solid mass and are needed in every cell, so they are very important. The body can manufacture some amino acids itself, but others, known as the "essential amino acids", must come from food. Animal protein contains almost all of these and is therefore known as "complete" protein.

With the exception of soy products, vegetable proteins are lacking or low in one or more amino acid. However, by eating certain foods together at the same meal any deficiency is overcome. This isn't as complicated as it sounds and usually happens automatically when menu planning. For example, cereals should be eaten with dairy products, pulses or nuts (muesli with yogurt or milk, chili beans with rice, nut roast made with breadcrumbs, peanut butter on toast). Pulses and nuts should be eaten with cereals or dairy products (dal with raita, nut burgers with a cream-based sauce).

VITAMINS
Vitamins are vital for proper body functioning. They can be divided into two categories – fat soluble and water soluble. As the name suggests, the fat soluble vitamins A, D, E, and K are found mostly in foods which

contain fat. They are stored in the body by the liver.

The water soluble vitamins C and B complex, dissolve in water and cannot be stored, so a regular supply is important.

A varied diet should supply all the vitamins our bodies need. Vegetarians and vegans should be careful to ensure that their intake of vitamins B_{12} and D is sufficient, although a deficiency of either is unlikely.

Vitamin B_{12}

Vitamin B_{12} is essential for the formation of healthy red blood cells; a deficiency causes a form of anaemia. As it is found only in animal foods (with the exception of uncertain amounts in seaweed and fermented soy products) it is the vitamin most likely to be lacking in a vegetarian or vegan diet. Vegetarians who eat milk, eggs, and cheese will get sufficient from these, but vegans should be careful to include some fortified foods in their diet. Yeast extracts, some brands of breakfast cereals, soy milk, and other products marketed for vegans (such as vegetable spreads and pâtés) are all good sources. Get into the habit of reading labels to identify fortified brands.

Vitamin D

Vitamin D is needed for the growth and formation of healthy teeth and bones. Most of the body's supply comes from the action of sunlight on the skin. The elderly or house-bound, whose exposure to sunlight is limited, and the young, whose bones grow at a much faster rate, could consider taking a supplement. Consult a doctor before doing so and do not exceed the stated dose. Good vegetarian sources of this vitamin are eggs and butter. Some margarines, milk powders, and yogurts are fortified; check the labels.

Make the Most of Vitamins

– For maximum vitamin retention, buy fruit and vegetables in peak condition, preferably from a store with a fast turnover. Eat them as soon as possible. Tough, old vegetables have a lower vitamin content than fresh.

– Store vegetables in a cool, dark place; light is destructive to vitamins, especially the vitamins B and C. Vitamin B_2 (riboflavin), in milk, is destroyed when exposed to ultra-violet light.

– Steam or boil vegetables until just tender using the minimum amount of water.

– Don't add baking soda to cooking water: Once the vegetables are cooked and drained, use the water for stocks, gravies, and soups.

– Don't prepare vegetables hours in advance and leave them soaking in water. Leave the skins on whenever you can.

– Eat plenty of raw vegetables and fruit.

– Vitamin losses continue after cooking, particularly when warm foods are left waiting around, so eat soon after cooking.

MINERALS

Minerals cannot be manufactured by the body and must be obtained from food. At present, 15 minerals have been identified as being essential to health and others are still under investigation. The majority of people obtain enough minerals provided a good variety of foods is eaten. Iron, calcium, and zinc are the three minerals most often discussed in relation to a vegetarian diet.

Iron

Iron is used to make the haemoglobin in red blood cells. Haemoglobin carries oxygen to every cell in the body and a shortage leads to anaemia. Iron deficiency is fairly common, particularly in women of child-bearing age, and teenage girls on weight-reducing diets. Vegetarians are susceptible to anaemia because meat is the best food source of iron, and because the body can absorb iron from meat more efficiently than it can from vegetarian foods.

Iron is found in many vegetarian and vegan foods, including leafy green vegetables, cereals, pulses, nuts, eggs, and dried fruits (especially apricots). The absorption of iron is greatly increased if vitamin C-rich foods are eaten at the same meal. It is decreased by the presence of tannin, which is found in large amounts in tea – so don't drink tea at meal times!

Calcium

Calcium is essential for the growth and development of bones, teeth and tissues. It is also needed for muscle contraction, nerve functioning, the action of several enzymes and for the normal clotting of blood. Because it is usually associated primarily with milk, eggs, yogurt, and cheese, vegans are considered to be at risk of deficiency. However, this is not a problem because calcium is also found in white or brown bread and flour, green vegetables, nuts, sesame seeds, dried fruits, and tap water in hard-water areas.

Zinc

Zinc is a trace mineral. Among other things, it's important for the functioning of enzymes and minerals. Recently it has received lots of attention in relation to a vegetarian diet. It has been suggested that zinc from plant sources is not readily absorbed by the body. However, there are so many other factors which affect zinc absorption and requirements, including age, sex, and hormonal balance, that it is highly unlikely that vegetarianism would be the cause of a deficiency. As long as a variety of food is included in the diet, a deficiency will be avoided. Good vegetarian sources are sesame seeds, cheese, nuts, pulses, and grains.

VEGETARIAN BABIES AND CHILDREN

Breast milk or infant formula contains all the vitamins and minerals a newborn baby needs for the first 4–6 months of life. Although breast milk is preferable for a number of reasons, commercial infant formula will provide complete nutrition. Babies should continue to drink breast or formula milk until they are 1 year old, but they can have store-brought milk on cereals and in cooked dishes from about 6 months. For vegan babies, special soy-based formulas are available; ordinary soy milk is not suitable since it is nutritionally inadequate.

Weaning should start between four and six months (although some larger, hungrier babies may be ready at 3 months – consult your doctor or clinic). Start with baby rice (check the packets for unsweetened brands) mixed with breast milk or formula, then try puréed and strained fruits and vegetables. Don't be discouraged if your baby refuses the new food; try again the next day. Introduce one new food at a time and wait three or four days before introducing another new food in case of an allergic reaction. Avoid wheat-based cereals until 6 months because gluten (a constituent of wheat grains) can cause an allergic reaction. Similarly, children under 1 year shouldn't be given egg white. It's used in the manufacture of some childhood vaccines so it's unwise to risk triggering off an allergy.

Try to give your child healthy food right from the start. Avoid making food very sweet (there's no need to add sugar to breakfast cereals) or very salty (don't add salt to vegetable cooking water). When buying baby foods, look for varieties without added sugar, salt and chemical additives.

From the age of 1, your child should be eating (or at least offered) three small meals a day, along with a mid-morning and a mid-afternoon snack (which could be something as simple as a glass of milk and a plain cookie).

From the age of 2, your child can eat much the same as the rest of the family and should be encouraged to eat a wide variety of foods. Avoid nuts unless they are ground into nut butter because there is danger of choking. Because of the risk of salmonella food poisoning, it is advisable not to give children soft cooked eggs. So make sure that poached eggs are cooked until the yolk is set, and avoid giving children soft scrambled eggs and runny omelets.

FEEDING A VEGETARIAN TEENAGER

Currently, the biggest growth of new vegetarians is in the 12 to 20 age group. For some families a non-meat-eater in their midst can cause problems at meal times. It's important to view this as a positive move for the family as a whole rather than as a problem. There's no doubt that the consumption of too much animal protein is unhealthy, so it's a good idea to use the opportunity to introduce more meat-free meals to all members of the household. Making meals based on rice, potatoes, and pasta is a good way to start. It's easy to cook simple nutritious vegetarian meals using these as a base combined with well flavored ingredients such as garlic, tomato, spices, herbs, and fresh vegetables. Creamy risottos, pilaffs, vegetable gratins, and stuffed baked potatoes are delicious and would usually be made without meat anyway. For particularly steadfast carnivorous members of the family, serve these with broiled meat or fish or sliced cold meat, as a last resort or until the appeal of vegetarianism sinks in!

Pizzas are surprisingly quick and easy to make. Piled high with vegetables and cheese, and served with a large mixed salad, they make a splendid supper. A chunky soup made from a mixture of vegetables served with hot garlic bread and followed by cheese and fruit makes a satisfying meal.

Meat substitutes such as soy products are useful additions to the new vegetarian cook's repertoire. Use them to make meat-free versions of traditional family favorites such as Lasagne, Spaghetti Bolognese, Kebabs, and Curry.

Adolescents need a nutrient-rich diet with lots of calories (girls about 2,300, boys about 2,800 per day). A varied vegetarian diet will easily provide this. Teenage girls may need to take an iron supplement. Encourage them to eat vitamin C and iron-rich foods together (see page 7). Vegan adolescents should eat cereals and yeast extracts fortified with vitamin B_{12} (see page 7).

THE VEGETARIAN STORECUPBOARD

Certain foods are particularly significant in a vegetarian diet, either because they contribute large amounts of a particular nutrient or because they require some explanation.

PULSES
The term pulse covers all the various beans, peas, and lentils which have been preserved by drying. Pulses are an important source of protein, carbohydrate, and fiber in a vegetarian diet. Most also contain significant amounts of iron, potassium, calcium, and some B vitamins. Soy beans are unique in that they contain complete protein (see page 6) as well as more calcium and iron than other pulses.

Store pulses in airtight containers in a cool, dark place. They keep well, but after about six months their skins begin to toughen and they take increasingly longer to cook, so buy them from a supplier with a fast turnover of stock.

Before cooking, all beans (with the exception of lentils and split peas) should be soaked overnight in a large bowlful of cold water. In the morning, drain them, bring to the boil in fresh water and boil rapidly for 10 minutes (to destroy the toxins present in some beans – although it is not strictly necessary for all beans it does them no harm and saves the problem of remembering which requires fast boiling), then simmer until the beans are tender (see chart overleaf). Add salt about 15 minutes before the end of the cooking time; salt added at the beginning of cooking tends to toughen the skins. The flavor can be subtly enhanced by the addition of a couple of bay leaves, or cloves of garlic, or a peeled onion studded with a few cloves to the cooking water.

To save time, there is a quick-soak method that works just as well. Put the beans into a saucepan, cover with cold water, and bring to the boil. Boil rapidly for 10 minutes, then remove from the heat. Cover the pan and leave the beans to soak in the same water for 3 hours. Drain and cook in fresh water for the usual time (see chart).

Although canned beans often have sugar and salt added, they're a good quick alternative to cooking your own. It's a good idea to empty them from the can directly into a colander or strainer and rinse them under cold running water before use. They tend to be quite soft, so add them to chili, casseroles, stews, and curries towards the end of the cooking time.

A 15 oz can of beans, drained, is roughly equivalent to ½ lb cooked beans, or ¼ lb dried (uncooked) beans. The weight of dried pulses approximately doubles during cooking, so if a recipe calls for ½ lb cooked beans you will need ¼ lb to start with. Drained, cooked pulses will keep for several days in a covered container in the refrigerator. Alternatively, freeze them in usable quantities. Thaw overnight and use as freshly cooked beans.

TYPE	APPEARANCE	COOKING TIME AFTER SOAKING	PRESSURE COOKING TIME★
Aduki beans	Round, red, very small	30–60 minutes	12 minutes
Black turtle beans	Kidney-shaped, black, shiny	1½ hours	20 minutes
Black-eye beans	Small, kidney-shaped, pale cream with black spot or 'eye'	1½ hours	12 minutes
Butter beans	Large, kidney-shaped, pale cream	1½ hours	17 minutes
Cannellini beans	White, like long haricots	1 hour	25 minutes
Chick-peas	Round with pointed top, ivory	1½–2 hours	20 minutes
Flageolet beans	Kidney-shaped, pale green	1 hour	15 minutes
Haricot beans	Kidney-shaped, pale cream	1–1½ hours	20 minutes
Lentils	Small and red or green or larger and greenish-brown, round, flattish	1 hour	15 minutes
Mung beans	Round, green, very small	40 minutes	12 minutes
Red kidney beans	Kidney-shaped, crimson red	1–1½ hours	20 minutes
Rose cocoa or borlotti beans	Long, pink with dark red flecks	1 hour	17 minutes
Soya beans	Small, round, ivory	3–4 hours	30 minutes
Split peas	Small, green or yellow, round	45–60 minutes	15 minutes

The cooking times given above are approximate and depend on the age of the beans and the soaking time. ★High (15 lb) pressure

To Cook Pulses in a Pressure Cooker

To cut down on lengthy cooking times, pulses can be pressure cooked (see chart for times). Overnight soaking is not necessary – just cover with boiling water and leave to soak for 1 hour. Drain, then transfer to the pressure cooker with 2½ cups water for every ½ lb beans (weighed after soaking). The cooker must not be more than one-third full.

Bring to the boil, then remove any skum that's risen to the surface. Lower the heat so that the beans are simmering gently, then put the lid on the pan. Bring up to pressure and cook for the time given. Reduce the pressure slowly. Season with salt while warm.

Do not cook mixtures of different types of pulses in the pressure cooker at the same time. This is potentially dangerous as overcooked beans can rise up in the pan and block the safety valves and air vents.

SPROUTING BEANS AND SEEDS

Although they can be grown from any type of bean, the best-known are usually grown from mung beans or alfalfa seeds. They are excellent in salads and stir-fries.

To grow them yourself at home, soak the beans or seeds in water overnight (start with about 3 tbsp). Drain, then transfer to a large clean glass jar. Cover with a piece of cheesecloth secured with an elastic band. Keep in a warm place (choose a dark place if you want pale sprouts; a light one for green sprouts) for about 4–7 days until the sprouts are about 3 inches long. During this time the beans must be rinsed each morning and evening. Simply fill the jar with warm water (through the cheesecloth), swirl the water around in the jar, then pour it out. Before serving, rinse again and drain thoroughly.

TOFU

Also known as soy bean curd, tofu is made from a paste of soy beans which has been pressed into blocks. It is often disregarded by vegetarians and meat-eaters because it's considered to be tasteless. In fact it is virtually tasteless but this can be an advantage – it can be marinated in flavors of your choice, both sweet and savory, which it readily absorbs. It really is worth experimenting with since it is an excellent source of vegetable protein and it contains no fat.

Silken tofu is soft and creamy and is useful for dressings, cheesecakes, sauces, and dips. It adds bulk and texture and greatly increases the nutritional value of these foods, taking on the flavorings of the other ingredients. Firm tofu has been pressed for longer and can be cut into chunks for frying, broiling, and inclusion in stews and curries, or it can be grated or chopped and made into burgers and roasts. You can also buy a smoked variety.

Store tofu in the refrigerator. Once the packet is opened, the block of tofu must be kept in a bowl of cold water in the refrigerator. It will remain fresh for a week if the water is changed daily.

TVP (Texturized Vegetable Protein)

TVP forms the bulk of most veggie burger and sausage mixes. It's made from soy flour which is extruded under pressure, then cut into chunks or small pieces to resemble ground meat. Unlike tofu, it has a slightly chewy, meat-like texture which makes it unappetizing to some vegans and vegetarians (although for the same reason it may appeal to some new vegetarians who miss the texture of meat). It is worth keeping a packet for emergencies because it's quite versatile, keeps well, and, like tofu, is an excellent source of low-fat protein.

MARGARINE

Choose your brand of margarine carefully. Some manufacturers add fish oils and whey (which contains animal rennet) to boost the vitamin content. Pure vegetable margarines are available from health food stores and supermarkets, as are hard vegetable fats and vegetarian suet. Check the labels on low-fat spreads – some contain gelatin.

CHEESE

Many cheeses are not completely vegetarian.

They contain rennet, an enzyme of animal origin added to clot the milk.

Some vegetarians have no objections to this; others prefer to eat cheese that is completely vegetarian. Vegetarian cheeses produced using vegetarian rennet are becoming more widely available. Vegetarian Cheddar is sold in some supermarkets and delis. Check labels as new varieties are coming into the shops all the time.

Soft cheeses, such as cottage and curd cheese, ricotta, low and full fat cream cheese, are usually manufactured without rennet, but check the labels.

WHITE OR WHOLEWHEAT?
There's no doubt that wholewheat flour, rice, bread, and pasta are fiber rich. In a varied vegetarian diet based on fruit, vegetables, and pulses, wholewheat foods of this kind are less significant in terms of fiber intake, than they might be in a meat-eater's diet.

We found that many people disliked the heavier, denser texture of wholewheat products and preferred pastries, pies, pasta, and cakes made with white flour or a mixture of white and wholewheat flours. Nutty brown rice and wholewheat bread make delicious accompaniments to hearty winter casseroles and stews, while a spicy vegetable korma is complemented by fragrant basmati rice. This is not a wholefood book; we prefer to use white or wholewheat products where appropriate. So, we've left the choice up to you. Throughout the book, where the recipes state flour in the ingredients, wholewheat or all-purpose white flour can be used. Likewise, white or brown rice or breadcrumbs, or wholewheat pasta, are suitable.

GELATIN
Gelatin is produced commercially from boiled beef bones so most vegetarians prefer not to use it. Alternative gelling agents include agar-agar and a product called Gelozone. Agar-agar is a tasteless white powder derived from seaweed. Unlike gelatin, which dissolves at a much lower temperature, agar-agar will only dissolve when it is boiled. It is available mainly from health food stores.

Gelozone contains carrageenan, guar gum and carob gum. Like agar-agar, it should be heated until dissolved. Both products can be used in sweet and savory dishes.

— One —

Appetizers

Here is a collection of tasty, mouth-watering recipes to get the taste buds tingling ready for the main event. Before choosing an appetizer, it's vital that you consider the other components of the meal. If you're planning on serving a heavy main course, a casserole or gratin perhaps, then the appetizer should be light and refreshing, while something more substantial will happily precede a light main course. The style and tone of the meal, and the event as a whole, are important, too. If it's to be a formal function, perhaps for a special occasion, then an impressive first course is probably called for. Something that looks pretty on the plate, such as Filo Purses with Stir-Fried Vegetables (page 25) or Spinach Parcels with Tomato Coulis (page 20), is ideal.

Start a casual, relaxed meal with something informal, perhaps something that's eaten with the fingers to get everyone in a party mood. Tomato Bruschetta (page 16) fits the bill, as does a dip with canapés. Guacamole and Hummus are here, but it's simple to whip up your own concoctions based on fromage blanc, sour cream, thick yogurt, mayonnaise, or silken tofu whizzed in the blender. Flavor one of these (or use a mixture of two) with crumbled blue cheese, whole-grain mustard, chopped fresh herbs, garlic, tahini, or a purée of fruits or vegetables.

If the main course is elaborate, requiring lots of last-minute attention, a cold appetizer that can be prepared in advance makes life easier. Hot appetizers which are cooked and served immediately can present problems if the main course is hot as well.

Soup makes a deliciously satisfying appetizer that needn't be reserved only for winter. See the recipes on pages 29–41.

CREAMY HUMMUS

The addition of thick yogurt makes this hummus deliciously creamy, and keeps the calories lower than if made conventionally with lots of oil. Tahini is a thick, creamy, paste, made from ground sesame seeds and sesame oil, which has long been popular in the Middle East. Light and dark varieties are available; the dark version is made from unhusked sesame seeds and has a much stronger, bitter flavor. For this recipe, it is preferable to use one of the lighter blends, but if you already have a jar of dark tahini in your cupboard, reduce the quantity to about 2 tbsp. Serve the hummus with Sesame and Cumin Bread Sticks (page 150).

14 oz can of chick-peas, drained, and rinsed	salt and pepper
1 garlic clove, skinned and crushed	**To serve**
⅓ cup light tahini	paprika
1 tbsp olive oil	lemon wedges
3 tbsp lemon juice	black olives
3–4 level tbsp thick yogurt	

1 Put the chick-peas in a food processor or blender with the remaining ingredients and 2 tbsp water. Blend until smooth, then taste, and adjust the seasoning if necessary. Spoon the hummus into a serving dish, cover, and chill for at least 20 minutes.

2 Sprinkle the hummus with paprika and serve accompanied by lemon wedges, black olives, and bread sticks.

SERVES 4

Mushroom Fritters

These deliciously spicy morsels are best served as soon as they emerge from the hot oil.

1 medium onion, skinned and finely chopped	1 level tsp cumin seeds
1½ cups chick-pea or gram flour	1 lb button or cremini mushrooms, wiped and trimmed
½ level tsp salt	vegetable oil for deep frying
¼ level tsp baking powder	**To garnish**
½ level tsp chili powder	lemon slices
2 level tsp dried fenugreek	chopped fresh coriander (cilantro)
2 tsp lemon juice	

1 Put all the ingredients, except the mushrooms and oil, in a bowl and mix well. Gradually add about ¾ cup cold water to make a batter the consistency of thick cream. Leave to stand for 10 minutes.
2 Heat the oil in a deep-fat fryer with a basket to 350°F. Check the temperature by dropping in a cube of bread; if the oil is hot enough, it should sizzle and turn golden brown in no more than 30 seconds.
3 Lower the basket into the hot oil. Drop the mushrooms into the batter and stir to coat. Remove a few at a time and drop them carefully into the oil. Fry for 2–3 minutes or until golden brown. Remove from the oil, drain on paper towels, and serve at once, garnished with lemon and coriander.
SERVES 6

Mushroom and Cashew Nut Pâté

Serve this protein-rich pâté with chunks of warm whole grain bread, or use it to top baked potatoes.

3 tbsp vegetable oil	½ level tsp cayenne pepper
2 oz unsalted cashew nuts	½ level tsp ground allspice
1½ lb medium open-cup mushrooms, chopped	7 oz silken tofu
2 garlic cloves, skinned and crushed	2 level tbsp chopped fresh parsley (optional)
1 level tsp dried thyme	salt and pepper

1 Heat the oil in a large, heavy-based frying pan and fry the cashews for 2–3 minutes or until browned on all sides. Remove from the oil with a slotted spoon and leave to cool.
2 Add the mushrooms, garlic, thyme, cayenne, and allspice to the pan and cook for about 10 minutes or until the mushrooms are very soft, stirring all the time. Cool slightly.
3 Meanwhile, put the nuts in a food processor and process until very finely chopped. Tip them into a bowl. Put the tofu in the food processor and process until smooth. Add the mushrooms and process until finely chopped. Add the nuts and parsley, if using, and season with salt and pepper and a little extra cayenne and allspice, if liked.
4 Spoon the pâté into a serving dish, cover and chill until ready to serve. Remove from the refrigerator 30 minutes before serving.
SERVES ABOUT 8

TOMATO BRUSCHETTA

Bruschetta is Tuscan garlic bread made with dense Italian peasant bread, rich green virgin olive oil and garlic. The success of this dish depends entirely on the ingredients; soggy sliced white bread and bland vegetable oil just will not do!

1½ lb very ripe, juicy tomatoes, roughly chopped	8–10 thick slices of good white peasant bread cut from a day-old loaf
a pinch of sugar	
salt and pepper	a few basil leaves
2–3 large garlic cloves, skinned	a few black olives (optional)
1 tbsp virgin olive oil	

1 Put the tomatoes in a bowl, add the sugar and season generously with salt and pepper. Crush one of the garlic cloves and add it to the tomatoes with the olive oil. Cover and leave to stand for 30 minutes–1 hour.
2 Lightly toast the bread on both sides until golden brown. Cut the remaining garlic cloves in half and rub all over both sides of the toast. (The more you rub, the stronger the garlic flavor will be.)
3 Arrange the toast on four individual serving plates. Spoon the tomatoes on top with a little of their juice. Tear the basil leaves into small pieces and sprinkle over the *bruschetta*. Scatter the olives, if using, on top and serve.
SERVES 4

AVOCADO WITH RASPBERRY VINEGAR

The sharpness of the raspberries perfectly offsets the rich avocados in this unusual appetizer.

½ pint fresh raspberries	salt and pepper
⅓ cup white wine vinegar	2 firm, ripe avocados
3 tbsp olive oil	a small head of radicchio
6 tbsp polyunsaturated oil (canola)	

1 Pick over the raspberries and place half in a small bowl. Reserve the remainder for garnish. Heat the vinegar until beginning to bubble, then pour over the raspberries. Leave to soak for at least 1 hour or overnight.
2 Strain the raspberries, pressing the fruit gently to extract all juices but not the pulp. Whisk the vinegar together with the oils, and season with salt and pepper.
3 Carefully halve and pit each avocado. Peel away the skin, then slice the flesh directly into the dressing. Stir gently until the avocado is completely covered in dressing. Cover tightly and chill in the refrigerator for 2 hours.
4 Meanwhile, separate the radicchio leaves, rinse and drain. Dry on paper towels, then put in a plastic bag and chill in the refrigerator.
5 To serve, place a few radicchio leaves on four individual plates. Spoon on the avocado mixture and garnish with the raspberries.
SERVES 4

Tomato Bruschetta

$\mathscr{S}$PINACH RICOTTA TERRINE

This terrine is cooked in a *bain-marie*, a French term used to describe a low-sided container which is half-filled with water kept just below boiling point. Delicate, usually egg-based, mixtures are cooked standing in it and the water prevents overcooking. No special container is needed; a roasting pan will do. Serve this terrine with Fresh Pear Dressing (see page 194).

½ lb fresh spinach	*salt and pepper*
1 tbsp olive oil	*Fresh Pear Dressing (page 194), to serve*
3 scallions, trimmed and finely chopped	***To garnish***
2 garlic cloves, skinned and crushed	*watercress sprigs*
1½ cups ricotta cheese	*pear slices*
3 free-range eggs	*toasted walnut pieces*
1¼ cups heavy cream	

1 Lightly grease a 1½ quart ovenproof terrine. Line the base and sides with wax paper, and lightly brush with oil.
2 Wash and drain the spinach and chop roughly. Heat the olive oil in a large saucepan. Add the scallions and garlic, and cook for 2–3 minutes. Add the spinach and continue to cook, stirring, until the spinach has wilted and all the excess liquid has evaporated.
3 Put the spinach mixture in a blender or food processor and add the ricotta cheese, eggs, and heavy cream. Add salt and pepper to taste and blend until smooth.
4 Pour the mixture into the prepared terrine and cover with greased foil. Stand the terrine in a roasting pan and pour in enough boiling water to come about halfway up the sides of the terrine. Cook in the oven at 350°F for 1½–2 hours or until a skewer inserted into the center of the terrine comes out clean. Remove from the oven and leave to cool in the *bain-marie*.
5 Pour any excess liquid off the terrine, then chill in the refrigerator for at least 2 hours. Turn the terrine out on to a plate, cut into thick slices, and serve garnished with sprigs of watercress, pear slices, and toasted walnuts. Spoon a little Fresh Pear Dressing around the slices and serve extra dressing separately.
SERVES 6

$\mathscr{C}$AULIFLOWER SOUFFLÉ TARTS

The cauliflower florets, sauce, and pastry cases can all be prepared in advance and stored separately in the refrigerator. Just whisk the egg whites at the last minute, fold into the sauce, and complete as directed.

2 cups self-rising wholewheat flour	*3 level tbsp all-purpose white flour*
1¼ cups Cheddar cheese, grated	*1¼ cups milk*
a pinch of paprika	*salt and pepper*
¾ cup vegetable margarine or butter	*2 free-range eggs, separated*
1 medium cauliflower (about 1¼ lb trimmed weight)	

1 Mix together the wholewheat flour, ½ cup cheese and the paprika. Rub in ½ cup of the margarine or butter, then add ¼ cup water and mix to a soft dough. Leave to stand for about 15 minutes.

2 Turn the pastry on to a lightly floured surface and knead until smooth, then roll out and use to line six 4½ inch tartlet pans. Chill in the refrigerator for 30 minutes.

3 Line the pastry cases with foil or wax paper and baking beans and bake blind in the oven at 400°F for 10–15 minutes or until just set but not browned.

4 Meanwhile, cut the cauliflower into small florets and steam or boil until just tender. Drain well.

5 Melt the remaining margarine or butter in a saucepan, add the all-purpose flour and cook for 1–2 minutes. Remove from the heat,

then gradually stir in the milk. Bring to the boil, stirring continuously, and cook until thickened. Season with salt and pepper.

6 When the pastry cases are cooked, remove them from the oven and remove the beans and foil or paper. Reduce the oven temperature to 375°F. Arrange a few cauliflower florets in each cooked pastry case. Place the remaining cauliflower, the sauce, egg yolks, and ½ cup of the remaining cheese in a food processor, and process until smooth. Pour into a bowl. Lightly whisk the egg whites and fold into the mixture. Spoon over the cauliflower florets and sprinkle with the remaining cheese.

7 Bake the tarts in the oven for about 20 minutes or until well risen and golden brown. Serve immediately.
SERVES 6

*B*AKED TOMATOES WITH CHEESE AND BASIL

If preferred, use any soft, creamy cheese instead of goats' cheese.

6 medium tomatoes	6 thick slices of bread
¼ lb mozzarella cheese	**To serve**
2 level tbsp finely chopped fresh basil	salad leaves
6 oz rindless goats' cheese	Vinaigrette Dressing (page 185)
salt and pepper	

1 Cut a thin slice from the bottom of each tomato and discard. Using a small, sharp knife or a teaspoon, carefully scoop out all the flesh and seeds, keeping the tomato shells whole. Strain the scooped-out tomato pulp and reserve the juices.

2 Coarsely grate or finely chop the mozzarella cheese and mix with the basil, goats' cheese, and enough reserved tomato juice to form a thick, creamy mixture. Season, then spoon into the tomato shells.

3 Using a plain, round 3½ inch pastry cutter,

stamp out six rounds from the bread slices. (The bread trimmings can be made into bread-crumbs and frozen for use in stuffings.) Toast the rounds on both sides, then place in a single layer in a lightly oiled ovenproof dish. Place a tomato on top of each toasted bread round.

4 Cook the tomatoes, uncovered, in the oven at 350°F for 20–25 minutes or until the cheese mixture looks melted and golden and the tomatoes are lightly cooked but not too soft. Serve with salad leaves and Vinaigrette.
SERVES 6

$\mathcal{G}$OATS' CHEESE AND ROASTED PEPPER SALAD

For a less substantial dish, omit the goats' cheese and serve the salad with the French bread rubbed with garlic. This would also make the dish into a suitable appetizer for a vegan meal.

6 large bell peppers (preferably a mixture of red, green and yellow)	⅓ cup olive oil
3–4 large garlic cloves	12 thin slices of French bread
1 level tsp Dijon mustard	6 small rindless goats' cheeses, each weighing about 2 oz
1 tsp honey	mixed salad leaves
salt and pepper	a few pine nuts, toasted
2 tbsp white wine vinegar or lemon juice	a few chopped fresh herbs (optional)

1 Broil the whole peppers and garlic cloves (still in their skins) under a very hot broiler for 10–15 minutes or until soft and blackened all over, turning occasionally. Leave until cool enough to handle.
2 Remove the skin from the garlic and squeeze the soft insides into a bowl. Add the mustard, honey, and plenty of salt and pepper. Beat together with a fork, mashing the garlic as you beat. Gradually beat in the vinegar or lemon juice followed by the oil. Taste and add more salt and pepper if necessary.
3 Carefully peel the blackened skin from the peppers, halve them, and remove the cores and seeds. Cut the flesh into strips and place in a shallow dish. Pour the dressing over the

peppers and leave to marinate for at least 1 hour.
4 Just before serving, toast the bread slices on both sides. Halve the cheeses and place one half on each slice of toast. Arrange on a baking sheet and bake in the oven at 350°F for 8–12 minutes or until the cheese is soft and warmed through, but not completely melted.
5 Meanwhile, arrange the salad leaves on six plates, and spoon over the peppers and marinade. Arrange the bread slices and baked cheeses on top and sprinkle with a few toasted pine nuts and fresh herbs, if using. Season with black pepper and serve immediately.
SERVES 6

$\mathcal{S}$PINACH PARCELS WITH TOMATO COULIS

These parcels are equally delicious served warm or cold. If spinach is not available, you could use a Boston lettuce instead.

¾ lb celery root, peeled and finely diced	a pinch of cayenne pepper
salt and pepper	1 bay leaf
¾ cup Cheddar cheese, grated	1 level tbsp chopped fresh basil
¼ cup full-fat soft cheese	1 level tsp sugar
1 tbsp olive oil	1–2 tbsp red wine
1 lb ripe tomatoes, chopped	⅔ cup vegetable stock
1 level tbsp tomato paste	16 medium fresh spinach leaves

1 For the filling, cook the celery root in boiling salted water for 12–15 minutes or until tender. Drain, mash, and beat in the cheeses. Season with salt and pepper and leave to cool.

2 Meanwhile, make the tomato coulis. Heat the olive oil in a saucepan, add the tomatoes, cover, and cook until soft. Uncover, bring to the boil, and add the tomato paste, cayenne pepper, bay leaf, basil, sugar, red wine, and stock. Simmer for 10–15 minutes. Remove the bay leaf, pour the mixture into a food processor, and blend until smooth. Strain, then season, and pour into a saucepan.

3 Wash the spinach leaves and steam for 4–6 minutes or until tender. As there will be a lot of filling in each parcel, steam a few extra leaves in case some tear or split. Drain well.

4 Lay two spinach leaves, slightly over-lapping, on a board and place one-sixth of the filling on top. Wrap the leaves around to enclose it. Repeat to make six parcels.

5 Steam the parcels gently for about 10 minutes or until heated through. Reheat the coulis and pour a little on to each of six warmed serving plates. Place a spinach parcel on each plate and serve immediately.
SERVES 6

DEEP-FRIED POTATO SKINS

Don't throw the scooped-out potato flesh away; use it to top Lentil Potato Pies (page 171), to make Potato Biscuits (page 154), or in any other recipe that calls for mashed potato. As these deep-fried skins are rather more-ish we're suggesting that this recipe will only serve 2–3. Serve a few vegetable crudités as well, if liked, to scoop up any excess dip, and to please those who are watching their weight! Make this appetizer to precede a low-calorie main course.

8 potatoes, each weighing about 4 oz	1 tbsp chili sauce
2 tbsp vegetable oil	⅔ cup sour cream
salt and pepper	2 level tbsp chopped fresh chives
¼ lb juicy ripe tomatoes, finely chopped	vegetable oil for deep frying
2 scallions, trimmed and finely chopped	chopped scallions or chives, to garnish

1 Scrub the potatoes clean and dry them with paper towels. Thread the potatoes on skewers, then brush them with the oil, and sprinkle with salt. Place directly on the oven shelf and bake at 400°F for 45 minutes–1 hour or until the potatoes feel soft when squeezed.

2 Meanwhile, make the dips: mix the tomatoes with the scallions and chili sauce and season with salt and pepper. In a separate bowl, mix the sour cream with the chives and season with salt and pepper. Cover the dips and chill in the refrigerator.

3 When the potatoes are tender, remove them from the oven and cut them in half lengthways. Scoop out the flesh, leaving a

layer of potato about ½ inch thick on the skin. Cut each skin in half lengthways.

4 Heat the oil in a deep-fat fryer to 375°F. Deep-fry the potato skins, a few at a time, for 30–60 seconds or until crisp. Remove with a slotted spoon and drain upside-down on paper towels.

5 As soon as all the potato skins are fried, sprinkle them with a little salt and serve immediately. Place the bowls of dip in the center of a large platter and arrange the potato skins around them. Garnish with chives or scallions.
SERVES 2–3

$\mathcal{F}$RIED ZUCCHINI WITH ROSEMARY AÏOLI

The quantities given in this recipe will make more aïoli than you need, but it's difficult to make a smaller amount. Leftover aïoli will keep well in a screw-top jar in the refrigerator for a week. You can serve it with baked potatoes, broiled and fried dishes, and salads. If fresh rosemary is unavailable, omit it and make plain garlic aïoli instead; dried rosemary is not suitable for this recipe.

1 level tbsp very finely chopped fresh rosemary	*freshly ground black pepper*
2–4 garlic cloves, skinned and crushed	*2 lb thin zucchini, trimmed*
¼ level tsp salt	*all-purpose flour for coating*
2 free-range egg yolks	*oil for deep frying*
2 tbsp lemon juice	*rosemary sprigs, to garnish*
1¼ cups olive oil	

1 To make the aïoli, put the rosemary, garlic, and a little of the salt in a bowl and mash with a fork until a paste is formed. (It won't be perfectly smooth because of the rosemary.) Add the egg yolks, the remaining salt, and 1 tsp of the lemon juice, and beat well.

2 Gradually add the olive oil, drop by drop, whisking all the time, until the mixture is thick and smooth. When all of the oil has been added, whisk in the remaining lemon juice. Season with pepper, cover, and leave to stand for at least 1 hour to allow the flavors to develop.

3 Just before serving, thinly slice the zucchini. Put some all-purpose flour in a bowl and season with salt and pepper. Add the zucchini and toss until coated.

4 Heat the oil in a deep frying pan or electric deep-fat fryer to 375°F. Put enough zucchini slices into the frying basket to quarter fill it, shaking off excess flour, and lower the basket into the oil. Cook for 3–4 minutes or until golden brown. Drain on crumpled paper towels and keep warm while cooking the remainder.

5 Pile the fried zucchini on to warmed individual serving plates and add a spoonful of rosemary aïoli. Garnish with sprigs of rosemary and serve immediately.
SERVES 4

GUACAMOLE WITH CRUDITÉS

Ripe avocados are essential to guacamole; a ripe avocado always "gives" slightly when pressed at the pointed end. A hard, under-ripe fruit will ripen in 1–2 days at room temperature if stored in a fruit bowl with ripe fruit, or in about a week in the refrigerator.

1 small onion, skinned and quartered	2 level tsp ground coriander
2–3 garlic cloves, skinned	2 level tsp ground cumin
1 inch piece of fresh ginger root, peeled	1 level tsp chili powder
4 large ripe avocados	2 ripe tomatoes, seeded and roughly chopped
finely grated rind and juice of 2 small limes	salt and pepper
¼ cup chopped fresh coriander (cilantro)	paprika, to garnish

1 Put the onion, garlic, and ginger in a food processor and process until finely chopped.

2 Halve, pit and peel the avocados, then chop roughly, and add to the mixture in the processor with all the remaining ingredients, except the tomato and seasoning. Process until almost smooth, then transfer to a bowl and stir in the tomato. Season with salt and pepper. Cover and chill in the refrigerator for 30 minutes to let the flavors develop. Garnish with paprika and serve with crudités.

Crudités to serve with Guacamole
Serve an assortment of crudités chosen and prepared to appeal to the eye as well as the taste buds. Baby vegetables, such as carrots, baby corn, cherry tomatoes, and button mushrooms can be served whole. Traditionally, crudités are cut into neat strips, all about the same size and arranged in tidy rows of color. You may prefer the wild approach, where vegetables are cleaned and trimmed to a manageable size, retaining their original shape. Arrange these in a more chaotic fashion on plain white china or a bed of crushed ice.

Sliced fresh fruit, such as apples, pears, nectarines, grapes, mangoes, star fruit, and fresh dates, as well as dried figs, dates, and apricots, all make good crudités.
SERVES 6–8

$\mathcal{W}$ ARM WINTER VEGETABLE SALAD

Serve with warm herb or garlic bread.

⅓ cup olive oil	15 ml (1 level tbsp) chopped fresh herbs, such as
1 tbsp finely chopped onion or shallot	coriander (cilantro), parsley, chives or thyme
1 garlic clove, skinned and crushed	¼ lb celery root or turnips, trimmed and peeled
2 tbsp hazelnut oil	½ lb carrots, trimmed and peeled
2 oranges	½ lb leeks, trimmed
1 tbsp lemon juice	orange sections, to garnish
1 tsp honey	

1 Heat 2 tbsp of the olive oil in a saucepan and sauté the onion or shallot and garlic for 3–4 minutes or until golden. Remove from the heat and add the remaining olive oil and the hazelnut oil.

2 Thinly pare the rind from one of the oranges and squeeze the juice from both. Add the rind and about ⅔ cup orange juice to the onion and garlic with the lemon juice, honey, and half the chopped herbs. Cover and leave at room temperature for at least 2 hours.

3 Meanwhile, thinly slice the celery root or turnips and carrots and cut into thin matchstick strips. Halve the leeks lengthways and cut into similar-sized strips. Blanch the vegetables separately in boiling salted water for about 5 minutes or until just tender. Drain well.

4 Strain the dressing mixture and reheat with the remaining herbs until warm. Arrange the warm vegetable strips in piles on six individual plates. Spoon over the dressing, garnish with orange sections and serve.
SERVES 6

$\mathcal{S}$ ATAY

This variation of the Indonesian classic is made with tofu. Choose the firm pressed type so it does not fall apart during cooking. The peanut sauce can be made well in advance and stored in the refrigerator; the tufo is marinated in advance. It then takes a mere 3–4 minutes' cooking to complete a delicious appetizer.

1 lb firm tofu	5 tbsp crunchy peanut butter
vegetable oil for broiling	2 tbsp soy sauce
For the marinade	1 level tsp brown sugar
2 garlic cloves, skinned and crushed	1 garlic clove, skinned and crushed
1 inch piece of fresh ginger root, peeled and grated	1 level tsp chili powder, or to taste
3 tbsp soy sauce	1 level tsp chopped fresh lemon grass or finely grated
2 level tsp brown sugar	lemon rind
For the peanut sauce	2 tbsp Crisp Fried Onions (see page 115), crumbled
2 oz creamed coconut, roughly chopped	(optional)

1 To make the marinade, mix all the ingredients together with 3 tbsp water in a large shallow dish. Cut the tofu into large chunks. Add the tofu and stir. Cover and leave to marinate in the refrigerator for 2–3 hours or overnight.

2 Meanwhile, to make the peanut sauce, pour ⅔ cup boiling water over the coconut and stir until dissolved. Add all the remaining ingredients and mix thoroughly. Cover and leave to stand.

3 Thread the tofu chunks on to 16 bamboo skewers and brush with a little vegetable oil. Cook under a very hot broiler for 3–4 minutes or until lightly browned, turning occasionally. Serve hot with the cold peanut sauce.

SERVES 4–6

$\mathcal{F}$ILO PURSES WITH STIR-FRIED VEGETABLES

These light, low-calorie parcels could be made ahead and baked just before serving. If you are making them in advance, brush them generously with melted margarine or butter, and keep them well covered to prevent the pastry drying out.

¼ lb celery, trimmed	½ cup bean sprouts
¼ lb carrots, trimmed	juice of 1 small lemon
3 oz scallions, trimmed	salt and pepper
6 tbsp vegetable margarine or butter	5 large sheets of filo pastry, each measuring about
1 inch piece of fresh ginger root, peeled and chopped	18 × 12 inches

1 Cut the celery, carrots, and scallions into thin shreds.

2 Heat 2 tbsp of the margarine or butter in a large frying pan. Add the ginger, vegetables, and bean sprouts, and stir-fry over a high heat for 3–4 minutes or until beginning to soften. Add the lemon juice and continue to stir-fry briskly until the vegetables are tender and most of the moisture has evaporated. Season and leave to cool.

3 Melt the remaining margarine or butter. Cut the pastry sheets in four to make a total of 20 rectangles. Layer the pieces in six stacks of three, using up the two spare rectangles on any thin or split pastry stacks and brushing each layer with melted margarine or butter.

4 Divide the vegetable mixture between the six stacks and draw the pastry edges up around the filling, pinching the tops together to form little 'money bags'. Place the pastries on a greased baking sheet and brush again with melted margarine or butter.

5 Bake in the oven at 400°F for about 20 minutes or until well browned and crisp. If necessary, cover the pastries lightly with parchment paper to prevent over-browning towards the end. Serve warm.

SERVES 6

EGGPLANT BLINIS

These are tiny, well flavored pancakes, topped with sautéed vegetables, and yogurt, crème fraîche or mayonnaise. If you increase the portion size, this makes a good main course.

1 eggplant, weighing about 1 lb
olive oil
1 cup all-purpose flour
1 level tsp baking powder
3 free-range eggs
2 garlic cloves, skinned and crushed

salt and freshly ground black pepper
about ¼ lb baby carrots, trimmed and scraped
¼ lb large mushrooms, wiped and thickly sliced
3 medium zucchini, thickly sliced
thick yogurt, crème fraîche, or flavored mayonnaise (see page 192), to serve

1 Prick the eggplant all over with a fork and rub the skin with a little olive oil. Bake in the oven at 400°F for about 30 minutes or until soft when pressed. Cool slightly, then halve, and scrape out the flesh.

2 Mash the eggplant flesh with a potato masher, then add the flour, baking powder, eggs, and one garlic clove. Mix well to make a fairly stiff batter. Season generously with salt and pepper and set aside.

3 Heat a little olive oil in a large saucepan, add the carrots and remaining garlic and fry over a high heat for 1–2 minutes. Lower the heat and continue to cook while frying the blinis.

4 To fry the blinis, heat a little olive oil in a large, heavy-based frying pan. Drop large tablespoons of batter into the oil and fry for 2–3 minutes or until firm and golden brown underneath. Turn the blinis and fry for a further 2–3 minutes or until the second sides are golden brown. Remove from the pan and keep warm while frying the remaining blinis. There should be enough batter to make about 20 blinis.

5 When all the blinis are cooked, increase the heat under the carrots, add the remaining vegetables and cook for 2–3 minutes or until the mushrooms and zucchini are just tender, shaking the pan continuously.

6 Arrange the blinis on warmed serving plates and top with the vegetables and a spoonful of yogurt, crème fraîche, or mayonnaise. Grind black pepper over the top and serve immediately.

SERVES 6

—Two—

*S*OUPS AND

*S*TOCKS

Good stock is essential for flavorsome soups. Unlike meat-based stock, vegetarian stocks are quick and pleasant to make – so there's no excuse for not making your own. Delicate chilled or fine-flavored soups, and dishes such as risotto, rely heavily on good strong stock to give a rich depth of flavor. However, for some heartier soups, such as Mixed Bean and Vegetable Soup (see page 30), or heavily spiced or curried dishes, it's possible to get away with using bouillon powder. Commercially prepared stocks, sold as cubes, powder, or tubs of concentrate, have improved dramatically in recent years, so it is well worth experimenting with different brands until you find a flavor that appeals. Vegans should scrutinize labels because some manufacturers add lactose – a milk sugar. For those worried about their salt consumption, low sodium brands are available.

On a practical note, both stocks and soups freeze well. Boil the strained stock vigorously in a large saucepan to reduce the volume, then freeze in ice-cube trays or in usable quantities in freezer bags. This intensely flavored stock is excellent for flavoring noodles, stuffed vegetables, and for making sauces.

Similarly, when making soups for the freezer, add less liquid to reduce the bulk, but remember to replace the missing liquid when reheating. Even with the help of a microwave, stocks and soups seem to take forever to thaw. They're best thawed overnight at cool room temperature; attempts to thaw quickly inevitably result in ruining the texture of chunky soups as it's impossible to resist mashing to try to speed up the process. Don't add cream, yogurt, fromage blanc, or eggs to soups for the freezer because they have a tendency to curdle when reheated.

Whether you're serving soup as an appetizer or a meal in itself, warm bread is the obvious but perfect accompaniment. Any of the breads featured in the chapter on page 143 are suitable as long as you choose appropriately. Nan-style Indian bread or poppadums are good with spicy lentil and bean soups, while something lighter and more delicate, like poppy seed-topped white bread rolls or crisp Melba toast, is better with subtly flavored soups like Vichyssoise (page 30) or Pea and Chervil Soup (page 35). If you haven't got the time or the ingredients to bake a loaf from scratch, commercially produced bread is easily transformed into something special. Garlic bread is the obvious choice but, following the same principle, why not flavor the butter or margarine with finely grated lemon rind and a squeeze of juice; chopped fresh herbs; chopped fresh chilies and a pinch of garam masala; or a little curry paste, pesto sauce or whole-grain mustard.

PICY BEAN AND ZUCCHINI SOUP

This soup is really quick and easy to make using canned beans. It makes an excellent supper dish served with crusty bread.

2 tbsp olive oil	½ lb potato, peeled and diced
1 medium onion, skinned and finely chopped	1 lb can red kidney beans, drained and rinsed
2 garlic cloves, skinned and crushed	1 lb can flageolet beans, drained and rinsed
2 level tsp ground coriander	1½ qt vegetable stock
1 level tbsp paprika	salt and pepper
1 level tsp mild curry powder	
1 lb zucchini, halved lengthways and sliced	

1 Heat the oil in a large saucepan, add the onion and garlic and cook for 2 minutes, stirring constantly. Add the spices and cook for 1 minute, stirring. Mix in the zucchini and potato, and cook for 1–2 minutes.
2 Add the remaining ingredients and season with salt and pepper. Cover and simmer for 25 minutes or until the potato is tender, stirring occasionally. Taste and adjust the seasoning, if necessary, before serving with crusty bread.
SERVES 4

NDALUSIAN SUMMER SOUP

Serve this version of gazpacho, the classic chilled tomato soup, at an *al fresco* lunch party, with bowls of finely chopped cucumber, onion, and green or red bell pepper, plus croûtons fried in olive oil (see page 34). Guests should help themselves to the accompaniments, sprinkling them over individual bowls of soup.

¼ cup olive oil	1 lb ripe tomatoes, roughly chopped
1 large onion, skinned and roughly chopped	2 tbsp wine vinegar
2 garlic cloves, skinned and roughly chopped	1 dried red chili, finely chopped
2 large red bell peppers, cored, seeded, and roughly chopped	salt and pepper
	¼ cup mayonnaise

1 Heat the oil in a large saucepan, add the onion and garlic and fry gently for 5 minutes or until soft but not colored.
2 Add the red peppers and fry for a further 5 minutes, stirring constantly, then add the tomatoes and stir to break them up. Add 3½ cups water, the wine vinegar, and chili. Season with salt and pepper.
3 Bring to the boil, then lower the heat, cover and simmer for 45 minutes.
4 Strain the soup or purée in a blender or food processor. If using a blender or processor, pass the puréed soup through a strainer to remove the tomato skins.
5 Put the mayonnaise in a large bowl and gradually whisk in the soup. Taste and adjust the seasoning, if necessary. Chill in the refrigerator for at least 4 hours before serving with chopped vegetables and croûtons.
SERVES 4–6

ℳIXED BEAN AND VEGETABLE SOUP

Use this basic recipe to make soup from any mixture of vegetables and beans available.
Freshly cooked beans could be used, but we've used cans to make the soup quick to cook.
Cut the vegetables into generous chunks to give the soup a good, hearty texture.

1 tbsp olive oil	*2 bay leaves*
1 medium onion, skinned and roughly chopped	*about 1 qt vegetable stock*
1 lb mixed root vegetables, including carrots, potatoes,	*1 lb can red kidney beans, drained and rinsed*
and parsnips, peeled and roughly chopped	*1 lb can black-eyed beans, drained and rinsed*
1 lb mixed vegetables, such as peppers, celery, and fennel,	*2 zucchini, trimmed and sliced*
prepared as necessary and roughly chopped	*3 level tbsp chopped fresh parsley or coriander*
1 garlic clove, skinned and crushed	*salt and pepper*
2 level tsp mild curry powder	

1 Heat the oil in a large heavy-based
saucepan. Add all the vegetables, except the
beans and zucchini, and cook over a high heat
for 4–5 minutes, stirring all the time. Add the
garlic, curry powder, and bay leaves and
continue cooking for 2–3 minutes.
2 Pour in the stock. (There should be enough
to cover the vegetables; if not, add a little
more.) Bring to the boil, then reduce the
heat, cover, and simmer for 20 minutes.

3 Add the beans and cook for a further
10 minutes. Remove the bay leaves. Purée
about half the soup in a blender.
4 Return the puréed soup to the saucepan
and bring to the boil, then add the zucchini
and herbs. Season to taste with salt and pepper
and simmer gently for 3–4 minutes or until
the zucchini are just tender. Add a little extra
stock, if necessary, to thin the soup.
SERVES 6 AS A MAIN COURSE

𝒱ICHYSSOISE

Serve this classic chilled soup with Melba toast for an elegant start to a celebration meal.

4 tbsp vegetable margarine or butter	*2 medium potatoes, peeled and thinly sliced*
4 leeks, trimmed and sliced	*salt and pepper*
1 onion, skinned and sliced	*¼ cup light cream*
1 qt vegetable stock	*snipped fresh chives, to garnish*

1 Melt the margarine or butter in a heavy-
based saucepan, add the leeks and onion, and
cook gently for about 10 minutes. Add the
stock and potatoes and bring to the boil.
2 Lower the heat, season with salt and pepper,
and cover. Simmer for about 30 minutes.

3 Strain the soup or purée in a blender or
food processor. Pour into a large serving bowl
and stir in the cream. Taste and adjust the
seasoning, if necessary. Chill for at least
4 hours before serving sprinkled with chives.
SERVES 4

Mixed Bean and Vegetable Soup

WINTER VEGETABLE SOUP

This is a really substantial soup, best served as a meal in itself, with crusty baguettes, garlic bread or warm granary rolls. Along with the bread, serve a bowl of grated sharp farmhouse Cheddar cheese or a wedge of Stilton, either of which would hold its own against the flavors in the soup.

2 tsp lemon juice	*6 tbsp vegetable margarine or butter*
½ lb Jerusalem artichokes	*¼ lb haricot beans, soaked overnight in cold water*
½ small cabbage, trimmed and washed	*bouquet garni*
1 lb carrots, trimmed and peeled	*Brown Onion Stock (see page 41) or water*
½ lb turnips, trimmed and peeled	*salt and pepper*
2 onions, skinned, or 2 leeks, trimmed and washed	*chopped fresh parsley, to garnish*
2–3 celery sticks, trimmed	

1 Fill a bowl with cold water and add the lemon juice. Peel the artichokes, slice them, then cut them into strips. Drop them into the acidulated water as you work, to prevent them from discoloring.
2 Shred the cabbage coarsely, discarding all thick or woody stalks. Cut the remaining vegetables into fairly small pieces.
3 Melt the margarine or butter in a large saucepan and add all the vegetables (except the cabbage and beans). Fry for about 10 minutes, stirring, until soft but not colored.

Drain the beans and add to the vegetables with the bouquet garni and enough stock or water to cover. Add plenty of pepper and bring to the boil, then lower the heat, cover with a lid, and simmer for 45 minutes–1 hour.
4 Add the cabbage and season with salt. Cook for a further 20–30 minutes, adding more liquid as required. When all the ingredients are soft, discard the bouquet garni and taste and adjust the seasoning. Serve hot, sprinkled with parsley.
SERVES 4

TUSCAN BEAN SOUP

This thick wholesome soup is a meal in itself. In Italy it comes in a number of guises, but always with cannellini beans and a variety of vegetables, depending on the season. Serve sprinkled with Parmesan cheese, or vegetarian Cheddar cheese, and accompanied by chunks of peasant bread.

¾ lb cannellini beans, soaked overnight in cold water	*1 lb tomatoes, skinned and roughly chopped*
¼ cup olive oil	*5 cups vegetable stock*
2 large onions, skinned and roughly chopped	*1 level tbsp chopped fresh thyme or sage*
6 celery sticks, trimmed and roughly chopped	*salt and pepper*
2 garlic cloves, skinned and crushed	*freshly grated Parmesan cheese, to serve*

1 Drain the beans and put them in a saucepan. Cover with fresh water, bring to the boil, and boil rapidly for 10 minutes. Lower the heat, cover and simmer for about 50 minutes or until the beans are tender. Drain, reserving the cooking liquor.

2 Put half the beans in a blender or food processor. Add 1¼ cups of the reserved cooking liquor and purée until smooth.

3 Heat the oil in a large saucepan. Add the onions, celery, and garlic and cook over a moderate heat for 5–10 minutes or until beginning to brown.

4 Stir in the tomatoes, stock, whole beans, and bean purée with the thyme or sage. Season with salt and pepper and bring to the boil. Reduce the heat, cover and simmer for about 40 minutes or until all the ingredients are tender. Serve hot, sprinkled with Parmesan cheese and accompanied by crusty bread.

SERVES 6

$\mathscr{S}$PICED DAL SOUP

Channa dal is a yellow pulse that is often mistaken for the yellow split pea. In fact it is the husked and split black chick-pea. It is a high-protein pulse with a slightly nutty flavor. If you find channa dal difficult to obtain, red lentils can be used instead.

¼ lb channa dal	2 tbsp vegetable oil or ghee (clarified butter)
1 level tsp cumin seeds	½ lb tomatoes, skinned and roughly chopped
2 level tsp coriander seeds	½ level tsp ground turmeric
1 level tsp fenugreek seeds	1 tbsp lemon or lime juice
3 dried red chilies	1 tsp black treacle
1 level tbsp shredded coconut	1 level tsp salt

1 Pick over the dal and remove any grit or discolored pulses. Put into a strainer and wash thoroughly under cold running water, then drain well.

2 Put the dal in a large saucepan, cover with 2½ cups water, and bring to the boil. Reduce the heat, cover, and simmer for at least 1 hour or until tender.

3 Finely grind the cumin, coriander, fenugreek, chilies, and coconut in a small spice mill or with a mortar and pestle. Heat the oil or ghee in a heavy-based frying pan, add the spice mixture and fry, stirring, for 1 minute. Remove from the heat and set aside.

4 Purée the dal with any remaining liquid in a blender or food processor and transfer to a large saucepan. Stir in the tomatoes, spice mixture, turmeric, lemon or lime juice, treacle, salt, and a further 1¼ cups water.

5 Bring to the boil, then lower the heat, cover, and simmer for about 20 minutes. Taste and adjust the seasoning. Serve hot.

SERVES 4–6

CARROT AND CORIANDER SOUP

Add extra flavor and crunch to this soup by serving it sprinkled generously with delicious home-made croûtons. Simply cut thick slices of bread into small dice and fry in olive oil or butter until golden. Drain on paper towels. Store in an airtight container until needed. Lower-fat croûtons can be made by toasting the bread instead of frying, but they aren't as delicious!

3 tbsp vegetable margarine or butter	salt and pepper
6 oz trimmed leeks, washed and sliced	⅔ cup plain yogurt or sour cream
1 lb carrots, trimmed, peeled and sliced	**To garnish**
2 level tsp ground coriander	fresh coriander (cilantro) leaves
1 level tsp all-purpose flour	croûtons (see above)
1 qt vegetable stock	

1 Heat the margarine or butter in a large saucepan. Add the vegetables, cover the pan, and cook gently for 5–10 minutes or until the vegetables begin to soften but not color.
2 Stir in the ground coriander and flour and cook for about 1 minute, then pour in the stock and bring to the boil, stirring all the time. Season with salt and pepper, reduce the heat, cover, and simmer for about 20 minutes or until all the ingredients are quite tender.
3 Leave the soup to cool slightly, then purée in a blender or food processor until quite smooth. Return the soup to the pan and stir in the yogurt or cream. Taste and adjust the seasoning, if necessary, and reheat gently, without boiling. Serve garnished with coriander and croûtons.
SERVES 6

SPINACH SOUP

When buying spinach, choose bright green leaves and avoid spinach that is yellow and wilted. Summer spinach is light green and fine textured, while winter spinach is darker and coarser.

1 lb fresh spinach, trimmed and washed	salt and pepper
3⅔ cups vegetable stock	1¼ cups buttermilk
1 tbsp lemon juice	a few drops of Tabasco

1 Place the spinach, stock, and lemon juice in a large saucepan. Season with salt and pepper and bring to the boil, then reduce the heat and simmer for 10 minutes.
2 Work the spinach through a strainer, or strain off most of the liquid and reserve, then purée the spinach in a blender or food processor until smooth.
3 Reheat the spinach purée gently with the cooking liquid, buttermilk, and Tabasco, to taste.
SERVES 4

$\mathscr{P}$ EA AND CHERVIL SOUP

Don't throw away empty pea pods – they can be used to make this light summer soup.
We've used fresh chervil to add a subtle aniseed flavor, but any herb will do.

1 tbsp vegetable oil	1 level tsp all-purpose flour
¼ lb scallions, trimmed and roughly chopped	3 cups vegetable stock
½ lb empty pea pods or snow peas, trimmed and roughly chopped	2 level tsp chopped fresh chervil
1 garlic clove, crushed	salt and pepper

1 Heat the oil in a large saucepan and stir in the scallions, pea pods and garlic. Cook for 2–3 minutes, stirring constantly.
2 Stir in the flour and stock and bring to the boil. Reduce the heat, cover and simmer gently for 25–30 minutes.

3 Cool the mixture slightly, then purée in a blender or food processor until quite smooth. Strain and return to the pan. Stir in the chopped chervil and season the soup well. Serve hot, or chilled with ice.
SERVES 2

Pea and Chervil Soup

SUMMER VEGETABLE SOUP

This summer soup can be served hot with chunks of French bread topped with grated cheese and broiled. Alternatively, try blending it to a smooth purée with a little yogurt and serving it chilled.

2 tbsp vegetable oil	2 oz button mushrooms, wiped and thinly sliced
¼ lb carrots, trimmed, peeled, and cut into matchsticks	1 qt vegetable stock
½ bunch of scallions, thinly sliced	¼ cup chopped fresh parsley
2 lb lima beans, shelled	salt and pepper
½ lb tomatoes, skinned, seeded, and roughly chopped	

1 Heat the oil in a large saucepan and add the carrots and scallions. Cook, stirring, for 1–2 minutes or until the vegetables are well browned.
2 Add the remaining vegetables and cook for a further minute. Add the stock and 3 level tbsp parsley. Season with salt and pepper.
3 Bring to the boil, then reduce the heat, cover and simmer for about 40 minutes. Garnish with the remaining parsley.
SERVES 4–6

SPICED LEEK AND POTATO SOUP

Mild curry paste is a useful item to keep in the storecupboard. The spices are already cooked so it can be stirred directly into soups, sauces, and dips to add a subtle, spicy flavor without any hint of the raw spice flavor associated with powdered spices.

2 tbsp vegetable margarine or butter	2½ cups Brown Onion Stock (see page 41)
½ lb trimmed leeks, roughly chopped	salt and pepper
1 medium onion, skinned and roughly chopped	⅔ cup light cream
½ lb potato, peeled and roughly chopped	chopped fresh coriander (cilantro), to garnish
1½ level tsp mild curry paste	

1 Melt the margarine or butter in a saucepan and sauté the vegetables with the curry paste for 2–3 minutes or until they start to soften and color. Add the stock and bring to the boil. Reduce the heat, cover, and simmer for 45 minutes or until all the vegetables are soft.
2 Purée the mixture in a food processor or blender until smooth. If you have time, push through a nylon strainer for a really smooth result. Season with salt and pepper. Serve hot or cover and chill for 2 hours or, preferably, overnight. Either stir in the cream or swirl it on top of the soup as a garnish with the fresh coriander.
SERVES 3–4

CREAM OF JERUSALEM ARTICHOKE SOUP

When buying Jerusalem artichokes, choose firm tubers with the smoothest surface available as they will be easier to peel. Use them as soon as possible after buying as they quickly lose their lovely creamy colour.

2 lb Jerusalem artichokes	1½ tbsp lemon juice
2 slices of lemon	2 level tbsp chopped fresh parsley
2 tbsp vegetable margarine or butter	⅔ cup light cream
1 medium onion, skinned and chopped	salt and pepper
1¼ cups milk	croûtons (see page 34), to serve

1 Wash the artichokes well and put them in a large saucepan with the lemon slices. Cover with 3½ cups cold water, bring to the boil, and cook for about 20 minutes or until tender. Drain off the water, reserving 2½ cups, and leave the artichokes to cool.
2 Peel the artichokes, then mash them roughly.
3 Melt the margarine or butter in a saucepan, add the onion, and cook gently for 5–10 minutes or until soft but not colored. Stir in

the reserved artichoke cooking water, the artichokes and milk. Bring to the boil, stirring, then simmer for 2–3 minutes.
4 Strain the soup or purée in a blender or food processor. Return to the rinsed-out pan and stir in the lemon juice, parsley, cream, and plenty of salt and pepper. Reheat gently and serve hot, sprinkled with croûtons.
SERVES 4

CELERY ROOT SOUP WITH DILL

Make sure that the soup is well blended to give a smooth texture, and don't forget the final touches just before serving.

2 tbsp vegetable margarine or butter	3 tbsp light cream
½ lb celery root, trimmed, peeled and sliced	lemon juice
1 medium onion, skinned and sliced	2 level tsp chopped fresh dill or a pinch of dried dill weed
3 cups vegetable stock	
salt and pepper	

1 Melt the margarine or butter in a saucepan, add the celery root and onion, and cook gently for 1–2 minutes, stirring constantly. Cover with a piece of damp parchment paper pressed down on to the vegetables, and a tight-fitting lid. Cook for about 10 minutes.
2 Remove the parchment paper and pour in the stock. Season with salt and pepper and bring to the boil. Reduce the heat, cover, and

simmer for about 30 minutes or until tender. Cool slightly, then purée in a blender or food processor until very smooth.
3 Return the soup to the pan and reheat, then remove from the heat and stir in the cream, a dash of lemon juice and the dill. Taste and adjust the seasoning, if necessary, before serving in warmed soup bowls.
SERVES 3–4

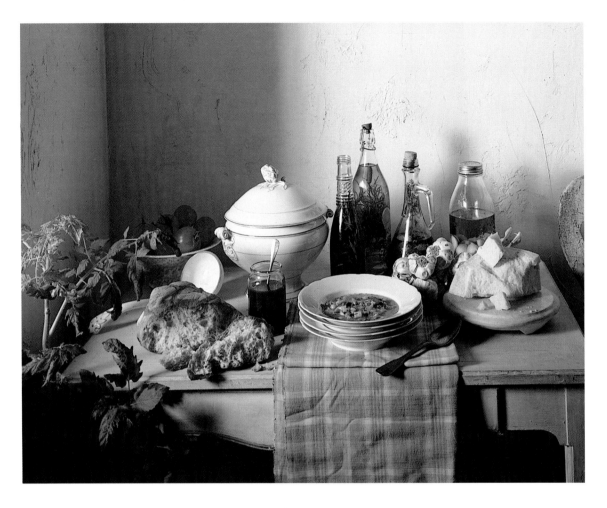

Minestrone

$\mathscr{B}$ROCCOLI AND STILTON SOUP

Served with chunks of hot crusty bread, this soup makes a delicious, filling supper dish.

2 tbsp vegetable margarine or butter	3 level tbsp split red lentils
1 large onion, skinned and chopped	3½ cups vegetable stock
½ lb broccoli, trimmed and chopped	2 oz Stilton cheese
a good pinch of cumin seeds	salt and pepper

1 Melt the margarine or butter in a large saucepan, add the onion, broccoli, and cumin and cook for 5 10 minutes or until beginning to soften.
2 Stir the lentils and stock into the vegetables. Bring to the boil, then reduce the heat, cover, and simmer for 20–30 minutes or until the lentils are soft. Leave the soup to cool slightly, then purée in a blender or food processor until smooth.
3 Return the soup to a saucepan and reheat gently. Crumble in the Stilton and season with salt and pepper. Serve hot.
SERVES 4

INESTRONE

The addition of Pesto and Pecorino or Parmesan cheese makes this a typical Genoese minestrone. It's really hearty, comforting food, perfect for a cold winter's evening.

6 oz dried cannellini beans, soaked overnight in cold water	¼ lb small pasta shapes
¼ cup olive oil	¼ lb shelled fresh or frozen peas
2 onions, skinned and chopped	6 oz green beans, topped, tailed, and sliced
3 garlic cloves, skinned and crushed	½ lb dark green cabbage, tough stalks removed and roughly chopped
2 carrots, trimmed, peeled and diced	5 level tbsp chopped fresh parsley
2 celery sticks, trimmed and diced	¼ cup Pesto (see page 193)
14 oz can chopped tomatoes	salt and pepper
2½ qt Brown Onion Stock (see page 41) or vegetable stock	**To serve**
	Pesto (see page 193)
¾ lb floury potatoes, peeled and diced	freshly grated Pecorino or Parmesan cheese

1 Drain the beans, put them in a very large saucepan and cover with fresh water. Bring to the boil and boil rapidly for 10 minutes, then cover, and simmer for 1 hour, then drain.
2 Heat the oil in a large saucepan, add the onions and garlic and fry for 5–10 minutes or until golden brown. Add the carrots and celery and cook for 2 minutes.
3 Stir in the beans, tomatoes, stock, potatoes, pasta, and fresh peas, if using. Bring to the

boil, then reduce the heat, half-cover and simmer for 1 hour.
4 Add the frozen peas, if using, green beans, cabbage, parsley, and Pesto. Season with salt and pepper and simmer for 30 minutes or until the vegetables are all tender. Serve immediately in a warmed soup tureen, with the Pesto and cheese in separate bowls for guests to stir into their soup.
SERVES 6–8 AS A MAIN COURSE

CED TOMATO AND BASIL SOUP

A refreshing chilled soup, best made when tomatoes are at their cheapest and most flavorsome. The pungency of fresh basil adds a delicious flavor.

1 lb tomatoes, chopped	1 level tbsp chopped fresh basil
1 small onion, skinned and chopped	2½ cups Brown Onion Stock (see page 41)
1 level tbsp tomato paste	salt and pepper

1 Put the tomatoes, onion, tomato paste and basil in a blender or food processor and purée until smooth. Pass through a strainer into a saucepan, then stir in the stock and heat gently to remove froth. Season with salt and pepper.

2 Remove from the heat and leave to cool, then chill in the refrigerator for at least 2 hours or overnight.
SERVES 4

PARSNIP AND APPLE SOUP

The velvety texture of a creamy soup is always welcoming, and the unmistakable flavor of parsnips, blended with a hint of tart apple, is very warming.

2 tbsp vegetable margarine or butter	⅔ cup light cream
1½ lb parsnips, trimmed, peeled, and roughly chopped	salt and pepper
1 tart apple, cored, peeled, and roughly chopped	**To garnish**
1 qt vegetable stock	fresh sage leaves or parsley
4 fresh sage leaves or ½ level tsp dried sage	croûtons (see page 34)
2 cloves	

1 Melt the margarine or butter in a large saucepan, add the parsnips and apple, cover, and cook gently for 10 minutes, stirring occasionally.
2 Pour in the stock, and add the sage and cloves. Bring to the boil, cover, then simmer for 30 minutes or until the parsnip is very soft.
3 Remove the sage leaves and cloves, leave the soup to cool slightly, then purée in a blender or food processor.
4 Return the soup to the saucepan, add the cream and reheat gently. Season with salt and pepper. Serve hot, garnished with the sage or parsley and croûtons.
SERVES 6

GINGERED DAL SOUP

Garlic and Scallion Sauce is a commercially prepared sauce, sold in bottles. You can sometimes find it in the specialty stores alongside the soy and chili sauces.

6 level tbsp instant coconut milk powder or 3 oz creamed coconut	3 tbsp Garlic and Scallion Sauce
	3 tbsp chopped fresh coriander (cilantro)
2 tbsp olive oil	salt and pepper
2 large garlic cloves, skinned and crushed	**To garnish**
1 inch piece of fresh ginger root, peeled and chopped	plain yogurt
14 oz split red lentils	chopped fresh coriander (cilantro)
7½ cups vegetable stock or water	

1 Pour 1¼ cups boiling water over the coconut and stir until dissolved.
2 Heat the oil in a large saucepan, add the garlic and ginger, and fry for 3 minutes or until soft and golden brown. Add all the remaining ingredients, including the coconut milk. Bring to the boil, cover, and simmer for 15–20 minutes or until the lentils are very tender. Season to taste with salt and pepper.
3 Cool slightly, then purée, in batches, in a food processor. Return to the saucepan and reheat gently. Taste and adjust the seasoning if necessary. Serve hot, topped with a swirl of yogurt and plenty of chopped fresh coriander.
SERVES 6

CHESTNUT AND ROASTED GARLIC SOUP

Dried chestnuts are available from good health food stores or European delis. This soup can also be made with two 1 lb cans peeled whole chestnuts in water, drained, but the flavor will not be as good.

½ lb dried chestnuts, soaked overnight in cold water	salt and pepper
4 large garlic cloves, unskinned	½ cup thick yogurt
3½ cups Brown Onion Stock (see below)	1 level tsp curry paste
3 tbsp dry sherry	fresh coriander (cilantro) leaves, to garnish
a pinch of freshly grated nutmeg	

1 Drain the chestnuts and put them in a saucepan. Cover with cold water, bring to the boil, and simmer for 20–30 minutes or until tender, then drain.
2 Put the garlic and chestnuts on a baking tray and roast in the oven at 400°F for 20 minutes or until the garlic is soft to the touch and the chestnuts are lightly browned. Cool slightly, then pop the garlic cloves out of their skins.

3 Put the garlic, chestnuts, and stock in batches in a blender or food processor and process until smooth. Pour into a saucepan, add the sherry, and season with nutmeg, salt, and pepper. Bring to the boil, then reduce the heat and simmer for 10–15 minutes.
4 Mix the yogurt with the curry paste. Serve the soup in warmed bowls, topped with yogurt and garnished with coriander leaves.
SERVES 8

BROWN ONION STOCK

Caramelizing the onions before adding the other ingredients produces a stock with a strong, slightly sweet flavor and a good brown color.

2 tbsp vegetable oil	a few sage leaves, thyme stalks and parsley stalks or 2 level tsp dried mixed herbs
2 large onions, skinned and roughly chopped	
2 garlic cloves, skinned and halved	2 bay leaves
2 celery sticks, washed and chopped	1 level tsp yeast extract (optional)
2 carrots, washed and chopped	salt

1 Heat the oil in a large, heavy-based saucepan. Add the onions and cook, stirring all the time, for about 10 minutes or until they turn a dark golden brown. Be careful not to let the onions burn. Add the remaining vegetables, herbs, and yeast extract, if using. Cook over a high heat for 4–5 minutes or until the vegetables are lightly browned.
2 Add 1 qt water to the pan and bring to the

boil. Season with salt, lower the heat and simmer gently for 30 minutes. Pass through a fine strainer into a bowl. The stock is now ready to use, or it can be returned to a clean saucepan and boiled rapidly to reduce the quantity and intensify the flavor. Cool and store in the refrigerator for 2–3 days or freeze for later use.
MAKES ABOUT 3½ CUPS

VEGETABLE STOCK

If using onion skins for color, remove them after 30 minutes or the stock will be bitter.

2 tbsp vegetable oil	vegetable trimmings, such as celery tops, cabbage leaves, Brussels sprouts leaves, mushroom peelings, tomato skins, and potato peelings
1 medium onion, skinned and finely chopped	
1 medium carrot, washed and diced	
2 oz turnip, washed and diced	onion skins (optional)
2 oz parsnip, washed and diced	bouquet garni
4 celery sticks, washed and roughly chopped	6 whole black peppercorns

1 Heat the oil in a large saucepan, add the onion and fry gently for about 5 minutes or until soft and lightly colored.
2 Add the other vegetables to the pan with any vegetable trimmings, outer leaves or peelings available. If a dark brown colored stock is required, add onion skins.
3 Cover the vegetables with 7½ cups cold water and add the bouquet garni and peppercorns. Bring to the boil.
4 Half-cover the pan and simmer the stock for 1½ hours, skimming occasionally with a slotted spoon.
5 Strain the stock into a bowl and leave to cool. Cover and chill in the refrigerator. This stock will only keep for 1–2 days, after which time it will begin to go sour.
MAKES ABOUT 1 QT

MUSHROOM STOCK

Dried mushrooms are expensive but they have a really strong flavor. Use this special stock for risottos, soups, and stir-fries.

1 tbsp vegetable oil	¼ oz packet dried porcini (cepe) mushrooms
¼ lb open-cap mushrooms, roughly chopped	a few fresh herb sprigs, such as thyme, rosemary, and parsley
1 onion, skinned and roughly chopped	
2 carrots, washed and roughly chopped	salt and pepper
½ head of fennel, roughly chopped	

1 Heat the oil in a large saucepan. Add the mushrooms, onion, carrots, and fennel and fry for 5 minutes or until softened. Add the dried mushrooms, the herbs and 7½ cups water. Bring to the boil and simmer for 45–50 minutes.
2 Pass the stock through a fine strainer into a bowl and season with salt and pepper. The stock is now ready to use, or it can be returned to a clean saucepan and boiled rapidly to reduce the quantity and intensify the flavour. Cool and store in the refrigerator for 2–3 days or freeze for later use.
MAKES ABOUT 1½ QT

—Three—

ALADS

The days when a salad consisted of tired lettuce leaves, a sliced tomato, and a limp piece of cucumber are over – or at least they should be. Market stalls and supermarkets now positively abound with brilliant displays of fruits and vegetables.

To start with, cast your eye over the varieties of lettuces now on offer. New, interesting, well flavored leaves are appearing all the time, from the ubiquitous Romaine and Iceberg, to exotica like the frilly leaved frisée or curly endive, or the russet brown Feuille de Chêne (Oak Leaf). Other interesting varieties worth looking out for are batavia, Lollo Rosso (Red Lollo) and Quattro Stagioni (Four Seasons) and the bitter, dark red radicchio.

Mâche, a delicate green leaf which is not a true lettuce, but a weed native to Europe, is now cultivated and makes a delicious addition to any salad bowl. Arugula, with its distinctive, peppery taste, is not a lettuce but a salad herb. It's experiencing a revival and makes a spectacular salad dressed simply with olive oil.

Whichever variety you choose, the leaves should be firm and crisp with no signs of browning or insect damage. To prepare, pull off and discard any damaged outer leaves and wash the lettuce thoroughly in plenty of cold water. Drain thoroughly and dry in a clean dish-towel or salad spinner. Transfer the clean leaves to plastic bags and store in the salad drawer in the refrigerator.

Not all salads are based on lettuce. Experiment with your own favorite combinations of vegetables, fruits, nuts, seeds, pulses, and pasta, tossed with one of the dressings on pages 181–194 to create your own masterpieces. If it's a salad based on robust ingredients like root vegetables, pulses, rice, pasta, dried fruit, seeds, nuts, and grains, add the dressing when everything is freshly cooked and still warm. Leave to cool, stirring occasionally, so that the flavors have time to be absorbed and mellow. Delicate leaf- and herb-based salads tend to flop if dressed too soon, so get everything ready and toss together at the last minute.

Finally, if you get the opportunity, take advantage of the ever-growing range of edible flowers that appears in stores in the summer. A few scattered on top of leafy salads make an eye-catching display.

HOT SPICED CHICK-PEA SALAD

Serve this hot salad with wholewheat bread for a light lunch or with baked potatoes or a rice dish as a main meal.

1 tbsp vegetable oil	two 1 lb cans cooked chick-peas, drained
1 medium onion, skinned and chopped	1 tbsp lemon juice
2 level tsp ground turmeric	¼ cup chopped fresh coriander (cilantro)
1 level tbsp cumin seeds	salt and pepper
1 lb tomatoes, roughly chopped	fresh coriander leaves, to garnish

1 Heat the oil in a saucepan, add the onion, and cook for 5–10 minutes or until golden brown, stirring constantly.
2 Add the turmeric and cumin seeds and cook, stirring, for 1–2 minutes. Add the

remaining ingredients. Cook for 1–2 minutes, stirring frequently.
3 Taste and adjust the seasoning, if necessary, before serving garnished with fresh coriander.
SERVES 4

ℬABY VEGETABLE AND PASTA SALAD

This salad is meant to be served lukewarm rather than hot or cold. However, if you would like to make it in advance and serve it cold, cool the vegetables and pasta completely and refrigerate until required. Let them come to room temperature before spooning them on top of the salad leaves.

¾ lb dried pasta shapes, such as ruotini, penne, conchiglie, or fusilli	¼ cup olive oil
salt and pepper	3 tbsp home-made or bought Pesto (see page 193)
1½ lb mixed baby vegetables, such as zucchini, patty pan squash, asparagus tips, sugar snap peas, and leeks	¼ lb black olives
	¼ lb cherry tomatoes
	a handful of mixed salad leaves
	a few chopped fresh herbs (optional)

1 Cook the pasta in boiling salted water for 5–10 minutes or until tender.
2 Meanwhile, prepare the vegetables, leaving them whole wherever possible. Any larger, slower cooking vegetables, such as patty pan squash, should be halved or quartered. Steam the prepared vegetables until just tender.
3 Whisk together the olive oil and Pesto.

Drain the pasta and put it in a large bowl with the Pesto mixture, the steamed vegetables, and the olives and tomatoes. Toss well together. Put the salad leaves in the bottom of a large serving bowl and spoon over the pasta mixture. Sprinkle with herbs, if using, and serve immediately.
SERVES 6

𝒢REEK SALAD

Feta, a Greek cheese, is available in supermarkets as well as Greek and Middle Eastern shops. Traditionally, feta is made from sheep's milk, but nowadays it is often made from cow's milk or a mixture of the two. It is milky white in color, with a crumbly texture and salty taste.

1½ lb beefsteak tomatoes	**For the dressing**
1 large cucumber	9 tbsp olive oil
2 medium red onions, skinned and thinly sliced	3 tbsp lemon juice
¼ lb black olives, stoned	3 level tbsp chopped fresh coriander (cilantro)
½ lb feta cheese	a good pinch of sugar
	salt and pepper

1 Cut the tomatoes into bite-sized chunks, discarding the cores. Cut the cucumber into bite-sized chunks.
2 Whisk the dressing ingredients together in a pitcher or shake together in a screw-top jar (go easy on the salt because of the saltiness of olives and feta cheese).

3 Put the tomatoes, cucumber, and onions in a large bowl, add the olives, and toss the ingredients together with your hands. Pour over the dressing and toss gently to mix, then crumble over the feta cheese. Serve as soon as possible.
SERVES 4–6

$\mathcal{T}$OMATO AND RED ONION SALAD

1½ lb mixed tomatoes, halved	4 tsp balsamic vinegar
1 large red onion, skinned and finely chopped	salt and pepper
¼ cup olive oil	

1 Combine the tomatoes and onion.
2 Whisk together the remaining ingredients and season with salt and pepper. Pour over

the tomatoes, toss well, and leave to marinate for at least 20 minutes before serving.
SERVES 6

$\mathcal{O}$RANGE AND GARLIC SALAD

Make the most of ready-prepared bags of salad with this delicious dressing.

2 garlic cloves, skinned and crushed	salt and pepper
¼ cup olive oil	a selection of mixed lettuce leaves, such as oak leaf, curly
1 tbsp red wine vinegar	endive, and lollo rosso
finely grated rind and juice of 1 small orange	

1 Put the garlic in a small bowl and mix to a paste with 1 tsp olive oil. Whisk in the vinegar, remaining olive oil, orange rind, and 3 tbsp orange juice. Season to taste.

2 Pour the dressing over the mixed salad leaves, toss well and serve immediately.
SERVES 4

$\mathcal{T}$OMATO AND ARTICHOKE SALAD

14 oz can artichoke hearts, drained and halved	3 tbsp olive oil
1 lb ripe tomatoes, quartered	2 level tbsp fromage blanc
1 large garlic clove, skinned and crushed	salt and pepper
4 tsp lemon juice	1 small onion, skinned and roughly chopped

1 Arrange the artichoke hearts and tomatoes in a serving dish.
2 Whisk together the garlic, lemon juice, oil, and fromage blanc. Season with salt and

pepper and stir in the roughly chopped onion.
3 Spoon the dressing over the vegetables, cover and chill for about 30 minutes.
SERVES 4

Tomato and Red Onion Salad *top*, Orange and Garlic Salad *bottom*

HERB OMELET SALAD

If available, use the classic *fines herbes* mixture of parsley, tarragon, chives, and chervil to flavor the omelets. See page 56 for more information about omelet-making.

4 free-range eggs, beaten	*1 large sweet green pepper, cored, seeded, and cut into strips*
2 tbsp chopped fresh herbs (see above)	
salt and pepper	*1 small head of fennel, trimmed and thinly sliced*
vegetable margarine or butter	*1 bunch of scallions, trimmed and cut into strips*
1 large sweet red pepper, cored, seeded, and cut into strips	*½ cucumber, cut into thin strips*
	1 quantity Vinaigrette Dressing (see page 185)

1 Beat the eggs with the herbs and 2 tbsp water. Season with salt and pepper. Heat a knob of margarine or butter in an omelet pan and use the eggs to make two thin, lightly set omelets. Turn out on to a sheet of parchment paper, roll up, and leave to cool slightly. Toss the remaining ingredients together.
2 Thinly slice the omelet and toss over the salad. Serve immediately.
SERVES 4

BULGAR WHEAT SALAD

This salad is excellent as part of a buffet and is simple to double up to serve larger numbers.

1¼ cups bulgar wheat	*2 level tbsp chopped fresh mint*
½ cucumber	*2 level tbsp chopped fresh parsley*
salt and pepper	*¼ cup olive oil*
½ sweet green pepper, cored, seeded, and diced	*3 tbsp lemon juice*
½ sweet red pepper, cored, seeded, and diced	*1 garlic clove, skinned and crushed*
1 bunch of scallions, trimmed and chopped	*1 lb tomatoes, sliced*
¼ lb feta cheese, diced	*¼ lb hazelnuts, toasted and skinned*

1 Soak the bulgar wheat in 1¼ cups boiling water for about 30 minutes or until the water has been absorbed, stirring occasionally.
2 Meanwhile, roughly chop the cucumber, sprinkle with salt, and leave for 15 minutes. Rinse, drain, and dry. Blanch the peppers in boiling water for 1 minute, then drain.
3 If necessary, drain the bulgar wheat. Mix with all the other ingredients, except the tomatoes and hazelnuts. Season with salt and pepper, cover, and refrigerate until required.
4 Serve on a bed of sliced tomatoes topped with the hazelnuts.
SERVES 6

SPICED CAULIFLOWER SALAD

In this recipe, the cauliflower is stirred into the dressing while it is still warm to gain maximum flavor from the spices.

1 bunch of scallions, trimmed	2 level tbsp mango chutney
6 tbsp vegetable oil	3 tbsp white wine vinegar
2 level tsp ground coriander	3 tbsp light cream
1 level tsp ground cumin	¼ cup chopped fresh parsley
1 level tsp ground turmeric	salt and pepper
2 oz unsalted cashew nuts	1 medium cauliflower

1 Cut the scallions into ½ inch lengths. Heat the oil in a small frying pan. Add the spices, scallions, and nuts and cook, stirring, for 2–3 minutes, then tip into a large bowl.
2 Roughly chop the mango chutney and stir it into the bowl with the vinegar, cream, and 3 level tbsp chopped parsley. Season with salt and pepper.
3 Divide the cauliflower into small florets and

cook in boiling salted water for 2–3 minutes only. Drain and, while still warm, stir into the dressing. Leave to marinate for several hours, turning occasionally. Taste and adjust the seasoning, if necessary.
4 To serve, spoon the salad into a glass bowl and garnish with the remaining chopped parsley.
SERVES 6

RAW VEGETABLES WITH GARLIC DRESSING

This vividly colored salad is excellent served with broiled and fried dishes (see pages 111–118), or as a starter served with warm lemon bread. Make lemon bread like garlic bread but omit the garlic and flavor the butter with grated lemon rind and a few chopped fresh herbs.

6 oz carrots, trimmed and peeled	2 tbsp wine vinegar
6 oz zucchini, trimmed	½ level tsp sugar
6 oz celery root, trimmed	½ level tsp mustard powder
1 tbsp lemon juice	1 garlic clove, skinned and crushed
6 oz raw beet, trimmed and peeled	salt and pepper
6 tbsp olive or vegetable oil	chopped fresh parsley, to garnish

1 Grate the carrots and zucchini into a bowl.
2 Peel and grate the celery root, toss immediately in the lemon juice, and add to the carrot and zucchini mixture. Lastly, grate the beet and add to the mixture.
3 Put the oil, vinegar, sugar, mustard, and garlic in a screw-top jar and season with salt

and pepper. Shake the jar until the dressing is thoroughly combined.
4 Pour the dressing over the vegetables and toss lightly just to coat. Serve immediately, garnished with chopped parsley.
SERVES 4

$\mathcal{B}$ROILED VEGETABLE SALAD

This cold vegetable dish is good as part of a summer barbecue or buffet.
The vegetables and dressing can be prepared separately well in advance and mixed just before
serving. The blanching water makes an excellent base for vegetable stock (see page 42).

1 sweet red pepper	
1 sweet green pepper	
¼ lb zucchini, trimmed	
about 6 whole garlic cloves	
1 bunch of asparagus, trimmed	
olive oil for brushing	
a few cherry tomatoes	
chopped fresh herbs, such as basil, marjoram, parsley, and chives	

For the dressing

2 tsp balsamic or garlic vinegar
1 tsp runny honey
1 level tsp Dijon-style mustard
5 tbsp olive oil
salt and pepper

1 Halve the peppers and remove the seeds and cores. Cut each half into four. Thickly slice the zucchini on the diagonal. Remove the loose, papery outer skins from the garlic cloves, but leave the inner skins attached.

2 Pour enough water to come to a depth of about 2 inches into a saucepan, and bring to the boil. When the water is boiling fast, add the peppers and the garlic. Bring back to the boil and boil for 1 minute. Remove the peppers with a slotted spoon (leaving the garlic in the water), refresh under cold running water and leave to drain. Repeat this process with the zucchini, using the same water. Remove the garlic from the pan and drain.

3 Steam the asparagus until just tender (see page 53). Drain, arrange on a serving plate, and leave to cool. Brush the blanched peppers, zucchini and garlic with a little olive oil and cook under a hot broiler until the vegetables are flecked with brown. Turn the vegetables over, brush with more oil, and cook the second side. Leave to cool, then arrange on the serving plate with the asparagus. Halve the tomatoes and scatter over the vegetables.

4 To make the dressing, put the vinegar, honey, and mustard in a small bowl, and whisk together with a fork until well blended. Gradually whisk in the olive oil to make a very thick dressing. Season with salt and pepper.

5 Just before serving, drizzle the dressing over the vegetables and sprinkle with herbs.
SERVES 3 AS A MAIN COURSE OR 4–6 AS AN ACCOMPANIMENT

WILD RICE AND THYME SALAD

If fresh lima beans are out of season, use frozen instead, or replace them with any cooked beans of your choice.

5 oz green beans, topped, tailed, and halved	*2 oz chanterelles, trompets des morts, or small button mushrooms, roughly sliced*
salt and pepper	*2 level tbsp chopped fresh thyme*
5 oz shelled lima beans	*2 tbsp walnut oil*
⅓ cup wild rice	*2 tbsp white wine vinegar*
1 cup long-grain white rice	*1 level tbsp Dijon-style mustard*
¼ cup vegetable oil	

1 Cook the green beans in boiling salted water for 10–12 minutes or until they are just tender. Drain, refresh under cold running water, and set aside to cool completely. Cook the lima beans in boiling salted water for 5–7 minutes. Drain and refresh under cold running water, slipping off their outer skins if wished, and set aside to cool completely.

2 Cook the wild rice in a large pan of boiling salted water for 25 minutes, then add the long-grain white rice. Boil together for a further 10 minutes or until both are just tender. Drain and refresh under cold running water. Stir together the green beans, lima beans, and rice in a large mixing bowl.

3 Heat the vegetable oil in a small frying pan and fry the mushrooms with the thyme for 2–3 minutes, stirring constantly. Remove from the heat and stir in the walnut oil, vinegar, and mustard. Season with salt and pepper, spoon into the rice mixture and stir well. Taste and adjust the seasoning, if necessary. Cool, cover, and leave to stand for at least 30 minutes before serving.
SERVES 6–8

$\mathscr{S}$WEET ONION SALAD

To make sure pearl onions stay whole when cooked, simply trim the root end when peeling – don't remove it completely. This salad is delicious with baked potatoes and nut burgers.

1 lb pearl onions	1 bay leaf
²⁄₃ cup red wine	2 level tbsp soft light brown sugar
⅓ cup olive oil	salt and pepper
3 level tbsp tomato paste	

1 Put the pearl onions in a large bowl and pour over enough boiling water to cover. Leave to soak for 3–4 minutes, then drain and peel.
2 Put the onions in a saucepan with all the remaining ingredients. Season with salt and pepper, cover, and simmer for 20 minutes or until the onions are tender but still retain their shape. Stir occasionally to prevent the sugar burning on to the pan.
3 Spoon the contents of the pan into a bowl, cool, cover, and chill in the refrigerator for 10–15 minutes before serving, or keep for up to 2 days.
SERVES 3–4

$\mathscr{S}$PINACH AND CORN SALAD

If fresh baby corn is not available, look for the precooked canned variety. Alternatively, toss sliced, boiled new potatoes into the salad instead.

¼ lb fresh young spinach, washed and dried	1 tbsp white wine vinegar
6 oz fresh baby corn	2 level tsp Dijon-style mustard
salt and pepper	1 level tsp sugar
¼ cup olive oil	¼ lb alfalfa sprouts or sprouted beans of your choice
1 garlic clove, skinned and crushed	1 head of endive, shredded

1 Remove any coarse stalks from the spinach. Halve the corn cobs lengthways and cook in boiling salted water for about 10 minutes or until just tender. Drain and refresh under cold running water.
2 Whisk together the olive oil, garlic, vinegar, mustard, and sugar. Season with salt and pepper.
3 Mix the spinach, corn, alfalfa sprouts, and endive in a salad bowl. Pour over the dressing, toss well, and serve immediately.
SERVES 6–8

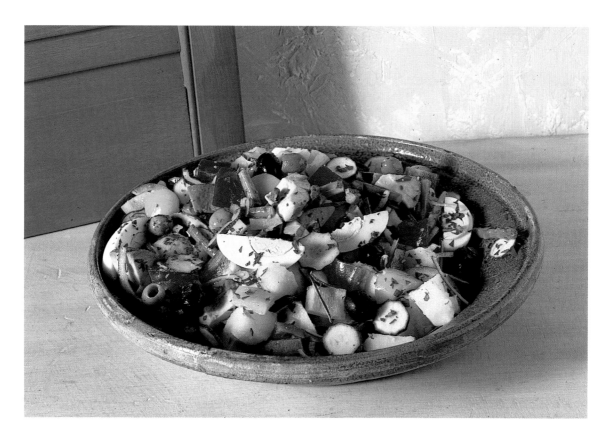

$\mathscr{P}$EASANT SALAD

This hearty, colorful salad makes a meal in itself. The best way to steam asparagus is to stand it, tied in a bundle, tips upwards, in about 2 inches of simmering salted water in a saucepan. Cover the tips with a tent of foil and cook for 5–8 minutes (depending on the thickness of the asparagus). The stems cook in the simmering water, while the delicate tips are gently steamed.

1½ lb potatoes	1 sweet yellow pepper, cored, seeded, and chopped
salt	chopped fresh parsley
3 free-range eggs	2 zucchini, trimmed and very thinly sliced
1 lb asparagus (or 1 large bundle), trimmed	2 oz green or black olives
1 avocado	3 tbsp capers
2 small red onions, skinned, halved, and thinly sliced	3 tbsp mayonnaise
1 sweet red pepper, cored, seeded, and chopped	1 quantity Mustard and Parsley Dressing (see page 185)

1 Cook the potatoes in boiling salted water for about 15 minutes or until tender. Cook the eggs in boiling water for about 10 minutes or until hard-boiled. Drain, cover with cold water, and leave to cool.
2 Steam the asparagus (see above).
3 Drain the potatoes. Leave to cool slightly, then peel off the skins, if preferred. Cut the potatoes into large chunks. Cut off the asparagus tips and reserve. Chop the stems into 1 inch pieces. Shell the eggs and cut into wedges. Peel and stone the avocado, and cut the flesh into chunks.
4 Mix all the ingredients together in a serving bowl. Whisk the mayonnaise into the dressing and pour over the salad. Toss together and serve immediately.
SERVES 8

*T*ZATZIKI

Different versions of this Greek dish are found in countries stretching from the Near East to India. The Turkish version is known as *cacik* and the Indian version is known as *raita*. It can be served as a salad, a sauce, or a dip, depending on the proportion of yogurt to solid ingredients used.

¼ cucumber	*2 tbsp chopped fresh mint or ½ tsp concentrated mint*
about 1¼ cups thick plain yogurt	*sauce*
1 garlic clove, skinned and crushed (optional)	*salt and pepper*
1 scallion, trimmed and finely chopped (optional)	*paprika*

1 If making a salad, halve the cucumber lengthways, then slice thinly into crescents. If making a sauce or a dip, finely chop the cucumber.
2 Mix the cucumber with the remaining ingredients and season with salt, pepper, and paprika.
VARIATIONS
Omit the garlic and scallion. Substitute fruit for the cucumber, such as one sliced banana or one finely chopped dessert apple. If liked, add one seeded and very finely chopped fresh green chili. Substitute chopped fresh coriander (cilantro) for the mint.

Raita is usually a much simpler mixture made with less cucumber and without garlic or scallion. Serve as a cooling accompaniment to curries and fried dishes.
MAKES ABOUT 1¼ CUPS

*M*USTARDY POTATO SALAD

Smooth-skinned waxy potato varieties, such as Maine or Long Island, make excellent potato salads.

1½ lb very small potatoes, thoroughly washed	*5 tbsp mayonnaise*
salt and pepper	*2 level tbsp whole-grain mustard*
1 cup fromage blanc	*2 level tsp Dijon-style mustard*

1 Cook the potatoes in boiling salted water for about 10 minutes or until tender. Meanwhile, mix together the remaining ingredients and season to taste with salt and pepper.
2 When the potatoes are cooked, drain them well, and add them to the mayonnaise mixture, mixing well so the potatoes are completely covered. Leave to cool before serving.
SERVES 4

—Four—

Omelets, Soufflés, and Pancakes

The perfect omelet, soufflé, or pancake is much easier to make than culinary myth would have us believe. In reality, once a few basic principles are grasped, no special skill is required for any of them.

An essential for both pancake- and omelet-making is a good heavy-based pan. Ideally, it should be kept solely for pancake- or omelet-making and should never be washed or scrubbed, just carefully wiped out with paper towels after use. It is also a good idea to store the pan wrapped, either in its original box or in paper towels, to prevent the surface becoming scratched. When buying a pan, choose one with a base that measures about 8–9 inches across, with or without a non-stick coating. The added advantage of a non-stick coating is that less fat is needed, making it the best choice if you're watching your weight.

A new pan should be "seasoned" before it is used for cooking. If available, follow the manufacturer's instructions; otherwise fill the pan with oil and heat it gently until hot. Repeat the process once or twice to seal the surface of the pan. Pour out the oil and the pan is ready for action. When cooking an omelet or pancake, heat the empty pan first so that the mixture begins to cook as soon as it is added to the pan; slow cooking makes them tough.

For soufflé-making, a deep, straight-sided soufflé dish with a perfectly smooth inside gives the most spectacular result. Grease it thoroughly to help the mixture glide up the sides. The basic soufflé mixture, or panada, is simply a very thick sauce mixture usually made with flour, butter, or margarine and milk. The egg yolks are always separated from the white and beaten into the panada, then the egg whites are whisked and folded in. The sauce must be cooled sufficiently first, or the yolks will scramble. Ideally, for the greatest volume, whisk the egg whites in a metal bowl; copper is best, but stainless steel is also good. Ensure that the whisk and bowl are spotlessly clean; if there is even a trace of grease lurking in the bowl the whites won't whisk to volume. When folding together the panada and whisked whites, a large metal spoon or a plastic spatula is best.

Finally, a word about eggs. Following recent scares involving the salmonella virus, it is prudent to treat eggs carefully. Free-range eggs are best. Buying from a farm shop or other reputable supplier with a fast turnover ensures that the eggs really are free-range and that they are fresh. Always check the date marked on the packet, store the eggs in the refrigerator (preferably in the egg box) and use within 2 weeks of purchase. To test an egg for freshness, put it in a bowl of water. If it floats it is bad; a fresh egg will sink. Bring eggs to room temperature just before using; eggs that are too cold are difficult to whisk to sufficient volume.

MELET

An omelet must be served immediately so have a warmed plate ready along with an
accompanying salad and warmed baguettes.

2–3 free-range eggs per person

salt and pepper

1 tbsp milk or water per person

vegetable margarine or butter for frying

1 Whisk the eggs just enough to break them
down; don't make them frothy as overbeating
spoils the texture of the finished omelet.
Season with salt and pepper and add the milk
or water.

2 Place an omelet or non-stick frying pan
over a gentle heat and, when it is hot, add a
generous knob of vegetable margarine or
butter, and heat until it is foaming but not
brown.

3 Add the beaten eggs. Stir gently with a fork
or wooden spatula, drawing the mixture from
the sides to the center as it sets and letting the
liquid egg in the center run to the sides.
When the eggs have set, stop stirring and
cook for another minute until the omelet is
golden brown underneath and still creamy on
top. Don't overcook or the omelet will be
tough.

4 If making a filled omelet, add the filling at
this point. Tilt the pan away from you slightly
and use a spatula to fold over a third of the
omelet to the center, then fold over the
opposite third. Slide the omelet out on to a
warmed plate, letting it flip over so that the
folded sides are underneath. Serve at once.

OMELET FILLINGS
Fines herbes Add 1 level tbsp finely
chopped fresh chervil, chives, and tarragon or
a large pinch of mixed dried herbs to the
beaten egg mixture before cooking.
Cheese Grate 1½ oz cheese. Put half of it in

the center of the omelet before folding.
Sprinkle the rest over the finished omelet.
Tomato Skin and chop 1–2 tomatoes and fry
in a little butter or vegetable margarine in a
saucepan for 5 minutes or until soft and pulpy.
Put in the center of the omelet before folding.
Mushroom Thickly slice about 2 oz
mushrooms and cook in vegetable margarine
or butter until soft. Put in the center of the
omelet before folding. (When available, wild
mushrooms make a delicious filling.)
Curried Vegetable Roughly chop leftover
vegetables, such as potato, green beans, lima
beans, or parsnips. Fry in oil with about
½ level tsp curry powder and a little garlic
until heated through.
Lovage and Blue Cheese Add 2 level tsp
finely chopped fresh lovage to the beaten egg
mixture. Cut 1–2 oz Blue Cheshire, Blue
Stilton, or Roquefort cheese into thin slices
and scatter over the omelet before folding.
Goats' Cheese Soften about 1 oz mild
goats' cheese and blend with a little fromage
blanc. Season with salt and pepper and put in
the center of the omelet before folding.
Soy Sauce For this Indonesian omelet, omit
the salt and flavor the eggs with 1–2 tsp soy
sauce. Serve with Peanut Sauce (see page 24).

A spoonful or two of Ratatouille (page 96),
Pesto (page 193) or steamed spinach seasoned
with nutmeg all make good omelet fillings.

$\mathscr{S}$PINACH AND MUSHROOM OMELET

Serve with warm crusty bread to mop up the delicious creamy mushroom sauce.

½ lb frozen chopped spinach, thawed and thoroughly drained	3 tbsp vegetable margarine or butter
4 free-range eggs	¼ lb button mushrooms, sliced
¼ level tsp grated nutmeg	2 level tsp whole-grain mustard
salt and pepper	⅔ cup sour cream

1 Pureé the spinach in a blender with the eggs, nutmeg, and salt and pepper to taste.
2 Melt half the margarine or butter in a frying pan, add the mushrooms and mustard, and cook for about 5 minutes or until soft. Add the sour cream, season with salt and pepper, and bring to the boil. Reduce the heat and simmer very gently.

3 Heat the remaining margarine or butter in a large non-stick frying pan. When foaming, add the spinach mixture. Cook until the base sets, then cook the top under a hot broiler.
4 Spoon the mushrooms on one half of the omelet and flip over the other half to enclose the mixture. Serve immediately.
SERVES 2

$\mathscr{T}$ORTILLA ESPAGNOLE

A Spanish tortilla, or omelet, should be much thicker than an ordinary omelet. Use a good heavy-based non-stick frying pan about 10 inches in diameter to get the right depth with this number of eggs.

about ¼ cup olive oil	6 large free-range eggs
1 lb waxy potatoes, peeled and diced	salt and pepper
2 medium onions, skinned and sliced	

1 Heat half the oil in a heavy-based, non-stick frying pan. Add the potatoes and onions and cook over a high heat for 1–2 minutes, stirring all the time, so that the potatoes are coated with oil and sealed on all sides.
2 Reduce the heat and cook for 5–10 minutes or until the potatoes are soft. Loosen any sediment at the bottom of the pan with a wooden spatula. Add a little extra oil, if necessary, and heat for a minute until very hot. Beat the eggs with a fork and season with

salt and pepper. Stir into the hot oil.
3 Cook over a high heat for 1–2 minutes, then reduce the heat and cook until the eggs are just set. Loosen the tortilla from the sides of the pan, then turn it out on to a serving plate.
4 Heat the remaining oil in the pan, then add the tortilla, browned side up, and cook for a further 1–2 minutes. Serve warm or cold, cut in wedges.
SERVES 4

Spinach and Mushroom Omelet

Plat du Jour

Omelette

Pommes frites

CARROT AND BUTTER BEAN SOUFFLÉS

Canned chick-peas could be used in place of the butter beans. If you prefer to use home-cooked beans, make sure that you cook them until really soft or they will spoil the texture of the soufflés.

1 lb carrots, trimmed, peeled and thinly sliced	3 oz Gruyère or Gouda cheese, grated
salt and pepper	3 free-range eggs, separated
2 tbsp vegetable oil	2 level tbsp chopped fresh coriander (cilantro)
1 level tbsp wholewheat flour	2 level tsp medium oatmeal or fresh brown breadcrumbs
1 lb can butter beans, drained and rinsed	

1 Cook the carrots in boiling salted water for 10–12 minutes or until well softened. Drain well, reserving ⅔ cup of the cooking water.
2 Heat the oil in a saucepan. Add the flour and cook, stirring, for 1 minute. Remove from the heat and gradually add the reserved water. Bring to the boil, stirring, then reduce the heat, and simmer for 2 minutes.
3 Put the carrots, sauce, butter beans, cheese and, egg yolks in a food processor. Process until well mixed and almost smooth. Season

with salt and pepper. Turn into a bowl and fold in the coriander. Whisk the egg whites until stiff and fold carefully into the mixture.
4 Spoon into four 2 cup capacity well-greased, deep, individual, ovenproof dishes. Sprinkle with the oatmeal or breadcrumbs.
5 Bake in the oven at 400°F for 20–25 minutes or until golden brown and just firm to the touch. Serve immediately.
SERVES 4

CHEESE SOUFFLÉ

Use a proper straight-sided soufflé dish to get the best rise. Run your finger around the edge of the mixture before it goes into the oven to achieve the classic "hat" effect.

1 level tbsp freshly grated Parmesan cheese	2 level tsp Dijon-style mustard
scant 1 cup milk	salt and pepper
slices of onion and carrot, 1 bay leaf, and 6 black peppercorns, for flavoring	cayenne pepper
2 tbsp vegetable margarine or butter	4 free-range eggs, separated
2 level tbsp all-purpose flour	3 oz mature Cheddar cheese, finely grated
	1 free-range egg white

1 Grease a 1½ quart soufflé dish. Sprinkle the Parmesan into the dish and tilt the dish, knocking the sides gently until they are evenly coated with cheese.
2 Put the milk in a saucepan with the flavoring ingredients. Bring slowly to the boil, then remove from the heat, cover, and leave to infuse for 30 minutes. Strain off and reserve

the milk.
3 Melt the margarine or butter in a saucepan and stir in the flour and mustard. Season with salt, pepper, and cayenne, and cook gently for 1 minute, stirring. Remove from the heat and gradually stir in the milk. Bring to the boil slowly and continue to cook, stirring, until the sauce thickens. Cool a little.

4 Beat the egg yolks into the cooled sauce one at a time. Sprinkle the Cheddar cheese over the sauce, reserving 1 level tbsp. (At this stage, the mixture can be left to stand for several hours if necessary.)

5 Stir in the cheese until evenly blended. Using a hand or electric mixer, whisk all the egg whites until they stand in stiff peaks.

6 Mix one large spoonful of egg white into the sauce to lighten its texture. Gently pour the sauce over the remaining egg whites and carefully fold the ingredients together. Do not overmix; fold lightly, using a metal spoon, until the egg whites are just incorporated.

7 Pour the soufflé mixture gently into the prepared dish. The mixture should come about three-quarters of the way up the side of

the dish. Sprinkle with the reserved cheese.

8 Stand the soufflé on a baking sheet and cook in the oven at 350°F for about 30 minutes. When cooked, the soufflé should be golden brown on the top, well risen and just firm to the touch, with a hint of softness in the center.
SERVES 4

VARIATIONS
Don't use too great a weight of filling or the soufflé will be heavy. Omit the cheese and add one of the following:
Blue Cheese Use a blue cheese, such as Stilton or Roquefort.
Mushroom 4 oz mushrooms, chopped and cooked in margarine or butter.

$\mathscr{S}$PINACH AND GRUYÈRE SOUFFLÉ

Gruyère or Emmenthal gives a good cheesy flavor but, of course, any other cheese can be used instead.

1 lb fresh spinach, cooked or ½ lb frozen leaf spinach, thawed	salt and pepper
4 tbsp vegetable margarine or butter	3 free-range eggs, separated
3 level tbsp all-purpose flour	¼ lb Gruyère or Emmenthal cheese, grated
scant 1-cup milk	1 free-range egg white

1 Grease a 1¼ quart soufflé dish. Put the spinach in a strainer and press to remove all moisture. Chop finely.

2 Melt the margarine or butter in a saucepan, add the spinach, and cook for a few minutes to drive off any remaining liquid.

3 Add the flour and cook gently for 1 minute, stirring. Remove the pan from the heat and gradually stir in the milk. Season with salt and pepper and bring to the boil slowly. Reduce the heat and continue to cook, stirring, until thickened. Cool slightly,

then beat in the egg yolks, one at a time, and 3 oz grated cheese.

4 Whisk all four egg whites together until stiff, then fold into the mixture. Spoon into the prepared soufflé dish and sprinkle with the remaining cheese.

5 Stand the dish on a baking sheet and bake in the oven at 375°F for about 30 minutes or until well risen and just set. Serve immediately.
SERVES 3–4

BASIC PANCAKES

Pancake batter should be left to stand for about 20 minutes to allow the starch granules to swell; the resulting pancake will be lighter. Use this basic recipe and the variations to create your own sweet or savory pancake dishes. Almost any mixture of cooked vegetables, pulses and nuts, moistened with one of the sauces in the chapter on page 181 can be used as a pancake filling.

1 cup all-purpose flour (all white or half wholewheat and half white)	1 free-range egg
	about 1¼ cups milk
pinch of salt	vegetable oil

1 Sift the flour and salt into a bowl. Make a well in the center.

2 Break the egg into the well and add a little of the milk. Mix the liquid ingredients with a wooden spoon, then gradually beat in the flour until smooth.

3 Add 1 tbsp oil and the remaining milk to obtain the consistency of thin cream.

4 Alternatively, the batter can be made by placing all the ingredients in a blender, and blending for a few seconds until smooth.

5 Cover the batter and leave to stand in the refrigerator for about 20 minutes.

6 Heat a pancake pan until hot, then brush with the minimum of oil, and wipe off any excess. Add a little extra milk to the batter if it has thickened. Pour a small amount of batter into the pan and swirl it around until it is evenly and thinly spread over the bottom of the pan. Cook over a moderate to high heat for about 1 minute or until the edges are curling away from the pan and the underside is golden. Flip the pancake over using a spatula and cook the second side.

7 Turn the pancake out on to a sheet of parchment paper (or wax paper if the

pancakes are to be frozen). Loosely fold a clean dish towel over the top.

8 Repeat until all the pancake batter has been used, lightly oiling the pan between pancakes.

MAKES ABOUT 8 PANCAKES

VARIATIONS

Buckwheat Pancakes Prepare as above, replacing half the flour with buckwheat flour. Don't sift the flour.

Spiced Chick-pea Pancakes Prepare as above, replacing the flour with 1 cup chick-pea (gram) flour. Toast 2 level tsp cumin seeds under the broiler, then grind to a powder. Add to the flour with ¼ level tsp ground turmeric. Replace ⅔ cup of the milk with water. Use a little more batter each time to make slightly thicker pancakes. Use more oil if necessary.

Sweet Pancakes Use the same basic mixture to make sweet pancakes. Serve sprinkled with sugar and lemon juice or drizzled with honey or maple syrup. Sweet pancakes can be filled with apple purée, bananas, or soft fruits, such as strawberries or raspberries, mixed with cream, yogurt or fromage blanc.

PANCAKE HINTS

1 To freeze pancakes, cool, then pack interleaved with wax paper, and freeze for up to 3 months. Thaw overnight at cool room temperature. Reheat wrapped in foil.

2 Pancakes can be wrapped and stored in the refrigerator for several days.

3 To warm pancakes, wrap small stacks in foil. Heat at 375°F for about 15 minutes.

4 Tortillas (see page 66) are a good vegan alternative to pancakes. They can be used in any of the following recipes.

Spinach-Filled Basic Pancakes

CRESPELLE

Crespelle, sometimes called *crespellini*, are Italian-style pancakes. They are similar to cannelloni in appearance but are made from a pancake batter rather than a pasta dough. Fillings can be as varied as those for cannelloni, so there is no reason to stick to this combination of cheese and spinach, which comes from Florence.

1 lb washed fresh spinach, cooked, or ½ lb frozen leaf spinach, thawed	⅔ cup freshly grated Parmesan cheese
	2½ cups Béchamel Sauce (see page 189)
4 tbsp vegetable margarine or butter	salt and pepper
1 small onion, skinned and finely chopped	8 Basic Pancakes (see left)

1 Drain the spinach well and chop finely.
2 Melt the margarine or butter in a saucepan, add the onion, and fry gently for 5 minutes or until soft but not colored. Stir in the spinach and cook for a further 2 minutes. Remove from the heat and stir in ½ cup Parmesan cheese and 6 tbsp béchamel sauce. Season with salt and pepper.
3 Spread an equal amount of the filling on each pancake, leaving a border around the edge. Roll up the pancakes loosely.
4 Arrange the pancakes in a single layer in a buttered ovenproof dish, then pour over the remaining béchamel sauce, and sprinkle with the remaining Parmesan cheese.
5 Bake in the oven at 425°F for 15–20 minutes or until golden brown.
SERVES 4

RATATOUILLE PANCAKES

Buckwheat pancakes, with their distinctive nutty flavor, make the most suitable partners for a ratatouille filling. If buckwheat flour is unavailable, pancakes made with half all-purpose and half wholewheat flour would be the next best thing. Serve with a crisp salad.

½ quantity Ratatouille (see page 96)	about ½ cup freshly grated Parmesan or Cheddar cheese
8 Buckwheat Pancakes (see page 62)	chopped fresh parsley

1 Divide the ratatouille between the pancakes. Fold to enclose the filling, then arrange in a single layer, seam-side down, in a lightly greased gratin dish.
2 Cover with foil and bake in the oven at 400°F for 20–25 minutes or until the pancakes are heated through. Sprinkle with the cheese and parsley and serve immediately.
SERVES 4–6

SPICY VEGETABLE PANCAKES

This filling can be made in advance, cooled and stored in the refrigerator ready for reheating when required. If you forget to warm the pancakes, fill them with the vegetable mixture, arrange them in a greased ovenproof dish, cover with foil, and bake in the oven at 400°F for 20–25 minutes.

2 level tbsp grated creamed coconut	½ lb potato, peeled and finely diced
2 tbsp vegetable oil	¼ lb tomatoes, skinned, seeded, and roughly chopped
½ lb onions, skinned and sliced	1 sweet green pepper, cored, seeded, and roughly chopped
1 garlic clove, skinned and crushed	
2 level tsp ground coriander	2 tbsp lemon juice
½ level tsp chili powder	salt and pepper
¼ level tsp ground turmeric	about 8 Spiced Chick-pea Pancakes (see page 62), warmed
¾ lb small cauliflower florets	

1 Dissolve the coconut in 1 scant cup hot water.
2 Heat the oil in a large frying pan. Add the onion and garlic with all the spices and cook, stirring, for 2–3 minutes or until the onions are just beginning to soften.
3 Add the cauliflower and the potato, cover and cook gently for 7–8 minutes or until just beginning to soften. Stir in the tomato and green pepper with the coconut water.
4 Cover and simmer gently for about 25 minutes or until the vegetables are tender and the liquid is reduced. Stir in the lemon juice and season with salt and pepper.
5 Divide the filling among the warm pancakes and serve immediately.
SERVES 4–6

$\mathscr{S}$OUFFLÉED BROCCOLI PANCAKES

The crispness of these baked pancakes complements the soft soufflé filling. Each pancake is fairly substantial so serve only with a simple salad.

¼ cup milk	⅓ cup all-purpose flour
1 slice each of onion and carrot for flavoring	3 free-range eggs, separated
4 black peppercorns	large pinch of grated nutmeg
1 bay leaf	2 oz mature Cheddar cheese, grated
½ lb broccoli florets	about 6 Buckwheat Pancakes (see page 62)
salt and pepper	2 level tbsp grated Parmesan cheese
4 tbsp vegetable margarine or butter	

1 Put the milk in a small saucepan with the onion and carrot slices, peppercorns, and bay leaf. Bring just to the boil, remove from the heat, cover, and leave to infuse for about 15 minutes. Strain and discard the flavorings.

2 Cook the broccoli in boiling salted water for 7–8 minutes or until tender, then drain.

3 Melt the margarine or butter in a saucepan, add the flour, and cook for 1–2 minutes. Remove from the heat and gradually stir in the flavored milk. Bring to the boil, stirring all the time; the mixture will be very thick. Allow to cool a little, then beat in the egg yolks.

4 Put the broccoli and sauce in a food processor or blender and blend until smooth. Transfer to a bowl, stir in the nutmeg and Cheddar cheese, and season with salt and pepper.

5 Whisk the egg whites until stiff, but not dry. Stir 2 level tbsp of the egg white into the broccoli mixture to lighten it, then carefully fold in the remainder.

6 Spoon a generous amount of the broccoli mixture down the middle of each pancake. Fold the two sides loosely over the top, then arrange the pancakes side by side in a shallow ovenproof dish. Sprinkle the Parmesan cheese over the top.

7 Bake in the oven immediately, uncovered, at 400°F for 15–20 minutes or until the soufflé mixture has risen and set and the pancakes are crisp.

SERVES 3–4

ENCHILADAS

If you find the tortillas have cooled too much and become stiff and dry after frying, then immerse each one in the sauce to make it pliable before filling. To make vegan enchiladas, omit the cheese and add an extra can of beans to the filling. Sprinkle the top with a few breadcrumbs.

1¼ cups wholewheat flour
1¼ cups all-purpose white flour
salt and pepper
4 tbsp white vegetable shortening
vegetable oil for frying
1–2 garlic cloves, skinned and crushed
1–2 fresh green chilies, chopped

1 sweet green pepper, cored, seeded, and chopped
1 lb cooked red kidney beans or two 1 lb cans red kidney beans, drained and rinsed
3 tbsp chopped fresh coriander (cilantro)
1½ quantities Tomato Sauce (see page 190)
a few drops of Tabasco
½ lb Cheddar cheese, grated

1 To make the tortillas, sift the flours and 1½ level tsp salt into a bowl, adding any bran left in the strainer. Rub in the vegetable shortening. Gradually stir in about ⅔ cup warm water, or enough to make a pliable dough.

2 Turn the dough on to a lightly floured surface and knead for a few minutes, then divide it into eight equal pieces. Roll out each piece into a 9 inch circle, keeping the remaining pieces of dough covered with a damp cloth.

3 Heat a large, heavy-based frying pan and brush lightly with oil. Cook the tortillas, one at a time, for 1–2 minutes on each side or until lightly flecked with brown and slightly puffed up. When all the tortillas are cooked, stack them between parchment paper.

4 To make the filling, heat about 2 tbsp oil in the frying pan and fry the garlic, chilies and green pepper for about 10 minutes or until the pepper is very soft. Meanwhile, mash the beans with ⅔ cup water, using a potato masher. Add them to the pan and keep frying and mashing until the mixture is very soft and mushy. Stir in the coriander and season with salt and pepper.

5 Heat the tomato sauce and flavor with Tabasco. Divide the fried bean mixture equally between the tortillas. Sprinkle with half the cheese, then roll up to enclose the filling. Arrange, seam-side down, in a gratin dish. Pour the sauce over the top and sprinkle with the remaining cheese. Bake in the oven at 400°F for 20–25 minutes or until piping hot.

SERVES 4–6

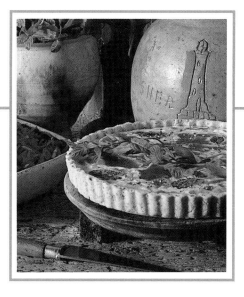

—FIVE—

$\mathscr{P}$ASTRIES, $\mathscr{P}$IES, AND

$\mathscr{T}$ARTS

The art of making good pastry lies in light, careful handling and accurate measuring. For most pastries, all-purpose white or wholewheat flour is best; self-rising gives an uneven, crumbly texture.

A good range of ready-made pastries is now available in the shops. Puff and flaky pastry are available frozen or in the chilled cabinet and produce such a good result without the time and effort involved in making them at home, that we have used the store-bought kind in the following recipes. Likewise, commercially-produced filo pastry is now so widely available, that home-made strudel pastry is a rarity. Vegans should read the labels on the packets carefully when buying ready-made pastry to check the ingredients are suitable.

We recommend that most tarts and some pies should be baked blind before the filling is added. This ensures that the pastry is cooked through and remains crisp. Make the pastry and line the tart pan or dish following the recipe, then, if you have time, chill the pastry in the refrigerator for about 30 minutes. This 'rests' the pastry and helps to prevent it shrinking when cooked. This is particularly important if you have over-stretched the pastry when lining the pan. Once chilled, prick the pastry base with a fork and line with a large piece of foil or parchment paper. Fill with ceramic 'baking beans' or dried pulses (retain some purely for this purpose). Bake in the oven at 400°F for 10–15 minutes or until the pastry is firm to the touch. Remove the beans and paper and bake for a further 5–10 minutes or until the base is firm and lightly colored. Pastry cases which need complete baking should be returned to the oven for a further 15 minutes or until firm and golden brown.

For small pastry cases, it should be sufficient to prick well with a fork before baking. Pastry cases which have been baked blind will keep for several days in an airtight tin, and freeze well.

PROVENÇALE PASTRY

This well flavored, crisp pastry is best for tarts and quiches. Vegans should omit the egg and increase the oil to 5 tbsp and the water to about 3–4 tbsp.

2 cups all-purpose white flour	¼ cup olive oil
large pinch of salt	lukewarm water
1 free-range egg, beaten	

1 Put the flour and salt in a bowl. Make a well in the center and add the egg, olive oil, and 2–3 tbsp lukewarm water. Mix vigorously with a fork or your fingers until the pastry forms a dough.

2 Knead the dough lightly, then form into a ball, cover with a damp dish towel, and leave to rest for 30 minutes before rolling out. Use and bake as directed in individual recipes.

VARIATIONS
Olive Pastry Follow the recipe and method for Provençale Pastry, but stir in 2 oz finely chopped black or green olives before adding the liquid.
Cumin Pastry Follow the recipe and method for Provençale Pastry, but fry 1 level tsp crushed cumin seeds in the oil for 2–3 minutes. Cool before adding to the flour.

$\mathscr{S}$HORTCRUST PASTRY

For shortcrust pastry, the proportion of flour to fat is two to one. Therefore, for a recipe using quantities of shortcrust pastry other than ½ lb, simply use half the quantity of fat to the flour weight specified. This basic pastry is suitable for most pies and tarts. To make a sweet pastry, add a little sugar to taste.

2 cups all-purpose white flour	*1 cup vegetable margarine or butter, chilled and diced*
pinch of salt	*chilled water*

1 Put the flour and salt in a bowl. Using both hands, rub the margarine or butter lightly into the flour until the mixture resembles fine breadcrumbs.

2 Gradually add 3–4 tbsp water, sprinkling it evenly over the surface. (Uneven addition may cause blistering when the pastry is cooked.) Stir with a round-bladed knife until the mixture begins to stick together in large lumps.

3 With one hand, collect the dough together to form a ball. Knead lightly for a few seconds to give a firm, smooth dough. Do not overhandle the dough.

4 To roll out, sprinkle a little flour on a work surface and the rolling pin (not on the pastry) and roll out the dough evenly in one direction only, turning it occasionally. The usual thickness is ⅛ inch. Do not pull or stretch the pastry.

5 The pastry can be baked straight away, but it is better if allowed to 'rest' for about 30 minutes in the pan or dish, covered with parchment paper or foil, in the refrigerator.

6 Bake at 400–425°F, except where otherwise specified, until lightly browned (see individual recipes).

VARIATIONS
Wholewheat Pastry (1) Follow the recipe and method for Shortcrust Pastry but use wholewheat flour instead of white. You will need to add a little extra water because wholewheat flour is usually more absorbent.

Wholewheat Pastry (2) Follow the recipe and method for Shortcrust Pastry, but replace half the flour with wholewheat flour.

Nut Pastry Follow the recipe and method for Shortcrust Pastry using white or wholewheat flour, or half and half, but stir in ½ cup very finely chopped walnuts, peanuts, cashew nuts, hazelnuts, or almonds before adding the water. When using salted nuts, do not add salt to the flour.

Cheese Pastry Follow the recipe and method for Shortcrust Pastry using white or wholewheat flour, or half and half, but stir in 4 oz finely grated Cheddar or other hard cheese, or 3 level tbsp freshly grated Parmesan cheese, and a pinch of mustard powder before adding the water.

Sesame Pastry Follow the recipe and method for Shortcrust Pastry using white or wholewheat flour, or half and half, but stir in ¼ cup toasted sesame seeds before adding the water.

Poppy Seed Pastry Follow the recipe and method for Shortcrust Pastry using white or wholewheat flour, or half and half but stir in 2 tbsp poppy seeds before adding the water.

Herb Pastry Follow the recipe and method for Shortcrust Pastry using white or wholewheat flour, or half and half, but stir in 3 level tbsp chopped fresh mixed herbs before adding the water.

ARTE PROVENÇALE

This delicious tart combines all the classic flavors of Provence – eggplant, green pepper, tomato, garlic, olives, marjoram, and basil.

1 quantity Provençale Pastry (see page 68)
2 level tbsp Dijon-style mustard
10 oz eggplant, very thinly sliced
1 small sweet green pepper, halved, cored, and seeded
olive oil for brushing
3 free-range egg yolks
1½ cups heavy cream

1 small garlic clove, skinned and crushed
6 oz mature Cheddar cheese, grated
salt and pepper
2 large tomatoes
a few black olives
a few chopped fresh herbs, such as parsley, marjoram and basil

1 Roll out the pastry on a lightly floured surface and use to line a greased shallow 11 inch round loose-bottomed, fluted tart pan. Spread the mustard over the pastry case, cover, and chill while preparing the filling.

2 Spread the eggplant in a single layer on an oiled baking sheet. Lay the green pepper halves, cut side down, on a chopping board, and cut into very fine slices. Sprinkle over the eggplant and brush with a little olive oil. Bake in the oven at 400°F for 20 minutes or until the vegetables are slightly softened and tinged with brown.

3 Beat together the egg yolks, cream, garlic, and cheese, and season with salt and pepper.

Slice the tomatoes thickly and, using a sharp knife, remove and discard the seeds from each slice.

4 Arrange the tomato slices in a single layer in the pastry case. Top with the eggplant and pepper slices and sprinkle with the olives. Carefully pour the custard mixture over the vegetables so that it just comes to the top of the pastry case. Stand the tart on a baking sheet and bake in the oven at 400°F for 30 minutes. Sprinkle with the herbs, then continue cooking for 15–20 minutes or until the custard has set. Serve warm or cold.
SERVES 6–8

ICH LEEK TART

This is a really rich, moist, filling tart packed with leeks, cream and cheese. It is everything that a savory tart should be.

Shortcrust Pastry made with 2 cups flour (see page 69)
4 tbsp vegetable margarine or butter
2½ lb leeks, trimmed, washed and thinly sliced
1¼ cups sour or heavy cream

8 oz Gruyère cheese, grated
3 free-range eggs, beaten
salt and pepper
freshly grated nutmeg

1 Roll out the pastry and use to line an oiled 9 inch springform cake pan or a very deep tart pan. Cover and chill while making the filling.

2 To make the filling, melt the margarine or butter in a large heavy-based saucepan. Add the leeks and cook over a high heat for 2–3 minutes or until the leeks start to soften, stirring all the time. Cover the pan with a lid, lower the heat, and cook for about 30 minutes or until the leeks are very soft. Shake the pan from time to time, but resist lifting the lid or you will lose the steam and the leeks will stick to the pan.

3 Add the cream, most of the cheese, and the eggs, and season with salt, pepper and nutmeg. Pour into the prepared pastry case and sprinkle with the remaining cheese.

4 Stand the tart on a baking sheet and bake in the oven at 425°F for 15 minutes, then reduce the temperature to 375°F, and cook for a further 35–40 minutes or until the filling is set and golden brown. Serve warm or cold.

SERVES 8

$\mathscr{S}$WEET PEPPER AND BASIL TART

Broiling the peppers makes the skins easy to remove. It also makes them more digestible.

Shortcrust Pastry made with 1½ cups flour (see page 69)	*2 free-range eggs*
2 large sweet red peppers (about ¾ lb total weight)	*2 level tbsp chopped fresh basil*
a few strands of saffron	*1 level tbsp chopped fresh parsley*
5 oz full-fat soft cheese with garlic and herbs	*salt and pepper*

1 Roll out the pastry on a lightly floured surface. Place an 8 inch plain tart ring on a flat baking sheet and line with the pastry. Cover and chill for 10–15 minutes. Line the pastry with foil or parchment paper weighed down with baking beans and bake blind in the oven at 400°F for 20 minutes or until just cooked through. Remove the beans and paper or foil.

2 Meanwhile, place the peppers under a hot broiler and cook for 10–15 minutes, turning frequently, until the skins are charred and black. Cool slightly, then peel off the skins.

Halve the peppers and remove the seeds. Cut into 2 inch pieces.

3 Grind the saffron with a mortar and pestle or in a small heavy bowl with the end of a rolling pin. Whisk together the cheese, eggs, herbs, and saffron. Stir in the peppers and season with salt and pepper.

4 Spoon the pepper mixture into the prepared tart case. Bake in the oven at 350°F for 25–30 minutes or until just set. Brown under a hot broiler for 1 2 minutes, if wished. Serve warm.

SERVES 4

GREEN TOMATO AND BASIL TART

Try this before your tomatoes ripen. Herb or Poppy Seed Pastry would be best.

Shortcrust Pastry made with 2 cups flour (see page 69)	*1 level tsp sugar*
1 tbsp vegetable oil	*3 level tbsp chopped fresh basil*
1 large onion, skinned and chopped	*1 cup mayonnaise*
1 lb firm green tomatoes, thinly sliced	*salt and pepper*
½ lb mature Cheddar cheese, grated	

1 On a lightly floured surface, thinly roll out the pastry and use to line the base and sides of a deep 9 inch round, loose-bottomed, fluted tart pan. Chill for 30 minutes.
2 Line the pastry case with foil or parchment paper weighed down with baking beans and bake blind at 350°F for 20–25 minutes or until dry and golden.
3 Meanwhile, heat the oil in a frying pan, add the onion, and cook for 3–4 minutes, stirring. Add the tomatoes and cook for a further 3–4 minutes or until beginning to soften.
4 Transfer to a bowl and stir in all the remaining ingredients. Spoon into the pastry case and bake at 350°F for 30–35 minutes or until lightly set and golden brown on top. Serve warm.
SERVES 6–8

AVOCADO PIE

The nutty, garlicky crust for this pie can be made in advance and frozen or stored in an airtight container for up to 2 days. However, the filling will discolor if left for too long, so make it no more than 2 hours before you intend to serve it.

2 cups wholewheat breadcrumbs	*1 tbsp tahini (see page 14)*
¼ cup cashew nuts, almonds or hazelnuts, chopped	*½ cucumber, finely chopped*
large pinch of dried thyme	*2 scallions, trimmed and finely chopped*
1 garlic clove, skinned and crushed	*2 firm tomatoes, chopped*
8 tbsp vegetable margarine or butter, melted	*1 level tsp sugar*
salt and pepper	*Tabasco or chili sauce, to taste*
2 large ripe avocados	*a few black olives*
1 tbsp raspberry vinegar or lime juice	*chopped fresh coriander (cilantro), chives, parsley, or mint*

1 To make the crust, mix together the breadcrumbs, nuts, thyme, garlic, and margarine or butter. Season with salt and pepper. Press over the bottom and sides of a 9 inch quiche dish or loose-bottomed tart pan. Bake in the oven at 400°F for 25–30 minutes or until golden brown and firm to the touch. Leave to cool.
2 To make the filling, halve, pit, and peel the avocados and mash the flesh. Mix with all the remaining ingredients, except the olives and herbs. Spoon into the pastry case and sprinkle the olives and herbs on top of the pie. Serve within 2 hours or the pie filling will discolor.
SERVES 6

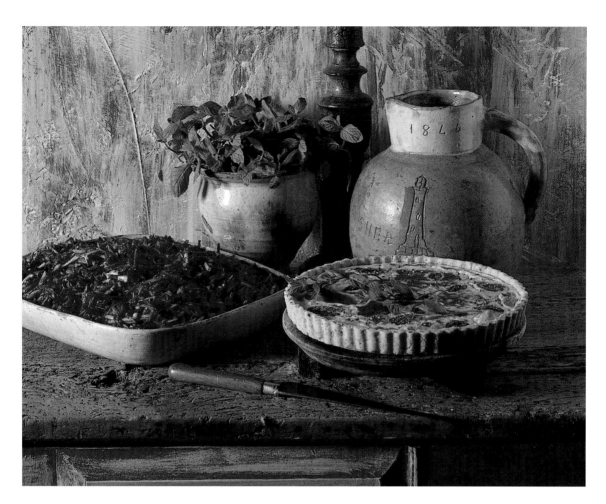

TARTE AU CHÈVRE ET MENTHE

This delicately flavored, creamy tart is delicious served for lunch with a salad, or in thinner slices as a starter, garnished with extra mint leaves.

Hazelnut Pastry made with 1½ cups flour (see page 69)	*2 free-range eggs*
6 oz mild fresh creamy goats' cheese (chèvre)	*salt and freshly ground black pepper*
1¼ cups fromage blanc	*a small handful of fresh mint leaves*

1 Roll out the pastry on a lightly floured surface and use to line a greased 9 inch shallow, loose-bottomed, fluted tart pan. Cover and chill while making the filling.

2 To make the filling, beat the cheese until smooth. Gradually beat in the fromage blanc, followed by the eggs. Season with salt and pepper.

3 Line the pastry case with foil or parchment paper weighed down with baking beans and bake blind in the oven at 400°F for 10–15 minutes, then remove the paper and beans, and bake for a further 5 minutes until the pastry base is cooked through.

4 Stir the filling, then pour it into the pastry case. Sprinkle with the mint leaves and grind a little black pepper over the top. Bake in the oven at 400°F for about 15 minutes or until firm to the touch. Cook under a hot broiler for 2–3 minutes until browned. Serve warm or cold.

SERVES 6

CATALAN PIE

When the recipes in this book were tested, this was one of the most popular. Based on a traditional Spanish pie, it is packed with flavor and texture. We liked it best served with a crisp mixed leaf salad. Before rolling out the pastry, check the size of your baking sheet. If the measurements given in the recipe are too large, make a shorter, squarer pie that will fit on your baking sheet.

1½ cups white bread flour, plus extra for sprinkling	*1 level tbsp mild chilli powder*
½ cup cornmeal (maize meal), plus extra for sprinkling	*1 lb ripe tomatoes, roughly chopped*
1 level tbsp sugar	*½ lb zucchini, trimmed and roughly chopped*
salt and pepper	*3 hard-boiled free-range eggs, peeled and chopped*
1 level tsp fast-action dried yeast	*3 tbsp raisins*
2 tbsp olive oil, plus extra for brushing	*2 tbsp capers*
¾ lb onions, skinned and roughly chopped	*¼ cup pine nuts*
2 large garlic cloves, skinned and crushed	

1 Put the flour, cornmeal, sugar, 1 level tsp salt, and the yeast in a bowl. Mix together, then make a well in the center and add ⅔ cup warm water. Stir together to make a dough, adding a little extra liquid if necessary.

2 Turn the dough on to a lightly floured surface and knead for 5–10 minutes or until smooth and elastic. Cover and leave to rise in a warm place for about 35 minutes or until doubled in size.

3 Meanwhile, heat the 2 tbsp olive oil in a heavy-based saucepan with a lid. Add the onions, garlic, and chili powder and cook over a high heat for 5 minutes, stirring all the time. Cover the pan, reduce the heat and cook for 15–20 minutes or until the onions are soft. Add the tomatoes and zucchini and cook for 5 minutes, stirring occasionally. If the mixture is very wet, cook over a high heat for a little longer to evaporate excess moisture. Add the eggs, raisins, capers, and pine nuts, season with salt and pepper, and leave to cool.

4 Turn the dough out on to a lightly floured surface and knead for 1–2 minutes. Divide it

in half and roll one half into a rectangle measuring about 13 × 10 inches. Transfer the dough to an oiled baking sheet and cover with the filling, spreading it almost to the edges.

5 Roll out the remaining dough to the same size and place on top of the filling. Twist the edges together to seal. Brush the pie with olive oil, cover loosely with a clean dish towel, and leave in a warm place until slightly risen.

6 Mark small indentations all over the pie with the end of a chopstick or your little finger. Sprinkle with cornmeal and bake in the oven at 450°F for about 20 minutes or until well risen and golden brown. Serve warm or cold.

SERVES 6

VARIATIONS

For a vegan version of this delicious pie, omit the eggs and replace with one of the following: 4 oz chopped tofu; 1 cup roughly chopped nuts; 4 oz cooked and slightly mashed red kidney beans; 4 oz cooked black-eyed beans.

*B*EAN AND POTATO PIE

Before rolling out the pastry, check that your baking sheet is large enough. If not, make the pie shorter and squarer to fit. Serve with a mixed salad or steamed fresh vegetables.

1 lb floury potatoes, peeled and roughly chopped	5 oz full-fat soft cheese with garlic and herbs
salt and pepper	½ lb cooked black-eyed beans or one 1 lb can black-eyed beans, drained and rinsed
2 tbsp vegetable oil	
1 large onion, skinned and chopped	freshly grated nutmeg
1 lb leeks, trimmed, washed and sliced	1½ lb frozen puff pastry, thawed
½ lb mushrooms, wiped and sliced	water, milk or beaten egg, to glaze
¼ lb fresh spinach, trimmed and washed	sesame seeds

1 Cook the potatoes in boiling, salted water for 10–15 minutes or until tender. Drain well and leave to cool.
2 Meanwhile, heat the oil in a large saucepan, add the onion and leeks, and fry for 5–10 minutes or until soft. Add the mushrooms and continue cooking until the mushrooms are soft. Add the spinach and cook for 1 minute or until the spinach is just wilted. Add the full-fat soft cheese, the beans, and potatoes and season generously with salt, pepper and nutmeg. Leave to cool.
3 Thinly roll out half the pastry on a lightly floured surface to a rectangle measuring about 13 inches long and 10 inches wide. Transfer the pastry to a baking sheet.
4 Spoon the filling on to the pastry, leaving a 1 inch border around the edges. Roll out the remaining pastry and use to cover the first. Brush the edges with water, milk or beaten egg and press together to seal. Lightly mark squares on the pastry with the back of a knife. Brush with milk or beaten egg and sprinkle with sesame seeds. Bake in the oven at 400°F for 30–35 minutes or until well risen and golden brown.
SERVES 6

*V*EGETABLE STRUDEL

Savory strudels are delicious. Vary the filling to make use of seasonal vegetables, or add a few cooked beans or nuts. Serve with steamed vegetables and one of the sauces on pages 181–194.

10 tbsp vegetable margarine or butter	1¼ cups fromage blanc
2 tbsp olive oil	ground mixed spice
1 lb waxy potatoes, peeled and diced	salt and pepper
1 lb parsnips, trimmed, peeled and diced	mild paprika
½ lb leeks, trimmed, washed and sliced	4 large sheets of filo pastry, each measuring 18 × 12 inches
1 small bunch of scallions, trimmed and chopped	
1 lb spring greens	¼ cup ground almonds
1 garlic clove, skinned and crushed	a few poppy seeds
15 ml (1 tbsp) lemon juice	

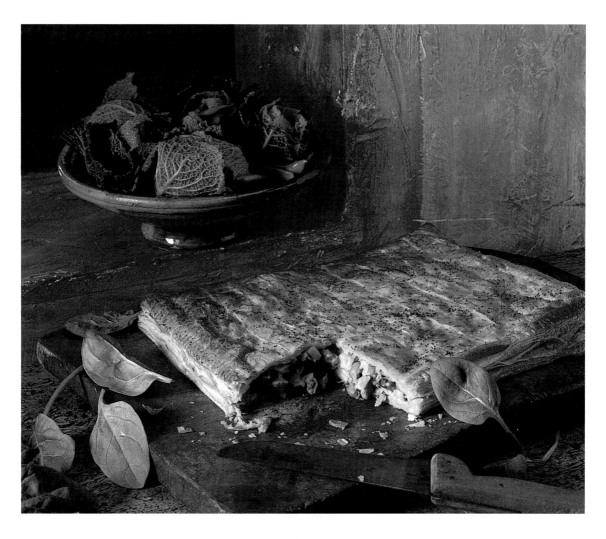

Vegetable Strudel

1 Melt 4 tbsp of the margarine or butter with half the olive oil in a large saucepan. Add the potatoes, parsnips, leeks, and scallions and fry for 4–5 minutes, stirring all the time. Add ¼ cup water, reduce the heat, cover, and cook gently for 10–15 minutes. Leave to cool.

2 Meanwhile, remove the tough stalks from the spring greens and discard. Finely shred the leaves. Heat 2 tbsp of the remaining margarine or butter with the remaining olive oil in a large frying pan, add the greens and garlic, and stir-fry for 2–3 minutes or until softened. Do not overcook. Stir in the lemon juice and leave to cool.

3 Stir the fromage blanc into the potato and leek mixture and season with a little mixed spice, salt, pepper, and paprika.

4 Melt the remaining margarine or butter. Lay one sheet of filo pastry on a clean work surface and brush lightly with melted fat.

Take a second sheet of pastry and place it so that it overlaps the first sheet to make an 18 inch square. Brush lightly with melted fat. Repeat with the remaining filo pastry to make a double thickness. Sprinkle the ground almonds evenly over the pastry.

5 Spoon half the potato mixture over the bottom quarter of the pastry, leaving a border around the edge. Top with the spring green mixture and the remaining potato.

6 Carefully fold the sides over the filling, then, starting from the filled end, roll the strudel up like a jelly roll. Carefully transfer to a baking sheet, seam-side down. Brush with melted fat, sprinkle with poppy seeds, and bake in the oven at 400°F for 20–25 minutes or until golden brown. Leave to stand for 5 minutes before serving.

SERVES 6

ROQUEFORT FEUILLETÉ

Roquefort is a little town in the northern hills of Languedoc in France and it is there, in the limestone caves, that this famous cheese gains its special flavor. Made from sheep's milk, it has a creamy texture and strong, salty taste.

2 tbsp vegetable margarine or butter	*freshly ground black pepper*
2 medium onions, skinned and sliced	*6 oz Roquefort cheese, crumbled*
¼ cup light cream	*½ lb frozen puff pastry, thawed*
1 level tbsp chopped fresh rosemary	*1 free-range egg, beaten*

1 Melt the margarine or butter in a frying pan, add the onion, and cook for 5–10 minutes or until it softens and begins to brown. Drain on paper towels and cool.
2 Whisk together the cream and rosemary, and season with pepper. Add the cheese.
3 Divide the pastry in half and roll out each piece thinly to an oblong about 12 × 8 inches. Place one on a baking sheet.
4 Spread the onion down the center of the pastry, leaving a clear border around the edge. Spoon over the cheese mixture. Brush the edges with beaten egg, then top with the second piece of pastry, sealing well. Trim and knock up the edges. Glaze the feuilleté with the remaining egg and decorate with strips made from pastry trimmings. Make a few holes in the top to allow steam to escape.
5 Bake in the oven at 425°F for 15 minutes or until well browned. Reduce the heat to 350°F, cover the feuilleté loosely with foil, and bake for a further 10 minutes. Cool slightly before serving.
SERVES 6

WILD MUSHROOM STRUDEL

This savory strudel relies on the use of wild mushrooms. Shiitake mushrooms are available fresh from some supermarkets and produce markets. Alternatively, replace them with fresh oyster mushrooms. If fresh wild mushrooms are not available, soak a small packet of dried *porcini* (cepe) mushrooms for 30 minutes in warm water, strain, and substitute for 2 oz of the total weight of mushrooms required.

1 cup long-grain brown rice	*2 level tsp chopped fresh oregano*
salt and pepper	*4 tsp soy sauce*
1 lb mixed mushrooms, such as shiitake, morel, flat, and field	*1 level tsp yeast extract*
	4 sheets of filo pastry, each measuring about 18 × 12 inches
5 tbsp vegetable margarine or butter	*sesame seeds*
1 lb leeks, trimmed, washed, and finely chopped	*Brandy and Celery Sauce (see page 194), to serve*
⅓ cup walnut pieces, finely chopped	

Wild Mushroom Strudel

1 Cook the rice in boiling salted water for about 20 minutes or until tender. Drain and cool. Finely chop the shiitake and morel mushrooms; roughly chop the flat and field mushrooms.

2 Melt 2 tbsp of the margarine or butter in a large frying pan. Add the leeks and fry for 1–2 minutes. Stir in the mushrooms and continue cooking for about 8 minutes or until quite tender and all excess moisture has been driven off. Mix in the walnuts, oregano, soy sauce, yeast extract, and rice. Season with salt and pepper, turn out into a bowl and leave to cool.

3 Melt the remaining margarine or butter. Layer up three sheets of pastry, brushing each sheet with melted margarine or butter. Cut in half crossways. You can leave the pastry whole here and make one long strudel, but we found shorter strudels were easier to roll up.

4 Spoon the filling over the two stacks of sheets, leaving a narrow border around the edge of each. Fold in the sides and roll up the strudels. Transfer to a lightly greased baking sheet and brush with melted margarine or butter. Crumple the remaining pastry decoratively on top, brush with the remaining margarine or butter, and sprinkle with sesame seeds.

5 Bake at 425°F for 25–30 minutes or until the pastry is crisp and golden. Serve accompanied by Brandy and Celery Sauce (see page 194).

SERVES 8

Tomato and Lentil Pie

This pie is light and moist in texture with a crumbly cheese crust. Serve hot, cold, or just warm with baked potatoes cooked in the oven at the same time as the pie.

¼ cup vegetable margarine or butter	1 level tsp dried basil
¼ lb leeks, trimmed, washed, and finely chopped	1 tbsp lemon juice
6 oz split red lentils	2 free-range eggs
1 garlic clove, skinned and crushed	salt and pepper
about 2 cups vegetable stock	2 cups all-purpose white flour
2 tomatoes, skinned and chopped	2 oz mature Cheddar cheese, finely grated

1 Melt 4 tbsp of the margarine or butter in a saucepan, add the leeks, and cook for about 10 minutes or until golden. Add the lentils and garlic and stir for 1–2 minutes to cover the lentils in fat. Add the stock, bring to the boil, then reduce the heat, half cover with a lid, and simmer for about 20 minutes or until the lentils are soft, stirring occasionally. (There should be little free liquid, so stir over a high heat to cook off any excess.) Cool slightly.
2 Remove the pan from the heat and add the tomatoes, basil, lemon juice, and 1 egg. Season with salt and pepper and leave to cool.
3 Meanwhile, make the pastry. Place the flour in a bowl and, using a fork, 'cut' in the remaining margarine or butter until the mixture resembles breadcrumbs. Stir in the cheese and add half the second egg, beaten, and about 3 tbsp cold water to form a soft dough.
4 Cover the pastry and chill for 15 minutes, then roll out two-thirds on a lightly floured surface and use to line an 8 inch quiche dish. Spoon in the cooled lentil mixture and level the surface. Roll out the remaining pastry and use to cover the pie, sealing the edges well. Brush with the remaining egg.
5 Bake in the oven at 400°F for 40 minutes or until golden brown.
SERVES 4–6

Spanakopittes

Serve these small triangular pastries with Tzatziki, Hummus, and olives to make a delicious Greek-style starter. They're also good for packed lunches or as part of a buffet (see the picture on pages 100–101).

2 tbsp olive oil	3 oz feta cheese, crumbled
1 small onion, skinned and chopped	1 egg, beaten
1 garlic clove, skinned and crushed	pepper
½ lb packet frozen chopped spinach, thawed and squeezed dry	6 oz filo pastry
	½ cup vegetable margarine or butter, melted

1 Heat the oil in a saucepan, add the onion and garlic, and fry gently for 5 minutes or until soft. Remove the pan from the heat and stir in the spinach, cheese, and egg. Season with pepper.
2 Cut the filo pastry sheets widthways into

2 inch strips. Cover with a slightly damp dish towel.

3 Brush one strip of the pastry with melted margarine or butter and place 1 tsp of the spinach mixture at the end of the strip.

4 Fold one corner of the strip diagonally over the filling, so the short edge lies on top of the long edge and forms a right angle.

5 Continue folding the pastry at right angles until you reach the end of the strip, forming a neat triangular package. Repeat with the remaining strips and filling to make about 50 triangles.

6 Place the packages, seam side down, in a large roasting pan, and brush with melted margarine or butter. Bake in the oven at 425°F for 15 minutes or until golden brown. Serve hot.

MAKES ABOUT 50

SPICY VEGETABLE PIE

Serve with steamed broccoli and green beans.

4 carrots, trimmed, peeled, and thinly sliced	*1¼ cups milk, plus 2 tbsp*
4 leeks, washed, trimmed, and thickly sliced	*4 oz Cheddar cheese, grated*
6 zucchini, washed, trimmed and thinly sliced	*¼ level tsp ground mace*
salt and pepper	*3 level tbsp chopped fresh coriander (cilantro) or parsley*
½ cup vegetable margarine or butter	*Wholewheat Pastry made with 1 cup flour (see page 69)*
1 onion, skinned and sliced	*beaten egg, to glaze*
2 level tsp ground cumin	*freshly grated Parmesan cheese*
½ cup wholewheat flour	*pinch of cayenne pepper or paprika (optional)*

1 Blanch the carrots, leeks, and zucchini in boiling salted water for 1 minute only. Drain.

2 Melt 3 tbsp margarine or butter in a heavy-based frying pan, add the onion and cumin, and fry gently for 5 minutes or until soft. Add the carrots, leeks, and zucchini, and fry for a further 5 minutes, stirring to coat in the onion mixture. Remove from the heat.

3 Melt the remaining margarine or butter in a separate pan, sprinkle in the flour, and cook for 1–2 minutes or until lightly colored, stirring constantly. Remove from the heat and gradually whisk in 1¼ cups milk. Return to the heat and simmer for 5 minutes or until thick and smooth, stirring constantly.

4 Stir in the Cheddar cheese and mace, and season with salt and pepper. Fold into the vegetables with the chopped coriander or parsley and 2 tbsp milk, then turn into a 1 quart ovenproof pie dish. Leave for 2 hours or until the pie filling is cold.

5 Meanwhile, make the pastry following the recipe on page 69. Cover and chill.

6 Remove the pastry from the refrigerator and roll it out on a lightly floured surface to a round or oval about 2 inches larger than the pie dish. Cut a strip from the outside edge of the pastry. Moisten the rim of the pie dish with water and place the pastry strip on the rim.

7 Use the remaining pastry as a lid. Moisten the strip of dough, then place the lid on top and press to seal. Trim, knock up, and flute the edge. Decorate the top with pastry trimmings. Brush the pastry with beaten egg and sprinkle with Parmesan and cayenne or paprika, if using. Bake in the oven at 375°F for 20–25 minutes or until the pastry is cooked. Serve hot.

SERVES 4

CHESTNUT PÂTÉ BRAID

A rich, well flavored filling enclosed by a plait of light, buttery brioche. If serving for a special occasion, such as Christmas, go to town on the decoration and make leaves and berries.

4 cups bread flour
2 level tsp fast-action dried yeast
2 level tsp salt
1 free-range egg, beaten
8 tbsp vegetable margarine or butter, melted
2 tbsp vegetable oil
1 level tsp dried thyme
2 celery sticks, trimmed and finely chopped
1 parsnip, trimmed, peeled, and finely chopped
1 onion, skinned and chopped
2 garlic cloves, skinned and crushed

1 lb can unsweetened chestnuts, drained and rinsed
½ lb open-cap mushrooms, wiped and finely chopped
¼ cup vegetable stock
1 tbsp hot horseradish relish
2 tbsp mushroom ketchup
salt and pepper
½ cup pitted prunes
⅓ cup shelled pistachios
2 tbsp chopped fresh parsley
beaten free-range egg, to glaze

1 Mix together the flour, yeast, and salt in a bowl. Make a well in the center, then pour in the egg, melted margarine or butter, and about 1 cup lukewarm water, or enough to make a soft, smooth dough. Beat thoroughly until the dough leaves the sides of the bowl clean.

2 Turn the dough on to a lightly floured surface and knead for about 10 minutes or until smooth and elastic. Put the dough in a large bowl, cover with a clean dish towel, and leave in a warm place for about 1 hour or until doubled in size.

3 Meanwhile, make the filling. Heat the oil in a large saucepan and fry the thyme, celery, parsnip, onion, and garlic for 5–10 minutes or until softened, stirring. Roughly chop half the chestnuts and add to the pan with the mushrooms, stock, horseradish relish, and ketchup. Cover the pan and cook for 15 minutes, stirring occasionally. Season generously with salt and pepper. Remove

from the heat and leave to cool.

4 Turn the dough on to a lightly floured surface and knead until smooth. Reserve a small piece for decoration and roll the remaining dough to a rectangle measuring 15 × 12 inches. Spoon the filling down the center of the dough, leaving a 3 inch border around the edges. Arrange the remaining chestnuts, the prunes, and pistachios down the center of the filling. Sprinkle with the parsley.

5 Cut the dough diagonally into ½ inch strips on either side of the filling. Fold each end over the filling, then braid the pastry over the filling to enclose it completely. Decorate with shapes cut from the reserved dough. Brush with beaten egg and transfer to a baking sheet. Bake in the oven at 400°F for about 30 minutes or until risen and firm to the touch. Leave to stand for 5 minutes, then remove, and transfer to a serving dish. Serve hot with Gravy (page 190).

SERVES ABOUT 6

Six—

Curries, Casseroles, and Stews

Here are beans, lentils, and vegetables combined with spices, flavorings, and herbs to make comforting, hearty meals. Influenced by the cuisines of several continents, the dishes in this chapter make cosmopolitan eating. Indian vegetarian food is always popular; a meal composed of several curry dishes, a delicately spiced basmati pilaff, Nan-style Bread (see page 155) served with chutney or raita is a good way to entertain a large group of people.

Chilled lager or lassi are the appropriate drinks to serve. In India, lassi is either sweet or salty. To make the salty version, mix equal quantities of plain yogurt and water in a blender or food processor. Add salt and toasted ground cumin or finely chopped fresh mint to taste. Sweet lassi is made in the same way but flavored with sugar, ground cardamom, or a little rosewater. Serve both salty and sweet lassi in tall glasses filled with crushed ice.

If you prefer something less spicy, try Rich Winter Casserole (see page 95), or Root Vegetable and Tahini Stew (see page 88). Serve these with good, old-fashioned accompaniments like dumplings, cobblers, and polenta (see page 142). Make dumplings by mixing 1 cup self-rising flour with 4 tbsp vegetable shortening. Add salt and chopped fresh mixed herbs to taste and enough water to mix to a smooth dough. Shape into small balls and add to the casserole or stew about 15–20 minutes before the cooking time is complete. Simmer gently on top of the stove or bake in the oven at 400°F unless otherwise stated. Don't let the liquid boil vigorously or the dumplings will disintegrate.

To make a cobbler topping, mix 2 cups self-rising flour with a pinch of salt and rub in 4 tbsp butter or margarine. Flavor with a few chopped herbs and a little cheese, then mix to a soft dough with milk. Knead together and roll out on a floured surface as if making biscuits. Cut out shapes and brush with milk. Arrange overlapping around the edge of the casserole, then bake in the oven at 425°F for 10–15 minutes or until golden brown.

Highly spiced or seasoned curries, casseroles, or stews tend to develop a faint 'musty' flavor after any length of time in the freezer. This is particularly true of strong garlic-flavored dishes, so if you're planning on long-term freezer storage it's wise to add the garlic when reheating. Casseroles thickened with flour may thin down on freezing, so it may be necessary to thicken the sauce again after reheating.

CAULIFLOWER IN CURRY SAUCE

This curry sauce can be used for other vegetables besides cauliflower. Potatoes, peas, okra, mushrooms, carrots, and eggplant can all be cooked in the same way as the cauliflower, although the cooking time will vary.

1 large cauliflower	1 level tsp salt
6 tbsp vegetable ghee or oil	1 level tsp ground turmeric
1 level tsp black mustard seeds	3 tomatoes, skinned and finely chopped
1 level tsp cumin seeds	1 small green chili, seeded and finely chopped
2 inch piece of fresh ginger root, peeled and finely chopped	½ level tsp sugar
	2 level tbsp chopped fresh coriander (cilantro)
1 small onion, skinned and finely chopped	

1 Divide the cauliflower into small florets, discarding the green leaves and tough stalks. Wash the florets well and dry on paper towels.
2 Heat the ghee or oil in a heavy-based saucepan or flameproof casserole. Add the mustard seeds and, when they begin to pop, stir in the cumin seeds, ginger, onion, salt, and turmeric. Fry for 2–3 minutes, stirring constantly.
3 Add the cauliflower and mix well to coat with the spice mixture. Stir in the tomatoes, chili, sugar, and half of the coriander. Cover the pan tightly with a lid and cook gently for 15 minutes or until the cauliflower is tender but not mushy.
4 Uncover the pan and boil rapidly for 1–2 minutes to thicken the sauce. Turn into a warmed serving dish and sprinkle with the remaining chopped coriander. Serve immediately.
SERVES 4 AS AN ACCOMPANIMENT

VEGETABLE CURRY

Don't be put off by this list of spices; mixing them yourself gives an infinitely better flavor than commercially prepared curry powder. Make coconut milk by mixing one 8 oz block of creamed coconut or one 3½ oz packet of instant coconut milk powder with 2½ cups boiling water. Serve this curry with plain boiled rice, pickles, and Nan-style Bread (see page 155) or Ajowan Parathas (see page 156).

1 medium onion, skinned and chopped	8 whole cloves
1 inch piece of fresh ginger root, peeled	8 green cardamom pods
1–2 garlic cloves, skinned	1 cinnamon stick
2 fresh green chilies, seeded	3 lb mixed vegetables, including cauliflower florets,
2 tbsp vegetable ghee or oil	carrots, potato, parsnip, turnip, and frozen peas,
2 level tsp ground turmeric	prepared as necessary and cut into large chunks
2 level tsp ground coriander	2½ cups coconut milk
2 level tsp ground cumin	salt and pepper
1 level tsp ground fenugreek	

1 Put the onion, ginger, garlic, and chilies in a blender or food processor and purée until almost smooth.
2 Heat the ghee or oil in a large, heavy-based saucepan, add the onion mixture, and fry for 5 minutes, stirring constantly. Add all the spices and cook over a high heat for 3–4 minutes, stirring all the time.
3 Add the vegetables to the pan and stir to coat in the spice paste. Gradually stir in the coconut milk and 1¼ cups water. Bring to the boil, then lower the heat, cover, and simmer for 45 minutes–1 hour or until the vegetables are just tender (the time depending on the type of vegetables used). Season with salt and pepper. Leave to stand for 5 minutes to let the flavors develop, then serve.
SERVES 4–6 AS A MAIN COURSE

VEGETABLE KORMA

This traditional southern Indian dish is extremely rich because it contains heavy cream and ground almonds. Serve it with a spinach curry, a rice pilaff, and a dal dish.

2 tbsp vegetable ghee or oil	2 level tsp ground turmeric
1 large onion, skinned and chopped	finely grated rind and juice of ½ lime or lemon
1–2 garlic cloves, skinned and crushed	½ cup ground almonds
1 inch piece of fresh ginger root, peeled and chopped	scant 1 cup heavy cream
1 tbsp coriander seeds	salt
1 tsp whole cloves	⅔ cup sliced almonds, toasted
2 tsp black peppercorns	3 tbsp chopped fresh coriander (cilantro) (optional)
6 green cadamom pods	
2 lb mixed vegetables, including some root vegetables, prepared as necessary, and cut into chunks	

1 Heat the ghee or oil in a large, heavy-based saucepan. Add the onion, garlic, and ginger and fry very gently, stirring frequently, for about 10 minutes or until soft and lightly colored.

2 Meanwhile, finely grind the whole spices and peppercorns in an electric grinder or using a mortar and pestle. Add to the pan and fry for 2 minutes, stirring all the time. Increase the heat, add the vegetables and turmeric, and fry for 1–2 minutes. Add the lime or lemon rind and juice, the almonds and 1¼ cups water. Cover and simmer gently for 30–40 minutes or until the vegetables are just tender (the time depending on the type of vegetables used).

3 Slowly stir in the cream and a little water if the korma is too dry. Season with salt and cook gently until heated through. Transfer to a warmed serving dish, sprinkle with the almonds and coriander, if using, and serve immediately.

SERVES 4–6 AS A MAIN COURSE

VARIATION

Tofu Korma (serves 3) Follow the above recipe up to adding the water in step 2. Bring to the boil, cover and simmer for about 20 minutes, stirring occasionally. Stir in the cream and ½ lb tofu and complete step 3.

PANEER

Paneer is a fresh, soft cheese frequently used in Indian dishes. It holds its shape well and cooks to a delicious golden brown color when fried or broiled. It's not widely available commercially, and there is no reasonable substitute, so it is worth making it at home. Use paneer in Indian dishes or chop it and sauté with spices, herbs, and vegetables of your choice. It's also good in stir-fries or in a sauce as a pancake filling. For a firm, creamy texture, use half and half; full-cream and low-fat give a softer result.

2½ quarts half and half full-cream or low-fat milk	about 5 tbsp strained lemon juice

1 Pour the half and half into a large, heavy-based saucepan and bring to a full rolling boil. Remove the pan from the heat and stir in the lemon juice.

2 Return to the heat and heat for about 1 minute until the curds and whey separate. If the curds do not separate after this time, return the pan to the heat and heat for 30 seconds more. If it still hasn't separated, add a little more lemon juice and heat again.

3 Line a colander with a double thickness of cheesecloth. Pour the mixture through the cheesecloth. Gather up the corners of the cheesecloth and squeeze all the liquid out of the curd.

4 Drain off the remaining whey by hanging the cheesecloth bundle from the faucets over the sink or from a suitable kitchen cabinet over a bowl. Leave it to drain for about 3 hours or until firm when squeezed. Paneer can be kept successfully in the refrigerator for up to 4 days.

MAKES ABOUT 10 OZ

VARIATIONS

Add any flavorings for paneer at the end of step 3.

Roasted Cumin Paneer Heat 1 tsp vegetable oil in a small frying pan. Add 2 level tsp cumin seeds and fry for 1–2 minutes, stirring all the time. Finely crush in a mortar and pestle.

Mixed Herb Paneer Add 2 level tbsp chopped fresh mixed herbs.

Garlic Paneer Add 1 small garlic clove, skinned and crushed.

Garlic and Herb Paneer Add 1 small garlic clove, skinned and crushed, and 2 level tbsp chopped fresh mixed herbs.

MUTTAR PANEER

Serve this dish as a main course, accompanied by Indian bread and a dal dish, such as Dry Moong Dal (see page 88).

10 oz Paneer (see left)	*1 level tsp garam masala*
vegetable oil for frying	*½ level tsp chili powder*
2 medium onions, skinned and roughly chopped	*¼ lb shelled fresh or frozen peas*
1 inch piece of fresh ginger root, peeled and roughly chopped	*4 small tomatoes, skinned and finely chopped*
1 garlic clove, skinned and crushed	*½ cup vegetable stock*
1 level tsp ground turmeric	*salt*
	2 level tbsp chopped fresh coriander (cilantro)

1 Cut the paneer into small cubes. Heat a little vegetable oil in a deep, heavy-based frying pan until very hot.

2 Add the cubes of paneer to the oil and fry until golden on all sides, turning once. Remove from the oil and drain on paper towels.

3 Pour off all but about ¼ cup of the oil. Add the onions, ginger, and garlic and fry gently, stirring frequently, for 10 minutes. Add the turmeric, garam masala, and chili powder and

fry for a further 2 minutes.

4 Add the peas and tomatoes to the pan and stir to combine with the spiced onion mixture. Add the stock, season with salt, then cover tightly, and simmer gently for 15 minutes or until the peas are tender.

5 Add the paneer and coriander. Shake the pan gently to mix the cheese with the peas. Simmer for a further 5 minutes before serving.

SERVES 3–4 AS A MAIN COURSE

ROOT VEGETABLE AND TAHINI STEW

This simple, earthy dish makes a satisfying meal on its own. Cut the vegetables into good-sized chunks to make sure the finished stew has plenty of texture.

2 tbsp vegetable oil	2 cups vegetable stock
½ lb carrots, trimmed, peeled, and sliced	2 bay leaves
½ lb parsnips, trimmed, peeled, and sliced	6 oz green beans, topped, tailed, and halved
½ lb all-purpose potatoes, peeled and roughly chopped	⅔ cup sour cream or fromage blanc
2 medium onions, skinned and chopped	3 tbsp sesame seeds, toasted
½ lb rutabaga, peeled and roughly chopped	salt and pepper
¼ cup tahini (see page 14)	

1 Heat the oil in a large heavy-based frying pan or flameproof casserole over a high heat. Add all the vegetables, except the green beans, and fry for 4–5 minutes or until they are just beginning to brown and soften.
2 Stir the tahini into the vegetable stock, then pour over the vegetables. Add the bay leaves. Bring to the boil, then reduce the heat, cover, and simmer for 15 minutes. Add the green beans, re-cover, and simmer for a further 20–25 minutes or until all the vegetables are tender.
3 Stir in the sour cream or fromage blanc and sesame seeds. Season with salt and pepper and serve immediately.
SERVES 4 AS A MAIN COURSE

DRY MOONG DAL

Serve this spicy, dry dal dish as part of an Indian-style meal. It's also delicious flavored with the finely grated rind of 1–2 lemons and crushed garlic, to taste.

½ lb moong dal (mung beans)	¼ level tsp ground turmeric
2 tbsp vegetable oil	pinch of cayenne pepper
2 level tsp ground cumin	salt
2 level tsp ground coriander	Crisp Fried Onions (see page 115), to serve

1 Pick over the dal and remove any grit or discolored pulses. Put into a strainer and wash thoroughly under cold running water. Drain well. Put the dal into a bowl and cover with cold water. Leave to soak for about 4 hours.
2 Drain the dal. Heat the oil in a large saucepan and stir in the cumin, coriander, turmeric, and cayenne. Add the drained dal and stir together. Add 1¼ cups water and season with salt.
3 Bring to the boil, then reduce the heat, cover, and simmer for 25–30 minutes or until the dal is tender and the water absorbed.
4 Turn the dal into a warmed serving dish and sprinkle with the onions. Serve hot.
SERVES 4–6 AS AN ACCOMPANIMENT

$\mathcal{B}$OSTON BAKED BEANS

There are many versions of this classic dark, rich New England dish and they all vary enormously, so much so that haricot beans and black molasses or treacle seem to be the only constants. The chili sauce and garlic are not particularly traditional and may be omitted if you prefer your beans less spicy. This recipe includes Worcestershire sauce, vegetarian brands of which are available. Check the label when buying.

1 lb dried haricot beans, soaked overnight in cold water	2 cups beer
2 onions, skinned and chopped	¼ cup tomato paste
2 level tbsp Dijon-style mustard	¼ cup vegetarian Worcestershire sauce
2 level tbsp dark brown sugar	2 tbsp chili sauce
5 tbsp black molasses	1 garlic clove, skinned and crushed
2 cups tomato juice	salt and pepper

1 Drain the beans. Put them in a large flameproof casserole and add enough fresh cold water to cover. Bring to the boil and boil rapidly for 10 minutes, then simmer for 45 minutes. Drain and return to the casserole with the remaining ingredients. Mix thoroughly together, season with salt and pepper, cover with a tightly fitting lid, and cook in the oven at 300°F for 4 hours or until the beans are very tender.

2 Check and stir the beans occasionally during cooking and add a little extra tomato juice or water, if necessary, to prevent them drying out. Taste and adjust the seasoning, if necessary, before serving.

SERVES 6–8 AS A MAIN COURSE

BEAN GOULASH

Use a mixture of beans of your choice for this dish, which is based on the Hungarian classic.

1 lb dried beans, such as black-eyed beans, kidney beans, or haricot beans, soaked overnight in cold water	1 level tbsp mild paprika
2 tbsp vegetable oil	1 level tsp sugar
1 lb onions, skinned and roughly chopped	2 level tbsp all-purpose flour
1 lb waxy potatoes, peeled and roughly chopped	1 quart vegetable stock
½ level tsp caraway seeds, crushed	1¼ cups sour cream or plain yogurt
¼ cup tomato paste	2 level tbsp chopped fresh parsley
	salt and pepper

1 Drain the beans and put them in a saucepan. Add enough fresh water to cover, then bring to the boil, and boil rapidly for 10 minutes.

2 Meanwhile, heat the oil in a large flameproof casserole and fry the onions and potatoes for about 10 minutes or until golden brown. Add the caraway seeds, tomato paste, paprika, and sugar and fry for 1–2 minutes.

Sprinkle in the flour and cook for 1 minute, then gradually add the stock. Bring to the boil, stirring all the time.

3 Drain the beans and add to the casserole. Bring back to the boil, cover, and simmer for 1–1½ hours or until the beans are tender. Stir in the sour cream or yogurt and parsley. Season with salt and pepper and serve.

SERVES 6 AS A MAIN COURSE

RED KIDNEY BEANS WITH GINGER AND CHILI

With their rich, creamy sauce, these red kidney beans are best served with plain boiled rice.

½ lb dried red kidney beans, soaked overnight in cold water, or two 1 lb cans red kidney beans, drained and rinsed	2 garlic cloves, skinned and crushed
2 tbsp vegetable ghee or oil	2–3 small green chilies, seeded and finely chopped
1 inch piece of fresh ginger root, peeled and finely chopped	⅔ cup light cream
	¼ cup tomato paste
	salt and pepper

1 Drain the dried beans and place in a large saucepan. Cover with plenty of fresh water, bring to the boil, and boil rapidly for 10 minutes. Reduce the heat, cover, and simmer for about 1½ hours or until tender, then drain.

2 Heat the ghee or oil in a heavy-based saucepan or flameproof casserole, add the ginger and garlic, and fry gently for 2

minutes. Add the chilies, the cream, and tomato paste. Add the cooked or canned kidney beans to the pan. Stir well to mix.

3 Cook over a gentle heat for 3–4 minutes or until thoroughly hot, but without boiling, stirring occasionally. Season with salt and pepper and turn into a warmed serving dish.

SERVES 4 AS A MAIN COURSE

Chick-peas Stewed with Tomatoes *left*, Ajowan Parathas *right (page 156)*

CHICK-PEAS STEWED WITH TOMATOES

Serve with boiled basmati rice flavored with cardamoms and cloves for a really nutrititious dinner.

½ lb dried chick-peas, soaked overnight, or two (1 lb) cans chick-peas, drained	1 level tbsp ground cumin
4 garlic cloves, skinned and crushed	1 level tbsp ground coriander
3 tbsp vegetable ghee or oil	1 level tsp garam masala
2 medium onions, skinned and finely chopped	4 ripe tomatoes, roughly chopped
2 small green chilies, seeded and finely chopped	2 level tbsp chopped fresh coriander (cilantro)
1 level tsp ground turmeric	1 level tbsp chopped fresh mint
1 level tsp paprika	salt and pepper

1 Drain the dried chick-peas and place in a large saucepan with half of the garlic. Cover with plenty of water, bring to the boil, cover, and simmer for 2–3 hours or until tender. Drain.

2 Heat the ghee or oil in a heavy-based saucepan, add the remaining garlic and the onions, and fry gently for about 5 minutes. Add the chilies and spices, and fry, stirring, for a further 1–2 minutes.

3 Add the tomatoes, coriander, and mint and cook, stirring, for 5–10 minutes or until the tomatoes turn to a purée.

4 Add the cooked or canned chick-peas and stir well. Simmer gently for another 5 minutes or until the chick-peas are heated through. Season with salt and pepper and serve hot.

SERVES 4 AS A MAIN COURSE

$\mathcal{P}$UY LENTILS COOKED WITH BAY

Puy lentils are tiny dark green lentils with a distinctive flavor. They hold their shape very well when cooked. Buy them in good stores and supermarkets. Here they are treated simply to enhance their delicious flavor.

1 medium onion, skinned	2 celery sticks or 1 carrot (optional)
about 8 whole cloves	salt and pepper
½ lb puy lentils	1 tbsp extra virgin olive oil
4 bay leaves	a splash of balsamic or red wine vinegar

1 Stick the cloves into the onion. Put this into a large saucepan with the lentils, bay leaves, and celery or carrot, if using. Cover with plenty of cold water and bring to the boil. Add plenty of salt. Reduce the heat, cover, and simmer gently for about 20–30 minutes or until the lentils are tender.

2 Drain the lentils, reserving the liquid for making stocks and sauces. Turn the lentils into a serving dish and season with pepper and a little salt if necessary. Toss with the olive oil and vinegar. Serve hot or cold.
SERVES 6–8 AS AN ACCOMPANIMENT

$\mathcal{T}$OFU AND VEGETABLES IN COCONUT SAUCE

This is best with firm tofu (see page 161). It also works well with Paneer (see page 86); cumin-flavored paneer is particularly good.

3 oz creamed coconut, chopped	½ level tsp chili powder
½ lb firm tofu (see page 161)	2 tbsp soy sauce
vegetable oil for deep frying, plus 3 tbsp	4 medium carrots, trimmed, peeled and cut into
6 scallions, trimmed and finely chopped	matchstick strips
1 inch piece of fresh ginger root, peeled and finely	2 cups cauliflower florets, separated into small sprigs
chopped	6 oz green beans, topped and tailed
1 garlic clove, skinned and crushed	6 oz bean sprouts
½ level tsp ground turmeric	salt and pepper

1 Put the creamed coconut in a measuring jug. Pour in boiling water up to the 900 ml 3⅗ cups mark. Stir until dissolved, then set aside.
2 Drain the tofu and cut into cubes. Pat dry thoroughly with paper towels. Heat the oil to 375°F in a wok or deep-fat frier. Deep-fry the cubes of tofu in the hot oil for 2–3

minutes or until golden brown on all sides, turning them frequently with a slotted spoon. Remove and drain on paper towels.
3 Heat the 3 tbsp oil in a heavy-based saucepan or flameproof casserole. Add the scallions, ginger, and garlic and fry gently for about 5 minutes or until softened.

4 Add the turmeric and chili powder and stir-fry for 1–2 minutes, then add the coconut milk and soy sauce and bring to the boil, stirring all the time. Add the carrots and cauliflower. Simmer for 10 minutes.

5 Add the green beans and simmer for a further 5 minutes, then add the tofu and bean sprouts and heat through. Season with salt and pepper, then serve immediately.
SERVES 4 AS A MAIN COURSE

VEGETABLE CHILI

Don't be put off by the length of this recipe. You will have a lot of the ingredients in your storecupboard, anyway, and they do make a difference to the finished flavor. It really is worth making a large batch of chili since it freezes well or can be kept in the refrigerator for up to 2 days. Serve it with boiled rice, topped with sour cream or thick plain yogurt, grated cheese, and a little extra chopped fresh coriander. Alternatively, use it to top baked potatoes, or to fill store-bought tacos. Simply warm the tacos in the oven (following the packet instructions), then fill with chili, shredded lettuce, sour cream or yogurt, and top with Guacamole (see page 23) or chopped avocado and grated cheese.

2 tbsp vegetable oil	1 large sweet green pepper, cored, seeded, and chopped
2 onions, skinned and chopped	2 lb mixed vegetables, including carrots, eggplant, parsnips, potato, and celery, prepared as necessary and cut into chunks
2 large garlic cloves, skinned and crushed	
1–2 fresh green chilies, seeded and chopped	
1 bay leaf	two 14 oz cans chopped tomatoes
1 cinnamon stick	½ lb dried red kidney beans, soaked overnight in cold water, then drained, and cooked (see page 10) or two 1 lb cans red kidney beans, drained and rinsed
4 cloves	
1 level tbsp mild paprika	
2 level tsp cumin powder	pinch of sugar
½ level tsp chili powder, or to taste	1 tsp malt vinegar
1 level tsp dried marjoram	3 level tbsp chopped fresh coriander (cilantro)
2 level tbsp tomato paste	salt and pepper
½ lb button mushrooms, wiped and sliced	

1 Heat the oil in a large saucepan or flameproof casserole. Add the onions, garlic, and chilies and fry for 3–4 minutes, stirring continuously. Add the bay leaf, all the spices, the marjoram, and the tomato paste, and fry for a further 2 minutes, stirring.
2 Add all the fresh vegetables and stir to coat in the spice mixture. Fry for 1–2 minutes, then add the tomatoes. Increase the heat and bring to the boil, stirring occasionally. Add enough water just to cover the vegetables, half cover the pan or casserole with a lid, and simmer for 35–45 minutes.

3 Add the kidney beans with the sugar, vinegar, and half the coriander. Add extra chili powder, if liked, and season with salt and pepper. Bring back to the boil, then lower the heat, and simmer for 15 minutes, stirring occasionally. If the chili looks very liquid, leave the lid off during this time. If it is dry, add a little extra water and cover completely.
4 Stir in the remaining coriander, then leave to stand for 5 minutes. Taste and adjust the seasoning, if necessary, before serving.
SERVES ABOUT 8 AS A MAIN COURSE

MIXED LENTIL CASSEROLE

This is a relatively low-calorie main dish. Serve topped with low-fat plain yogurt to keep the calorie content low.

1 level tsp cumin seeds	1 lb button mushrooms, wiped and halved if large
1 level tbsp coriander seeds	2 garlic cloves, skinned and crushed
1 level tsp mustard seeds	1 oz piece of fresh ginger root, peeled and grated or finely chopped
3 tbsp olive oil	¼ level tsp ground turmeric
¼ lb onions, skinned and sliced	6 oz split red lentils, rinsed and drained
1 lb carrots, trimmed, peeled, and sliced	2 oz brown or green lentils, rinsed and drained
¼ lb trimmed leeks, sliced	salt and pepper
¼ lb daikon (white radish), peeled and roughly chopped	¼ cup chopped fresh coriander (cilantro)

1 Crush the cumin, coriander, and mustard seeds in a mortar with a pestle or in a strong bowl with the end of a rolling pin.

2 Heat the oil in a very large flameproof casserole. Add the onions, carrots, leeks, and daikon, and fry for 2–3 minutes, stirring constantly. Add the mushrooms, garlic, ginger, turmeric, and crushed spices, and fry for a further 2–3 minutes, stirring.

3 Stir the lentils into the casserole with 3 cups boiling water. Season with salt and pepper and return to the boil. Cover and cook in the oven at 350°F for about 45 minutes or until the vegetables and lentils are tender. Stir in the fresh coriander and taste and adjust the seasoning, if necessary, before serving.
SERVES 6 AS A MAIN COURSE

ROOT VEGETABLE STEW

This simple combination of root vegetables makes an ideal dinner dish served with baked potatoes and salad.

1 lb carrots, trimmed and peeled	2 garlic cloves, skinned and crushed
1 lb parsnips, trimmed and peeled	¼ lb button mushrooms, wiped
¼ lb celery root	2 cups vegetable stock
lemon juice	salt and pepper
2 tbsp vegetable margarine or butter	¼ cup light cream
2 medium onions, skinned and sliced	2 level tbsp chopped fresh parsley

1 Cut the carrots and parsnips into ¼ inch thick slices. Trim the celery root and chop into large chunks. Drop immediately into cold water lightly acidulated with lemon juice.

2 Melt the margarine or butter in a large flameproof casserole. Add the onions and

garlic and fry for 2–3 minutes or until beginning to soften, stirring constantly. Stir in the carrots, parsnips, and mushrooms and fry for a further 4–5 minutes, stirring, then add the stock and season with salt and pepper. Bring to the boil, cover, and cook in the oven at 325°F for 50 minutes or until the vegetables are tender.

3 Meanwhile, remove the celery root from the acidulated water and cook in boiling salted water for about 35 minutes or until very tender. Drain and purée in a blender or food processor with a little of the casserole juices. Stir the celery root purée into the casserole, return to the boil, taste, and adjust the seasoning, if necessary. Stir in the cream and parsley just before serving.

SERVES 6 AS A MAIN COURSE

RICH WINTER CASSEROLE

Vary the mixture of beans and vegetables in this casserole according to availability and personal taste. Plump, herby dumplings (see page 84) are an excellent accompaniment.

¼ lb red kidney beans, soaked overnight in cold water	6 oz button mushrooms, wiped
¼ lb black-eyed beans, soaked overnight in cold water	6 oz pearl onions, skinned
4 tbsp vegetable margarine or butter	2 celery sticks, trimmed and chopped
1 small onion, skinned and chopped	3 large carrots, trimmed, peeled, and sliced
1 garlic clove, skinned and chopped	1 lb mixed vegetables of your choice, prepared as necessary, and cut into large chunks
3 level tbsp all-purpose flour	bouquet garni
2½ cups Brown Onion Stock (see page 41)	salt and pepper
1¼ cups red wine	

1 Drain the beans and put them in a saucepan. Add enough fresh water to cover, bring to the boil and boil rapidly for 10 minutes, then drain.

2 Meanwhile, melt the margarine or butter in a flameproof casserole, add the onion and garlic, and fry for 5–10 minutes or until softened and slightly tinged with brown. Sprinkle with the flour and cook for 1–2 minutes, stirring all the time. Remove from the heat and gradually stir in the stock and wine. Bring to the boil, stirring all the time.

3 Add the remaining ingredients to the casserole with the drained beans. Cover and cook in the oven at 350°F for 2–2½ hours or until the beans are tender. Season with salt and pepper and remove the bouquet garni before serving.

SERVES 4 AS A MAIN COURSE

RATATOUILLE

The addition of lots of chopped fresh herbs is what gives this ratatouille its authentic Provençale flavor. Serve it as a main course with beans, rice, pasta, or warm bread, or as an accompaniment to nut roasts, burgers, or baked potatoes.

¼ cup olive oil	1 sweet red pepper, cored, seeded, and roughly chopped
2 medium onions, skinned and thinly sliced	1 level tbsp chopped fresh basil
1 large garlic clove, skinned and crushed	2 level tsp chopped fresh thyme
¾ lb eggplant, halved or quartered lengthways and thinly sliced	2 level tbsp chopped fresh parsley
1 lb small zucchini, trimmed and thinly sliced	2 level tbsp tomato paste
1 lb tomatoes, skinned, seeded, and roughly chopped	pinch of ground or crushed aniseed
1 sweet green pepper, cored, seeded, and roughly chopped	salt and pepper

1 Heat the oil in a large saucepan, add the onion and garlic, and fry for about 5 minutes or until soft but not brown.
2 Add the eggplant, zucchini, tomatoes, peppers, herbs, tomato paste and aniseed. Season with salt and pepper. Fry for 2–3 minutes, stirring, then cover tightly, and simmer for 30–40 minutes or until all the vegetables are just tender. Stir well.
3 If the vegetables produce a great deal of liquid, boil, uncovered, for 5–10 minutes until reduced. Taste and adjust the seasoning, if necessary. Serve hot or cold.
SERVES 4 AS A MAIN COURSE

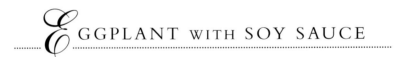

EGGPLANT WITH SOY SAUCE

This is delicious served with Fragrant Coconut Rice (see page 134).

3 tbsp vegetable oil	salt and pepper
1 medium onion, skinned and chopped	14 oz can chopped tomatoes
2 garlic cloves, skinned and crushed	2 tbsp dark soy sauce
large pinch of hot chili powder	1 level tbsp dark brown sugar
1¼ lb eggplant, trimmed and roughly chopped	

1 Heat the oil in a saucepan and fry the onion, garlic, and chili powder for 2–3 minutes or until the onion is soft. Add the eggplant and continue cooking for 2–3 minutes, stirring frequently.
2 Add the remaining ingredients, cover, and simmer gently for 10–15 minutes or until the eggplant is tender but still retains its shape. Taste and adjust the seasoning, if necessary, before serving hot.
SERVES 2–3 AS A MAIN COURSE

—SEVEN—

BAKES AND GRATINS

In this chapter you will find down-to-earth, hearty dishes, such as Gratin Dauphinoise, Tian of Zucchini and Jerusalem Artichoke Gratin – comforting food to be served on cold wintry days with the simplest of accompaniments. Here, too, is Lentil Loaf, Vegetarian Roast, Baked Potatoes, and Stuffed Peppers, dishes which have traditionally been the mainstay of vegetarian cuisine.

Most of these creations are based on fresh vegetables. To get the best results, it is essential that you buy good quality produce at the peak of freshness. Leafy vegetables should be bright green with no sign of yellowing or browning. Leaves should be undamaged, not slimy or wilted. Root vegetables should be firm with no discolored patches or damage to the skin. Tomatoes, sweet peppers, eggplant and zucchini should be firm and heavy with no sign of mold or shrivelling.

All vegetables are best eaten as soon as possible after purchase as far as flavor and vitamin retention are concerned (see page 7). However, root vegetables will keep quite well in a cool, dark place for about a week. More delicate vegetables last longer if stored in the refrigerator.

It's possible to turn almost any mixture of vegetables into a tasty gratin. Simply mix lightly cooked vegetables with a few cooked lentils, beans, or grains, season, then add enough tomato, cheese, Béchamel, or one of the other sauces on pages 181–194 to moisten. Turn into a gratin dish, sprinkle with an equal mixture of breadcrumbs and grated cheese and bake in the oven at 400°F until the top is golden and bubbling.

Alternatively, make a savory crumble topping by rubbing margarine or butter into all-purpose flour until the mixture resembles fine breadcrumbs. A proportion of half fat to flour is about right, as when making shortcrust pastry. Add a few chopped nuts or oats for extra crunch and season with chopped herbs and salt and pepper. Sprinkle on top of the vegetable mixture and bake like a gratin. Incidentally, garlic or flavored butters make particularly more-ish crumbles.

$\mathcal{N}$UT AND CREAM CHEESE BAKE

Some brands of cream cheese are made without animal rennet; check the labels.

2 tbsp vegetable oil	½ cup walnut halves, chopped
1 lb onions, skinned and chopped	⅔ cup shredded coconut
1 lb zucchini, trimmed and sliced	2 level tbsp tomato paste
6 oz mushrooms, wiped and sliced	a few drops of Tabasco
6 oz wholewheat breadcrumbs	½ level tsp each of dried rosemary, sage, and marjoram
1½ cups full-fat soft cheese	salt and pepper
½ cup unsalted cashew nuts, chopped	

1 Heat the oil in a large frying pan, add the onions and zucchini and fry for 5–10 minutes or until the onion is transparent, stirring frequently. Add the mushrooms and continue to fry for 1–2 minutes.

2 In a large bowl, combine the vegetable mixture with the remaining ingredients until evenly mixed. Season with salt and pepper. Turn into a 1½ quart ovenproof dish. Cover with foil and bake at 375°F for 40 minutes. About 15 minutes before the end of cooking, remove the foil to brown the top. Serve straight from the dish.

SERVES 6

TIMBALLO DI RISO

Timballo is an Italian dish from the region around Naples and there are many different versions. The basic risotto mixture which forms the case for the filling is usually the same, but the filling varies from one cook and one occasion to another – you literally fill your timballo with whatever you have to hand! Sautéed vegetables or cooked pulses of your choice can all be used, and the tomato sauce for serving suggested here can be changed to a cream, cheese, or herb sauce, whichever complements the filling best. It can also be made with leftover risotto.

6 tbsp vegetable margarine or butter	2 garlic cloves, skinned and crushed
1 onion, skinned and finely chopped	2 tsp chopped fresh basil or 1 tsp dried
2 cups Arborio (risotto) rice	¼ cup dried breadcrumbs
⅔ cup dry white wine	⅔ cup freshly grated Parmesan cheese
about 1 quart hot vegetable stock	2 free-range eggs, beaten
salt and pepper	3 hard-boiled free-range eggs, shelled and sliced
2 tbsp olive oil	½ lb Mozzarella cheese, sliced
½ lb mushrooms, wiped and sliced	Tomato Sauce (see page 190), to serve

1 First make the risotto. Melt 4 tbsp of the margarine or butter in a heavy-based saucepan. Add the onion and fry gently for 5 minutes or until soft but not colored.

2 Add the rice and stir until coated in the fat, then pour in ⅔ cup of the wine and bring to the boil. Simmer, stirring, until the rice has absorbed all the liquid.

3 Pour in about ⅔ cup stock, add 1 tsp salt and simmer and stir as before until all the liquid is absorbed. Continue adding stock in this way until the rice is just tender; this should take 15–20 minutes.

4 Meanwhile, heat the oil in a separate pan, add the mushrooms and garlic, and fry gently until the juices run. Stir in the remaining wine and the basil. Season with salt and pepper and remove from the heat.

5 Sprinkle the breadcrumbs over the base and up the sides of a well-buttered 8 inch spring-form cake pan or mold, making sure there are

no gaps.

6 Remove the risotto from the heat and stir in the Parmesan cheese with the beaten eggs, the remaining margarine or butter, and salt and pepper to taste.

7 Press three-quarters of the risotto over the base and up the sides of the lined pan. Arrange about one-third of the hard-boiled egg slices in the bottom, then sprinkle over about one-third of the mushrooms. Top with one-third of the Mozzarella slices.

8 Repeat these layers until all the eggs, mushrooms and Mozzarella are used up, then press the remaining risotto firmly on top.

9 Cover the pan with foil and bake in the oven at 375°F for 1 hour or until firm. Leave to rest in the pan for 5 minutes, then turn out on to a warmed serving platter. Serve immediately, with Tomato Sauce.
SERVES 8

Overleaf, from left to right, Tomato Herb Foccacia *(page 151),* Bulgar-stuffed Tomatoes *(page 103)*
Baby Vegetable and Pasta Salad *(page 45)*
Creamy Hummus *(page 14),* Guacamole *(page 23),* Spanakopittes *(page 80),* Sesame and Cumin Bread Sticks *(page 150)*

*V*EGETABLE AND NUT ROAST

This recipe makes a "loaf" which slices well and can be served hot or cold. Any type of chopped nuts can be used, such as almonds, Brazil nuts, or unsalted peanuts, but it's worth buying mature Cheddar specially, as it adds a mouthwatering depth of flavor.

¾ cup long-grain brown rice
salt and pepper
1 tbsp vegetable margarine or butter
1 medium onion, skinned and chopped
1 garlic clove, skinned and crushed
2 carrots, trimmed, peeled, and grated

¼ lb mushrooms, wiped and finely chopped
1½ cups fresh wholewheat breadcrumbs
1 cup nuts, finely chopped
¼ lb mature Cheddar cheese, grated
2 free-range eggs, beaten
Tomato Sauce (see page 190) or chutney, to serve

1 Cook the rice in boiling salted water for 30–35 minutes or until tender. Drain well.
2 Meanwhile, heat the margarine or butter in a frying pan and fry the onion, garlic, carrots, and mushrooms for 5–10 minutes or until softened, stirring frequently. Remove from the heat, then stir in the breadcrumbs, nuts, cooked rice, cheese, and eggs. Season with

salt and pepper and mix thoroughly together.
3 Pack the mixture into a greased 1½–2 quart loaf pan and bake in the oven at 350°F for 1–1¼ hours or until firm to the touch and brown on top. Serve sliced, hot or cold, with Tomato Sauce or chutney.
SERVES 4–6

*T*IAN OF ZUCCHINI

Use up leftover cooked rice or pre-cooked frozen rice to make this simple supper dish.

2 thick slices of white bread
1¼ cups milk
¾ lb long-grain rice
salt and pepper
2 free-range eggs

olive oil
2 oz Gruyère cheese, grated
1 small garlic clove, skinned and crushed (optional)
1½ lb small zucchini, trimmed and thinly sliced
freshly grated Parmesan cheese (optional)

1 Remove the crusts from the bread and discard. Tear the bread into small pieces and place in a large bowl. Pour over the milk and leave to soak.
2 Meanwhile, cook the rice in boiling salted water until tender. Drain well.
3 Beat the eggs and 2 tbsp olive oil into the bread mixture with about a quarter of the cheese and the garlic, if using. Season generously with salt and pepper.

4 Carefully fold the zucchini and rice into the milk and bread mixture, and pour into a greased gratin dish. Sprinkle with the remaining Gruyère cheese and a little Parmesan, if using. Drizzle with a little extra olive oil. Bake in the oven at 400°F for 35–40 minutes or until golden brown and firm to the touch. Leave to cool in the dish for 10 minutes before serving.
SERVES 3–4

$\mathscr{B}$ULGAR-STUFFED TOMATOES

Serve these stuffed tomatoes as part of a summer lunch with a selection of salads. They are equally delicious served hot.

⅔ cup bulgar wheat	salt and pepper
4 large beefsteak tomatoes, each weighing about 6 oz	**To serve**
¼ cup nuts, such as hazelnuts, peanuts or cashews, toasted and chopped	plain yogurt
	Pesto (see page 193), Creamy Hummus (see page 14) or Guacamole (see page 23)
½ cup stoned black olives, roughly chopped	chopped fresh basil
2 tbsp Pesto (see page 193)	
3 level tbsp chopped fresh basil	

1 Put the bulgar wheat in a bowl and pour over ⅔ cup boiling water. Leave to soak for 30 minutes or until the water has been absorbed and the bulgar has softened.
2 Cut the tops off the tomatoes and reserve. Scoop out the tomato centers with a spoon and finely chop half the tomato flesh. (Discard the remainder.)

3 Add the chopped tomato to the bulgar wheat with the remaining ingredients and season with salt and pepper. Use to fill the tomato shells. To serve, top each tomato with a spoonful of yogurt and a little Pesto or a spoonful of hummus or Guacamole. Sprinkle with basil and replace the tomato tops.
SERVES 4

$\mathscr{G}$RATIN DAUPHINOISE

For this unorthodox version of a classic dish, it is vital that the potatoes are sliced wafer-thin, so that they cook until melt-in-the-mouth tender. Cooking them in milk first speeds up the oven cooking time (without this they can take up to 4 hours to cook properly). Use potatoes with a 'waxy' texture or they will break up when boiled.

2 lb waxy potatoes, peeled	salt and pepper
5 cups milk	freshly grated nutmeg
1 small garlic clove, skinned and halved	¼ lb Gruyère cheese, grated
2½ cups heavy cream	

1 Cut the potatoes into very thin slices, using a very sharp knife. Put them in a large saucepan and add the milk. Bring to the boil and simmer very gently for 10–12 minutes or until just soft. Drain well and reserve the milk.
2 Grease a large gratin dish and rub the bottom and sides of the dish with garlic. Put the cream in a saucepan and bring to the boil.
3 Arrange the potatoes in the prepared dish

in an even layer. Cover the potatoes with the cream, adding a little of the reserved milk. Season generously and sprinkle with the nutmeg and grated cheese.
4 Bake, uncovered, in the oven at 350°F for 1–1½ hours or until the potatoes are very tender and the top is brown. Leave to stand for 15 minutes before serving.
SERVES 6

BAKED POTATOES AND FILLINGS

Baked potatoes are the perfect informal meal, providing hot and filling high-fiber food with minimum effort. They are delicious topped simply with grated or cottage cheese, a spoonful of plain yogurt, and a generous sprinkling of black pepper, or piled high with one of the fillings suggested below. Alternatively, serve them with Ratatouille (see page 96), Creamy Hummus (see page 14) or Vegetable Chili (see page 93).
If you have a microwave oven, save time by cooking the pricked potatoes on HIGH for 12–14 minutes or until the potatoes feel soft when squeezed, turning them over once during cooking. To crisp the skins, put them into a very hot oven for about 10 minutes.

4 large potatoes, each weighing about 6 oz
vegetable oil (optional)
Avocado and Smoked Cheese Filling
2 large ripe avocados
⅔ cups plain yogurt
lemon juice, to taste
¼ lb smoked hard cheese, cubed
salt and pepper
Carrot, Peanut, and Alfalfa Filling
5 tbsp plain yogurt
3 tbsp peanut butter
3 tbsp mayonnaise
4 large carrots, trimmed, peeled, and coarsely grated
¼ cup roasted peanuts

1½ cups alfalfa sprouts
a squeeze of lemon juice
black pepper
Hot Chili Bean Filling
14 oz can chopped tomatoes
2 level tsp tomato paste
2 garlic cloves, skinned and crushed
½ level tsp chili powder
½ level tsp dried oregano
1 lb cooked red kidney beans (see page 10) or 1 lb can red kidney beans, drained and rinsed
2 level tbsp chopped fresh coriander (cilantro) or parsley
salt and pepper

1 Wash and scrub the potatoes and prick all over with a fork. If you prefer baked potatoes with softish skins, rub the potatoes all over with a little oil; for very crunchy skins, put them into the oven while still wet.

2 Bake the potatoes in the oven at 450°F for about 1 hour or at 400°F for about 1½ hours or until the potatoes feel soft when gently squeezed, turning them over once during cooking. (They can be cooked at a lower temperature if, for example, you are cooking a casserole in the oven at the same time, but of course they will take much longer.)

3 While the potatoes are cooking, make the required filling (see right).

4 When the potatoes are cooked, cut them in half and mash the flesh lightly with a fork. Pile the prepared filling on top and serve.
SERVES 4

FILLINGS
Avocado and Smoked Cheese Cut one of the avocados in half, remove the pit, and scoop out the flesh. Mash with a fork or purée in a blender or food processor with the yogurt and lemon juice. Halve, pit, and peel the remaining avocado and cut into cubes. Fold into the puréed mixture with the cheese, and season with salt and pepper. Use to fill the potatoes.

Carrot, Peanut, and Alfalfa Beat the yogurt, peanut butter, and mayonnaise together, then gradually fold in the carrots, peanuts, and alfalfa. Season with lemon juice and black pepper, and use to fill the potatoes.

Hot Chili Bean Put all the ingredients into a saucepan, season with salt and pepper, and bring to the boil. Cook vigorously for 15–20 minutes or until reduced and thickened. Use to fill the potatoes.

$\mathscr{I}$MAM BAYILDI

This traditional Turkish dish is usually served cold, but it could be served lukewarm if you prefer. Serve with crusty bread or toasted pitta bread, and perhaps a Greek Salad (see page 45).

6 small eggplant	¼ cup chopped fresh parsley
salt and pepper	¼ level tsp ground allspice
scant 1 cup olive oil	1 level tsp sugar
1 lb onions, skinned and finely sliced	2 tbsp lemon juice
3 garlic cloves, skinned and crushed	chopped fresh parsley, to garnish
14 oz can tomatoes, drained or 1 lb tomatoes, skinned and chopped	

1 Halve the eggplant lengthways. Scoop out the flesh and reserve. Leave a substantial shell so they do not disintegrate.

2 Sprinkle the insides of the eggplant shells with salt and put upside-down on a plate. Leave for 30 minutes to drain away the juices.

3 Heat 3 tbsp olive oil in a saucepan, add the onions and garlic, and fry gently for about 15 minutes or until soft but not coloured. Add the tomatoes, reserved eggplant flesh, parsley, and allspice. Season with salt and pepper. Simmer gently for about 20 minutes or until the mixture has reduced.

4 Rinse the eggplant and pat dry with paper towels. Spoon the filling into each half and place them side by side in a shallow ovenproof dish. They should fit quite closely together.

5 Mix the remaining oil with ⅔ cup water, the sugar, and lemon juice. Season with salt and pepper. Pour around the eggplant, cover and bake in the oven at 300°F for about 1 hour or until tender.

6 When cooked, remove from the oven, uncover, and leave to cool for 1 hour. Chill in the refrigerator for at least 2 hours before serving garnished with parsley.
SERVES 6

*L*ENTIL LOAF

This makes a soft-textured, mildly flavored loaf. Serve with a crisp salad.

6 oz split red lentils	1 garlic clove, skinned and chopped (optional)
1¼ cups vegetable stock or water	6 oz farmhouse Cheddar cheese, grated
1 bay leaf	1½ cups wholewheat breadcrumbs
1 tbsp vegetable oil	2 level tbsp chopped fresh parsley
1 medium onion, skinned and finely chopped	1 tbsp lemon juice
2 celery sticks, trimmed and finely chopped	1 free-range egg, beaten
1 sweet red pepper, cored, seeded, and finely chopped	salt and pepper
¼ lb mushrooms, wiped and finely chopped	Tomato Sauce (see page 190), to serve

1 Put the lentils, stock or water, and bay leaf in a saucepan, bring to the boil, then reduce the heat, cover, and simmer gently for 15–20 minutes or until the lentils are very soft.

2 Meanwhile, grease and line a 1 quart loaf pan. Heat the oil in a large saucepan, add all the vegetables and the garlic, if using, and fry for 2–3 minutes, stirring all the time. Reduce the heat, cover the pan, and cook for 10 minutes or until the vegetables are softened.

3 Mix the vegetables with the lentil mixture. Add half the cheese and the remaining ingredients and season generously with salt and pepper. The mixture should be moist but not sloppy.

4 Spoon the mixture into the prepared pan and bake in the oven at 350°F for about 1 hour or until firm to the touch in the center. Sprinkle over the remaining cheese. Increase the oven temperature to 400°F and cook for a further 8–10 minutes or until the cheese melts. Cool in the pan for 10 minutes before turning out. Serve hot or cold, thickly sliced and accompanied by Tomato Sauce.
SERVES 4–6

*S*UMMER GRATIN

The cheese and oats are sprinkled around the edges of the dishes to produce an attractive border for the gratin.

6 oz dried butter beans, soaked overnight in cold water, or 1 lb can butter beans, drained and rinsed	2 tbsp vegetable oil
1 lb tomatoes, skinned and quartered	1 medium onion, skinned and thinly sliced
2 level tbsp tomato paste	1 garlic clove, skinned and crushed
½ level tsp ground cumin	¼ lb button mushrooms, wiped and halved
salt and pepper	2 oz red Leicester cheese, grated
14 oz broccoli, trimmed and cut into small florets	⅓ cup rolled oats

1 If using soaked dried beans, drain them and place in a saucepan. Cover with fresh water, bring to the boil and boil rapidly for 10 minutes, then reduce the heat, cover, and simmer for about 30 minutes. Drain well.

2 Place half the beans, the tomatoes, tomato paste and cumin in a food processor. Season with salt and pepper and purée until smooth.

3 Cook the broccoli in boiling salted water for about 5 minutes or until just tender. Drain.

4 Heat the oil in a large frying pan, add the onion, garlic, mushrooms, and remaining beans, and stir over a high heat for 3–4 minutes or until beginning to soften.

5 Gently stir in the broccoli and cook for a further 1 minute, then spoon the mixture into six individual ovenproof serving dishes, and spoon over the puréed mixture.

6 Mix the cheese and oats together, then sprinkle around the edge of each dish. Bake at 400°F for about 25 minutes or until thoroughly hot, golden brown, and bubbling.
SERVES 6

$\mathscr{S}$PINACH AND LENTIL ROULADE

Make sure that the spinach is really thoroughly drained before adding it to the sauce. It's a good idea to wrap it in a double thickness of cheesecloth or a clean dish towel and to wring it out over the sink to remove all traces of water.

6 tbsp vegetable margarine or butter	6 oz split red lentils, rinsed
1/4 lb frozen chopped spinach, thawed and thoroughly drained	1/2 cup chopped scallions
1/2 cup all-purpose flour	salt and pepper
1 1/4 cups milk	2 level tbsp tomato ketchup
2 free-range eggs, separated	1 level tbsp creamed horseradish

1 Grease and line a 13 × 9 inch jelly roll tin with wax paper.

2 Melt 4 tbsp margarine or butter in a saucepan and stir in the spinach and flour. Cook for 1 minute, then add the milk. Bring to the boil, stirring, and simmer for 2–3 minutes. Remove from the heat and beat in the egg yolks. Stiffly whisk the egg whites and fold into the mixture. Spoon into the prepared tin and spread evenly. Bake in the oven at 425°F for about 15 minutes or until well risen and firm to the touch.

3 Meanwhile, cook the lentils and scallions in boiling salted water for 15–20 minutes or until tender. Drain well, then beat in the tomato ketchup, horseradish, and remaining margarine or butter. Season with salt and pepper.

4 Turn out the roulade on to a sheet of wax paper and peel off the lining paper. Spread the lentil mixture over the surface and roll up like a jelly roll, using the paper to help. Serve immediately.
SERVES 4

$\mathcal{J}$ERUSALEM ARTICHOKE GRATIN

Serve this warming supper dish with a salad and some crusty bread.

2 lb Jerusalem artichokes	*¼ level tsp grated nutmeg*
salt and pepper	*3 medium leeks, trimmed and thickly sliced*
½ lb small pearl or pickling onions	*½ lb shelled fresh or frozen peas*
6 tbsp vegetable margarine or butter	*⅔ cup heavy cream*
1 tbsp olive oil	*3 oz Gruyère cheese, grated*
2 garlic cloves, skinned and crushed	*3 oz Cheddar cheese, grated*
⅔ cup dry white wine or vegetable stock	*¼ cup breadcrumbs*

1 Parboil the Jerusalem artichokes in salted water for 10 minutes. Remove with a slotted spoon and leave until cool enough to handle. Peel off the skins and slice the flesh thickly.
2 Add the pearl onions to the water and boil for 2 minutes, then remove with a slotted spoon. Peel off the skins, leaving the root ends intact so that the onions remain whole.
3 Heat 4 tbsp of the margarine or butter with the oil in a heavy-based saucepan, add the onions and garlic, and toss over a moderate heat until the onions are well coated in the fat.
4 Pour in the wine or stock and ⅔ cup water and bring to the boil. Add the nutmeg, cover, and simmer for 10 minutes. Add the artichokes, leeks, and peas and continue simmering for 5 minutes or until all the

vegetables are tender. With a slotted spoon, transfer the vegetables to a flameproof gratin dish.
5 Boil the cooking liquid rapidly until reduced to about half of its original volume. Reduce the heat and stir in the cream. Mix the two cheeses together. Stir half into the sauce. Season with salt and pepper and stir until the cheeses have melted.
6 Pour the cheese sauce over the vegetables in the dish. Mix the remaining cheese with the breadcrumbs, then sprinkle on top.
7 Dot the remaining margarine or butter over the gratin, then bake in the oven at 425°F for about 10 minutes or until the topping is golden brown.
SERVES 4

$\mathcal{S}$TUFFED SWEET PEPPERS

For extra flavor, stir a little Hazelnut and Coriander Pesto (see page 193) into the cooked rice mixture. Alternatively, serve the finished peppers with Harissa Sauce (see page 184).

3 sweet green peppers	*1 level tbsp tomato paste*
3 sweet red peppers	*¼ lb mushrooms, wiped and sliced*
4 tbsp vegetable margarine or butter	*salt and pepper*
1 onion, skinned and finely chopped	*¼ cup pine nuts or sliced almonds, roasted and*
1 garlic clove, skinned and crushed	*chopped*
1 inch piece of fresh ginger root, peeled and chopped	*2 tsp soy sauce*
¼ cup long-grain rice	*2 tbsp vegetable oil*
1¼ cups vegetable stock	

1 Cut a 1 inch lid from the stem end of each sweet pepper. Scoop out the seeds and membranes and discard. Blanch the shells and lids in boiling water for about 2 minutes. Drain and cool.

2 Melt the margarine or butter in a saucepan and gently fry the onion, garlic, and ginger for 5 minutes or until softened. Stir in the rice and cook for 1–2 minutes.

3 Add the stock, tomato paste, and mushrooms. Bring to the boil and simmer for 13–15 minutes or until the rice is tender and all the stock has been absorbed.

4 Season well with salt and pepper, and stir in the nuts and soy sauce. Use this mixture to fill the peppers.

5 Replace the lids, then put the peppers in a deep ovenproof dish and pour over the oil. Cover with foil and bake in the oven at 375°F for 30 minutes or until tender.
SERVES 6

MELANZANA PARMIGIANA

Salting the eggplant draws out some of the moisture, thus reducing the amount of oil absorbed during cooking. (It is also thought to extract any bitterness, but the quality of eggplant has improved so much that salting for this reason is no longer necessary.) However, if you are short of time, or not concerned about calories, this step can be omitted. Serve with a crisp mixed green salad and plenty of crusty bread.

2 lb long medium eggplant	*½ lb Mozzarella cheese, drained and cubed*
salt and pepper	*a handful of fresh basil leaves, marjoram, or oregano*
olive oil	*(optional)*
1¼ cups Tomato Sauce (see page 190)	*freshly grated Parmesan cheese*

1 Trim off the ends of the eggplant and discard. Cut the eggplant lengthways into thin slices. Sprinkle the slices generously with salt and leave to drain in a colander for at least 30 minutes.

2 Rinse the eggplant and pat dry with paper towels. Heat a little olive oil in a non-stick frying pan and fry the eggplant, in batches, for 3–4 minutes each side, or until golden brown and just cooked through, brushing the frying pan with more olive oil between each batch. Drain well on crumpled paper towels.

3 Spread half the Tomato Sauce in the base of a large gratin dish. Cover with half the eggplant slices and scatter over the Mozzarella. Cover with the remaining eggplant slices and sprinkle with herbs, if using. Season with salt and pepper.

4 Spread the remaining Tomato Sauce over the eggplant and sprinkle with Parmesan cheese. Bake in the oven at 400°F for 30–35 minutes or until golden brown and bubbling. Leave to cool for 5 minutes before serving.
SERVES 4–6

$\mathscr{P}$OTATO AND SPINACH ROLL

This is another filling Italian dish. The method is rather laborious, but the finished product is well worth the effort.

1 lb all-purpose potatoes, peeled
salt and pepper
2 lb fresh spinach, trimmed and washed or 1 lb packet frozen spinach
2 tbsp olive oil
1 large onion, skinned and chopped
¼ lb curd cheese

⅔ cup freshly grated Parmesan cheese
pinch of freshly grated nutmeg
2 free-range eggs
1 level tsp baking powder
about 1¼ cups all-purpose white flour
4 tbsp vegetable margarine or butter
Tomato Sauce (see page 190), to serve

1 Cook the potatoes in boiling salted water for about 20 minutes or until tender.

2 Meanwhile, make the filling. Put the spinach in a saucepan with a very little water and cook gently for 5–10 minutes (or until thawed if using frozen spinach). Drain well and chop finely.

3 Heat the oil in a frying pan, add the onion, and fry gently for 3–4 minutes or until soft but not colored. Add the spinach and cook for a further 2 minutes.

4 Turn the spinach into a bowl and add the curd cheese, ⅓ cup Parmesan cheese, the nutmeg, and one egg. Season with salt and pepper and beat well together.

5 Drain the potatoes, then push them through a strainer into a bowl. Make a well in the center and add the remaining egg, the baking powder, and most of the flour. Beat well together.

6 Knead the mixture on a work surface, adding more flour if necessary, for about 5 minutes. The dough should be smooth and slightly sticky. Shape into a ball.

7 Roll out the dough to a rectangle measuring about 14 × 12 inches. Spread the spinach mixture over the dough, leaving a 1 inch border.

8 Roll up the dough like a jelly roll. Wrap tightly in a cheesecloth and tie the ends with string.

9 Bring a large flameproof casserole, roasting tin, or fish kettle of salted water to the boil and place the roll in it. Return to the boil, then reduce the heat, and simmer, partially covered, for 30 minutes. Remove the roll from the water, unwrap, and leave to cool for 2 hours.

10 Cut the roll into 1 inch thick slices and arrange the slices, slightly overlapping, in an ovenproof dish.

11 Melt the margarine or butter and pour over the slices. Sprinkle with the remaining Parmesan cheese and bake in the oven at 400°F for about15 minutes or until golden. Serve hot, with Tomato Sauce.
SERVES 8

-EIGHT-

BROILED AND FRIED DISHES

There has been a marked decline in the popularity of deep-fat frying in recent years as we all strive for lower-fat, healthier diets. However, providing it is done correctly, the amount of fat absorbed during cooking can be kept to a minimum. It's preferable to use oil that is high in polyunsaturates; canola, safflower, sunflower, corn, or soy oil are all suitable. Cooking oils are stable at high temperatures but some molecular changes do take place when oil is heated, so change it after two or three uses.

An electric deep-fat fryer is a good investment since it ensures that the fat reaches the correct temperature and it has a lid to keep smells to a minimum.

Pans of hot oil are notoriously dangerous,

so, of course, never leave a pan unattended on the stove. Push the pan to the back of the stove and leave it to cool completely before straining the oil. Thoroughly drain the fried food on crumpled paper towels.

Broiling is a healthier option. Always preheat the broiler until hot before cooking to ensure that the food has a good crisp surface. Anything suitable for broiling can be cooked on the outdoor grill in summer.

This eclectic collection of dishes meets all requirements. Some, like Felafel (see page 114), and Onion Pakoras (see page 116), are suitable appetizers or could also be served as part of a tapas-style meal, with salad and vegetable based dishes, chunks of bread, and chilled beer or red wine.

BEAN BURGERS WITH MANGO CHUTNEY

Make sure that you mash the beans thoroughly in step 3 or the mixture will not hold together when it is cooked. The chutney makes a delicious and unusual accompaniment.

½ cup brown rice
salt and pepper
8 oz cooked beans, such as red kidney, black-eyed or aduki (see page 10), or a 1 lb can of beans, drained and rinsed
1–2 garlic cloves, skinned and crushed
½ level tsp curry paste
2 level tsp tomato paste

½ inch piece of fresh ginger root, peeled and grated
½ cup medium oatmeal
vegetable oil for frying or broiling
For the Mango Chutney
1 small ripe mango
2 level tbsp shredded coconut
finely grated rind and juice of 1 lime

1 Cook the rice in boiling salted water for about 30 minutes or until tender.
2 Meanwhile, make the mango chutney. Peel the mango and cut the flesh away from the pit. Cut the flesh into small pieces and mix with the remaining ingredients. Set aside.
3 When the rice is cooked, drain, and leave it to cool slightly. Put the beans in a bowl and mash thoroughly with a potato masher. Add the garlic, curry paste, tomato paste, ginger, and rice. Season with salt and pepper and beat

thoroughly until the mixture clings together.
4 Shape the mixture into eight burgers. Spread the oatmeal on a plate and press the burgers into it to coat lightly.
5 Heat some vegetable oil in a frying pan and fry the burgers for 2–3 minutes on each side or until golden brown. Alternatively, brush the burgers lightly with oil and broil for 2–3 minutes on each side or until golden brown. Serve with the chutney.
SERVES 4

Curried Tofu Burgers *left*, Wild Rice and Thyme Salad *right (page 51)*

CURRIED TOFU BURGERS

Adding tofu to vegetarian burgers ensures that they remain moist. It also produces burgers that are lower in fat than those based entirely on nuts.

1 tbsp vegetable oil	*½ lb block tofu*
1 large carrot, trimmed, peeled, and finely grated	*⅓ cup wholewheat breadcrumbs*
1 large onion, skinned and finely grated	*¼ cup mixed nuts, finely chopped*
2 level tsp coriander seeds, finely crushed (optional)	*salt and pepper*
1 garlic clove, skinned and crushed	*all-purpose flour*
1 level tsp curry paste	*vegetable oil for frying or broiling*
1 level tsp tomato paste	

1 Heat the 1 tbsp oil in a large frying pan. Add the carrot and onion and fry for 3–4 minutes or until the vegetables are softened, stirring all the time. Add the coriander seeds, if using, garlic, curry paste, and tomato paste. Increase the heat and fry for 2 minutes, stirring all the time.
2 Mash the tofu with a potato masher, then stir into the vegetables with the breadcrumbs and nuts. Season with salt and pepper, and beat thoroughly until the mixture starts to

stick together. With floured hands, shape the mixture into eight burgers.
3 Heat some oil in a frying pan and fry the burgers for 3–4 minutes on each side or until golden brown. Alternatively, to broil the burgers, brush them lightly with oil and cook under a hot broiler for about 3 minutes on each side or until golden brown. Drain on paper towels and serve hot.
MAKES 8

ELAFEL

Serve these spicy chick-pea balls as a main course with Tzatziki (see page 54) and a fruit and nut pilaff, or as an appetizer with a bowl of yogurt flavored with chopped fresh coriander or mint for guests to dip the felafel into.

½ lb chick-peas, soaked overnight in cold water, then drained and cooked (see page 10) or two 1 lb cans chick-peas, drained and rinsed	*1 garlic clove, skinned and crushed*
1 level tsp ground cumin	*2 tbsp tahini (see page 14)*
1 level tsp ground turmeric	*½ cup fresh breadcrumbs*
1 level tsp cayenne pepper	*3 level tbsp chopped fresh coriander (cilantro)*
1 level tsp salt	*all-purpose flour for coating*
	vegetable oil for frying

1 Put all the ingredients, except the flour and oil, in a food processor or blender and process until the chick-peas are finely chopped but not puréed.
2 Turn the mixture into a large bowl and add about 2 tbsp water. Knead the mixture with your hands until it begins to cling together, adding a little extra water, if necessary.
3 With floured hands, shape the mixture into

20 walnut-sized balls. Slightly flatten each ball with the palm of your hand and coat in flour.
4 Heat the oil in a deep-fat fryer to 375°F or until a 1 inch cube of bread will brown in the hot oil in 40 seconds. Fry the felafel in the hot oil, a few at a time, for 2–3 minutes or until golden brown. Drain on crumpled paper towels and serve hot.
SERVES 4–6

ROILED GOATS' CHEESES WITH LAVENDER

Serve as an appetizer, a light lunch or as part of a barbecue menu with a tomato, olive, and onion salad.

1 level tsp chopped fresh lavender blossom	*eight 1–1½ oz fresh soft goats' cheeses*
1 level tbsp chopped fresh herbs, such as parsley and thyme	*8 fresh grape leaves*
	olive oil

1 Mix together the lavender and herbs, then roll the goats' cheeses in the mixture until lightly coated.
2 Drop the grape leaves in boiling water and leave for 1–2 minutes. Drain and refresh under cold running water. Dry with paper towels.
3 Brush both sides of the leaves with olive

oil. Wrap each cheese in a leaf and secure with a wooden toothpick.
4 Cook the parcels under a medium broiler for 4–5 minutes, keeping them 3–4 inches from the heat. The leaves should be just beginning to turn brown. Serve immediately.
SERVES 8

CRISP FRIED ONIONS

These delicious, flavorsome morsels are invaluable for adding extra color, texture, and flavor to pilaffs, birianis, curries, salads, and casseroles. They can be stored for up to 2 weeks in an airtight container in the refrigerator.

2 medium onions, skinned

vegetable oil for frying

1 Cut the onions in half lengthways, then cut into thin slices.
2 Heat about ¼ inch oil in a frying pan. When hot, add the onions and fry for about 10 minutes or until golden brown, stirring all the time. Remove the onions from the pan with a slotted spoon and drain on paper towels. Leave to cool and become crisp before using as desired.

VEGETABLE TEMPURA

This dish of crisp, raw vegetables, quickly fried in a light, semi-transparent batter, sums up the Japanese feeling for food. Ingredients should be at their natural best and cooking should be kept to a minimum, so that flavor, texture, and aroma can all be enjoyed to the full.

1 oz fresh ginger root, peeled and grated

¼ cup sake or dry sherry

3 tbsp soy sauce

½ cup all-purpose flour, plus 2 level tbsp

2 level tbsp cornstarch

2 level tbsp arrowroot

salt and pepper

¼ lb cauliflower florets

2 large carrots, trimmed

16 button mushrooms

2 medium zucchini

2 sweet red peppers

vegetable oil for deep-frying

1 First make the dipping sauce. Put the ginger in a bowl and add the sake or sherry, the soy sauce and scant 1 cup boiling water. Stir well to mix, then set aside while preparing the vegetables and batter.
2 Sift the ½ cup all-purpose flour, the cornstarch, and arrowroot into a large bowl with a pinch each of salt and pepper. Gradually whisk in 1¼ cups ice cold water to form a smooth, thin batter. Chill.
3 Divide the cauliflower into tiny sprigs, discarding any thick, woody stalks. Peel the carrots and cut into thin sticks. Wipe the mushrooms and trim the stalks, if necessary. Trim and slice the zucchini.

4 Cut the red peppers in half, remove the cores and seeds, and slice the flesh into thin strips. Toss the vegetables in the 2 level tbsp all-purpose flour.
5 Heat the oil in a wok or deep-fat fryer to 375°F or until a 1 inch cube of bread will brown in the hot oil in 40 seconds. Dip the vegetables in the batter in batches, then remove with a slotted spoon, taking up a lot of the batter with the vegetables. Deep-fry for 3–5 minutes or until crisp, then remove with a slotted spoon. Drain on paper towels. Serve immediately, with the dipping sauce.
SERVES 4

ONION PAKORAS

In northern India, these more-ish morsels are served as an afternoon snack, while in southern and western India they are known as *bhaijas* and are served as part of a main meal.

1 lb onions, skinned	*1 level tsp chili powder*
½ cup gram or wholemeal flour	*1 level tsp ground caradamom*
¼ cup self-rising flour	*2 level tbsp chopped fresh mint or coriander (cilantro)*
1 level tsp garam masala	*salt and pepper*
1 level tsp ground turmeric	*vegetable oil for frying*

1 Halve the onions, then cut into very thin crescent-shaped slices. Mix the onions with the remaining ingredients, season with salt and pepper, and add 6–8 tbsp water, or enough to make a fairly stiff paste. Divide into eight and shape roughly into rounds with your fingers and a tablespoon.

2 Heat some vegetable oil in a frying pan and fry the pakoras in batches for about 3 minutes on each side or until well browned. Drain on paper towels and serve hot.

MAKES 8

SPICED DAL CROQUETTES

The moong dal in these croquettes are not cooked before being ground to a paste. For this reason, it is essential to soak them for the full 24 hours or they will not be soft enough.

½ lb moong dal (mung beans)	*salt and pepper*
1 level tsp caraway seeds, crushed	*about ¼ cup vegetable oil*
½ level tsp chili powder	*1¼ cups plain yogurt*
1 level tsp garam masala	*2 level tbsp chopped fresh mint*
½ level tsp ground turmeric	

1 Pick over the dal and remove any grit or discoloured pulses. Put into a strainer and wash thoroughly under cold running water. Drain.

2 Put the dal in a bowl and cover with cold water. Leave to soak for 24 hours.

3 Drain the dal, then process in batches in a food processor until ground to a fine paste. Add the spices and ½ level tsp salt and work again until thoroughly mixed in.

4 Heat a little oil in a heavy-based frying pan until smoking hot. Add spoonfuls of the croquette mixture and fry for 2–3 minutes on each side until lightly colored.

5 Remove the croquettes with a slotted spoon, then drain well on paper towels while frying the remainder.

6 Put the yogurt in a blender or food processor with the mint. Season with salt and pepper, and process to a thin sauce.

7 Put the hot croquettes in a shallow serving dish and pour over the yogurt sauce. Cover the dish and chill for at least 2 hours before serving.

SERVES 4

Muttar Paneer (page 87) left, Onion Pakoras right

STIR-FRIED VEGETABLES

Vegetable stir-fries are delicious made with whatever vegetables you have to hand, though it's important to cut them all into pieces of a similar size. Add tougher, slower-cooking vegetables, such as baby corn, carrots, green beans, onions, sweet peppers, celery, fennel, and radish, first. Delicate fast-cooking vegetables, such as bean sprouts, Chinese lettuce, pak choi, and spinach, need only 2–3 minutes in the hot oil. Once you've grasped the basic technique, it has endless possibilities. When cooked, the vegetables should be served right away, so make sure that any accompanying noodles or rice are almost cooked when you begin stir-frying.

¼ cup peanut (groundnut) or vegetable oil
2 garlic cloves, skinned and crushed
1 inch piece of fresh ginger root, peeled and sliced
1–2 fresh chilies, seeded and chopped (optional)
1 cup cashew nuts, peanuts, or almonds
2 lb mixed vegetables, prepared as necessary and cut into thin strips or slices

1 tbsp light soy sauce
1 tbsp dry sherry
1 level tsp sugar
1 level tsp five-spice powder (optional)

1 Heat the oil in a wok or very large, deep frying pan. Add the garlic, ginger, and chilies, if using, and stir-fry for 1–2 minutes. Add the nuts and cook for 2 minutes, stirring all the time. Remove the pan from the heat, remove the nuts with a slotted spoon and set aside.
2 Reheat the oil, then sprinkle in any slow-cooking vegetables. Cook over a very high heat for 3–4 minutes, stirring all the time. Add the remaining vegetables and cook for a further 2–3 minutes or until heated through but still very crisp.
3 Add the soy sauce, sherry, sugar, and five-spice powder, if using. Cook for a further 1 minute, then transfer to a warmed serving dish, sprinkle with the nuts and serve immediately.
SERVES 4–6

VARIATIONS
Stir-fried Vegetables with Coconut Milk Omit the nuts, soy sauce, sherry, sugar, and five-spice powder. Dissolve 6 oz creamed coconut in 1¾ cups boiling water. Mix with 1 level tsp ground cumin and 2 tbsp chopped fresh coriander (cilantro). Cook the vegetables as above, then, when the vegetables are cooked, remove them from the pan with a slotted spoon, and set aside. Add the coconut mixture to the hot oil and cook for 1 minute, stirring all the time. Return the vegetables to the pan and reheat for 1–2 minutes. Serve immediately.

Stir-fried Vegetables with Tofu Marinate ½ lb diced tofu in 2 tbsp soy sauce and 2 tbsp dry sherry with 1 skinned and crushed garlic clove for at least 30 minutes before cooking. Drain the tofu and stir-fry in hot oil for 2–3 minutes. Remove from the pan and set aside. Cook the vegetables as above and add the soy sauce mixture as in the main recipe, or the coconut mixture. Stir in the tofu at the end and reheat for 1–2 minutes before serving.

— NINE —

PASTA AND GNOCCHI

It's difficult to remember what we did for fast, satisfying meals before pasta became so readily available in this country. Because it's quick and easy to cook, cheap, nutritious, and tasty, pasta has become one of our most popular foods.

There are many excellent dried pastas available, but the best are made from durum wheat. Most packets give cooking instructions, but much depends on the shape of the pasta, how much water you put in the pan, and how you like it cooked, so it's advisable to taste as you go. The most important thing to remember is that pasta requires lots of fast boiling water; a small pan with insufficient water will produce unevenly cooked, stodgy pasta.

This applies to cooking fresh pasta, too. It's much easier to buy fresh pasta now and it cooks in just a few minutes. Most supermarkets stock a good selection in their chilled cabinets and, of course, good Italian delicatessens make their own. Once you get it home, store it in the refrigerator for up to 2 days, or put it in the freezer (and cook from frozen). We found it almost impossible to estimate portion sizes for pasta, partly because our tasters would invariably eat as much as they could cram on to their plates, and partly because a lot depends on how rich the sauce is. So, as a very rough guide, for an appetizer allow approximately 2–3 oz dried pasta per person and, for a main course, allow 4–6 oz dried pasta or 5–6 oz fresh.

Cooked pasta should be served hot and steaming straight from the pan, so have warmed bowls or plates to hand and hungry guests ready and waiting. Should you find yourself with leftovers, the only satisfactory method of reheating it is in the microwave. Both dressed and plain pasta can be reheated in this way without losing texture or flavor. If you don't own a microwave, toss plain leftover pasta with one of the dressings on pages 181–194, mix with a few cold cooked beans and vegetables, and serve as a salad.

For want of a better description, gnocchi are like small dumplings which are cooked in boiling water and served with a sauce, like pasta. They may be made with flour, semolina, cornmeal, or potato. The same mixture may also be spread in a dish, left until cold and then cut into rounds or squares, arranged in a dish, coated with Tomato or Béchamel Sauce (see pages 190 and 189), sprinkled with cheese, and baked in the oven until heated through, golden brown, and bubbling. In Italy, gnocchi is usually served as a first course. It makes a very substantial dish unless served in minute quantities, so we suggest serving it as a main course with a crisp, lightly dressed salad.

Parmesan cheese is a must for serving with both pasta and gnocchi. A lump of cheese bought from a delicatessen or good supermarket and freshly grated at home is infinitely superior to the ready-grated varieties, and it doesn't cost much more. It will keep, wrapped, in the refrigerator for up to 2 weeks.

In addition to the recipes in this section, chapter fifteen (page 181) includes lots of other sauces suitable for serving with pasta and gnocchi, including the classic Genoese Pesto (see page 193).

$\mathcal{S}$PAGHETTI WITH GARLIC

Increase or decrease the quantity of garlic and chili used in this recipe according to your taste. It's an intensely flavored dish, so a small amount of spaghetti goes a long way. Serve with a crisp mixed leaf and watercress salad dressed lightly with a sharp vinaigrette.

about 1 lb dried spaghetti	*1 chili, seeded and chopped*
salt and pepper	*2 level tbsp chopped fresh parsley, coriander (cilantro) or*
5 tbsp virgin olive oil	*basil (optional)*
2 garlic cloves, skinned and crushed	

1 Cook the spaghetti in boiling salted water for 8–10 minutes or until *al dente* (tender but still firm to the bite).
2 Meanwhile, heat the oil in a heavy-based saucepan, add the garlic and chili, and fry for 3–4 minutes, stirring occasionally. Don't let the garlic and chili become too brown or the oil will taste bitter. Remove from the heat and set aside until the pasta is cooked.
3 Drain the pasta thoroughly. Reheat the oil over a very high heat for 1 minute, then pour over the pasta with the herbs, if using. Season with salt and pepper and serve immediately.
SERVES 6

$\mathcal{B}$OLOGNESE SAUCE

This is our vegetarian version of the classic pasta sauce, with apologies to the Italians! Use it to dress pasta, fill lasagne, or as a base for cottage pie.

2 tbsp olive oil	*1 bay leaf*
1 celery stick, trimmed and finely chopped	*1 bouquet garni*
2 carrots, trimmed, peeled, and finely chopped	*1 level tsp yeast extract*
1 medium onion, skinned and finely chopped	*1 level tsp sugar*
¼ lb mushrooms, wiped and finely chopped	*salt and pepper*
2 garlic cloves, skinned and crushed	*freshly grated nutmeg*
3 level tbsp tomato paste	*1 cinnamon stick*
two 14 oz cans chopped tomatoes	*6 oz TVP*
1¼ cups dry red wine	*3 tbsp chopped fresh parsley*
2½ cups vegetable stock	

1 Heat the oil in a large, heavy-based saucepan, add the celery, carrots, onion, mushrooms, and garlic and fry for about 5 minutes or until softened. Add the tomato paste and fry for 1 minute, then add all the remaining ingredients except the parsley. Bring to the boil, then reduce the heat, cover, and simmer gently for 30–45 minutes or until very tender.
2 Stir in the parsley and season with more salt, pepper, and nutmeg, if necessary. Remove the cinnamon stick, bay leaf, and bouquet garni before serving.
SERVES 8

$\mathscr{S}$PRING VEGETABLE PASTA

The beauty of this recipe is its versatility. Try experimenting with different combinations of herbs and vegetables as they come into season. Alternative types of pasta may also be used.

¼ lb fresh asparagus or green beans, trimmed

½ lb leeks, trimmed and thinly sliced diagonally

salt and pepper

6 oz creamy goats' cheese or full-fat soft cheese with garlic and herbs

5 oz mascarpone cheese or ⅔ cup extra-thick heavy cream

4 tbsp vegetable margarine or butter

2 tbsp olive oil

1 medium onion, skinned and finely chopped

¼ lb carrots, trimmed, peeled, and thinly sliced diagonally

½ lb cremini mushrooms, wiped and thinly sliced

½ cup dry white white

1½ cups crème fraîche

¼ cup chopped fresh herbs, such as parsley, thyme, and sage

¼ lb frozen petits pois

1-1½ lb dried penne

mascarpone cheese, to serve

1 Cut the asparagus or green beans into 2 inch lengths and blanch with the leeks in boiling salted water for 3–4 minutes. Drain thoroughly. Mix together the goats' cheese and mascarpone cheese or cream.

2 Heat the margarine or butter with the oil in a large frying pan. Stir in the onion and cook, stirring, for 3–4 minutes. Add the carrots and mushrooms and continue to cook for 2–3 minutes or until beginning to soften.

3 Stir in all the remaining ingredients, except the cheese mixture, pasta, and mascarpone,

and simmer very gently until thickened.

4 Meanwhile, cook the pasta in boiling salted water for about 10 minutes or until *al dente* (tender but still firm to the bite).

5 Remove the sauce from the heat and gently stir in the cheese mixture. Season with salt and pepper.

6 Drain the pasta thoroughly and transfer to a warmed serving dish. Spoon on the hot sauce and serve immediately, topped with a spoonful of mascarpone.

SERVES 4

SPINACH AND RICOTTA CANNELLONI

It's much easier to make cannelloni using lasagne noodles than it is to make it with cannelloni tubes. If you cannot buy fresh lasagne noodles, use dried, but cook them first according to packet instructions and reduce the final cooking time to about 20 minutes.

¼ cup olive oil
2 small onions, skinned and finely chopped
2 level tbsp tomato paste
1 level tsp mild paprika
two 14 oz cans chopped tomatoes
pinch of dried oregano
1¼ cups dry red wine or vegetable stock
large pinch of sugar

salt and pepper
1 garlic clove, skinned and crushed
1 lb frozen leaf spinach, thawed and drained
1 lb ricotta cheese
freshly grated nutmeg
18 small sheets of fresh lasagne noodles
freshly grated Parmesan cheese or a few breadcrumbs

1 To make the sauce, heat half the oil in a heavy-based saucepan, add half the onion, and fry for 5–10 minutes or until very soft. Add the tomato paste and paprika and fry for 2–3 minutes. Add the tomatoes, oregano, red wine or stock, and sugar, and season with salt and pepper. Simmer for 20 minutes.
2 Heat the remaining oil in a large saucepan, add the garlic and remaining onion and cook for 5 minutes, stirring all the time. Add the spinach and cook for 2 minutes. Cool slightly,

then add the ricotta cheese. Season with nutmeg, salt, and pepper.
3 Lay the lasagne sheets on a work surface and divide the spinach mixture between them. Roll up the sheets to enclose the filling and arrange, seam-side down in a single layer, in a greased ovenproof dish. Pour the sauce over and sprinkle with Parmesan cheese or breadcrumbs. Bake in the oven at 400°F for 30 minutes.
SERVES 4–6

PASTA WITH MUSHROOM AND HUMMUS SAUCE

Store-bought hummus makes the basis for a very quick and easy pasta sauce.

2 tbsp olive oil
½ lb button mushrooms, wiped and sliced
1 bunch of scallions, trimmed and chopped
pinch of cumin seeds

1 cup hummus
2 tbsp milk
½ lb dried spaghetti or tortellini
salt and pepper

1 Heat the oil in a saucepan. Add the vegetables and cumin seeds and fry for 2–3 minutes, stirring constantly.
2 Add the hummus and milk. Cover and simmer for 5–10 minutes.

3 Meanwhile, cook the pasta in boiling salted water for 8–10 minutes or until *al dente* (tender but still firm to the bite). Drain well.
4 Stir the pasta into the sauce and season.
SERVES 2

TAGLIATELLE with SUN-DRIED TOMATO SAUCE

For an occasional treat, serve the pasta and sauce topped with a spoonful of crème fraîche and a generous amount of coarsely grated Pecorino or Parmesan cheese. The sauce is equally good served with spaghetti or another type of pasta.

2 tbsp olive oil (preferably from the jar of sun-dried tomatoes)	*1 garlic clove, skinned and crushed*
2 tbsp vegetable margarine or butter	*14 oz can chopped tomatoes*
1 small onion, roughly chopped	*¼ lb drained sun-dried tomatoes, finely chopped*
3 oz celery, roughly chopped	*½ cup dry white wine*
3 oz carrot, roughly chopped	*salt and pepper*
	1–1½ lb dried tagliatelle

1 Heat the oil and margarine or butter in a large saucepan. Add the onion, celery, carrot, and garlic and cook, stirring, for 8–10 minutes or until beginning to soften.
2 Stir in the canned tomatoes, sun-dried tomatoes, and wine. Season with salt and pepper, cover, and simmer for about 30 minutes, stirring occasionally.
3 Meanwhile, cook the tagliatelle in boiling salted water for 8–10 minutes or until *al dente* (tender but still slightly firm to the bite).
4 Pour about half the sauce into a food processor or blender and purée until quite smooth. Stir into the remaining sauce and reheat if necessary.
5 Drain the tagliatelle thoroughly and transfer to a warmed serving bowl. Pour over the sauce and serve immediately.
SERVES 4

*P*ASTA WITH LEEKS AND FROMAGE BLANC

Use a hot variety of horseradish relish to give the sauce a good 'kick'.

3 tbsp olive oil	salt and pepper
½ lb leeks, trimmed, washed thoroughly, and sliced	1¼ cups fromage blanc
⅔ cup vegetable stock	1 tbsp horseradish relish
8–10 oz pasta of your choice	chopped fresh parsley, to garnish

1 Heat the oil in a saucepan. Add the leeks and cook over a low heat for 4–5 minutes or until the leeks begin to soften. Add the stock, bring to the boil, then reduce the heat, cover, and simmer for 15–20 minutes or until the leeks are very soft.

2 Meanwhile, cook the pasta in boiling salted water for 8–12 minutes or until *al dente* (tender but still firm to the bite).

3 Stir the fromage blanc and horseradish into the leek mixture. Season with salt and pepper and heat gently, without boiling and stirring all the time. Drain the pasta and transfer to a warmed serving bowl. Pour over the sauce, toss together and serve immediately, sprinkled with parsley.

SERVES 2

*S*TUFFED BAKED PASTA SHELLS

You will need very large pasta shells for this recipe, measuring about 1½ inches long before cooking; once cooked they are even bigger. Don't be tempted to use smaller shells – you will run out of patience trying to stuff them! Serve with a mixed salad.

7 tbsp vegetable margarine or butter	24 large dried pasta shells
1¼ cups salted cashew nuts, roughly chopped	⅓ cup all-purpose flour
6 oz button mushrooms, wiped and roughly chopped	3 cups milk
1 small onion, skinned and roughly chopped	1 bay leaf
2 oz celery, trimmed and roughly chopped	10 oz Cheddar cheese, coarsely grated
½ lb fresh spinach	3 level tbsp chopped fresh parsley
salt and pepper	1 free-range egg

1 Melt 4 tbsp margarine or butter in a large frying pan. Add the cashew nuts, mushrooms, onion, and celery, and fry for about 10 minutes or until golden and any excess liquid has evaporated, stirring occasionally.

2 Wash the spinach, put in a saucepan, cover, and cook over a low heat until just wilted. Drain well, then roughly chop. Stir into the

mixture, season and leave to cool.

3 Cook the pasta shells in boiling salted water for about 10 minutes or until just tender. Drain well. Fill the shells with the nut mixture and place in a single layer in a large, shallow ovenproof dish.

4 Melt the remaining margarine or butter in a small saucepan. Add the flour and cook, stirring, for 1–2 minutes, then remove from the heat, and gradually blend in the milk. Add the bay leaf, then bring to the boil and simmer, stirring, for 2–3 minutes. Remove from the heat and discard the bay leaf, then beat in the cheese, parsley, and egg. Season

with salt and pepper and spoon evenly over the pasta.

5 Bake at 350°F for about 40 minutes or until golden and bubbling.

SERVES 4–6

MUSHROOM LASAGNE

The preparation of lasagne is always lengthy, but the benefit is that it can be frozen or finished a day ahead ready for last-minute baking.

½ lb frozen leaf spinach, thawed
salt and pepper
olive oil
about ¼ lb fresh lasagne or ½ lb dried lasagne noodles
2 lb mixed mushrooms, such as button, flat and cremini, wiped
8 tbsp vegetable margarine or butter
2 tbsp lemon juice

¼ cup all-purpose flour
2½ cups milk
2½ cups vegetable stock
freshly grated nutmeg, to taste
2 large garlic cloves, skinned and crushed
6 oz Gruyère cheese, grated
⅓ cup fresh white breadcrumbs

1 Drain the spinach and squeeze out any excess liquid. Chop finely.

2 Bring a large saucepan of salted water to the boil. (Use two if necessary.) Add a dash of olive oil to each, followed by the lasagne. Cook according to packet instructions, stirring occasionally. When the pasta is tender, drain it in a colander, and immediately run cold water over it. This will stop the pasta from cooking further and will rinse off some of the starch. Spread the pasta out on clean dish towels and cover with a damp dish towel until required.

3 Quarter or slice the mushrooms, or leave them whole, depending on their size. Melt half the margarine or butter in a large saucepan. Add the mushrooms and lemon juice, and season with salt and pepper. Cover and cook over a fairly high heat for 4–6 minutes or until the mushrooms are tender. Remove from the pan with a slotted spoon, then bubble the juices to evaporate any excess moisture until

there is only fat left in the saucepan.

4 Melt the remaining margarine or butter in the same saucepan. Carefully stir in the flour and cook for 1–2 minutes before slowly blending in the milk and stock. Gradually bring to the boil, making sure that you keep stirring all the time, and cook for 1–2 minutes or until boiling and thickened. Mix in the nutmeg, garlic, and spinach. Taste and adjust the seasoning if necessary.

5 Spoon a little of the sauce into the base of a 3 quart ovenproof dish. Top with a layer of pasta followed by a layer of mushrooms. Spoon over more of the sauce, then continue layering the ingredients, finishing with the sauce, making sure that it completely covers the ingredients underneath. Sprinkle over the Gruyère cheese and breadcrumbs.

6 Stand the dish on a baking sheet and cook at 400°F for 45 minutes–1 hour.

SERVES 6

PENNE WITH TOMATO AND CHILI

This simple sauce is equally delicious if made in advance, cooled and then reheated when required. It is also good served with baked potatoes, nut roasts, burgers, or a different type of pasta. Should you need to make it in a hurry, from storecupboard ingredients, some or all of the vegetables may be omitted.

2 tbsp olive oil
2 celery sticks, trimmed and finely chopped
1 small carrot, trimmed, peeled, and finely chopped
1 medium onion, skinned and finely chopped
1–2 garlic cloves, skinned and crushed
2 level tbsp tomato paste
1 level tsp dried herbes de Provence

1–2 fresh red chilies, seeded and chopped
two 14 oz cans chopped tomatoes
⅔ cup dry red wine or vegetable stock
a handful of fresh parsley (including some stalks), chopped
salt and pepper
1 lb dried penne

1 Heat the oil in a large heavy-based saucepan. Add the celery, carrot, onion, and garlic and cook over a high heat for 2–3 minutes, stirring all the time. Lower the heat and continue cooking for about 5 minutes or until the vegetables are beginning to soften without browning.
2 Add the tomato paste, dried herbs, and chilies, increase the heat and fry for 1–2 minutes. Add the tomatoes, red wine or stock, and half the parsley. Season with salt and pepper and bring to the boil, then lower

the heat, cover, and simmer for 45 minutes.
3 Cook the pasta in boiling salted water for about 10 minutes or until *al dente* (tender but still firm to the bite).
4 While the pasta is cooking, remove the lid from the sauce, increase the heat, and cook vigorously until it is reduced and thickened. Add the remaining parsley, taste and adjust the seasoning, if necessary.
5 Drain the pasta and tip it into the sauce. Toss together to mix and serve immediately.
SERVES 4

VEGETABLE LASAGNE

Sheets of fresh lasagne are available in the chilled cabinet of most supermarkets today. If using pre-cooked dried lasagne noodles, add a little extra liquid (stock or water) to the vegetable mixture. Serve with a crisp green salad.

2 tbsp olive oil
1 garlic clove, skinned and crushed
1 carrot, trimmed, peeled, and chopped
1 large onion, skinned and sliced
1 sweet red pepper, cored, seeded, and chopped
1 level tbsp mild paprika
2 level tsp dried oregano or marjoram
1 large eggplant, trimmed and cut into large chunks
½ lb button mushrooms, wiped and sliced

2 large zucchini, trimmed and sliced
two 14 oz cans chopped tomatoes
2 level tbsp tomato paste
2 bay leaves
about ¼ lb fresh lasagne or ½ lb dried
salt and pepper
3¼ cups Béchamel Sauce (see page 189)
Parmesan or Cheddar cheese, grated (optional)

1 Heat the oil in a large saucepan. Add the garlic, carrot, onion, and sweet pepper and fry for 1–2 minutes or until beginning to soften. Add the paprika, herbs, and eggplant and fry for a few minutes more.

2 Add the remaining vegetables to the pan with the tomatoes, tomato paste, and bay leaves. Bring to the boil, then reduce the heat, cover, and simmer for 30 minutes.

3 Meanwhile, if using dried lasagne that needs pre-cooking, cook it in boiling salted water according to packet instructions. Drain and leave to dry on a clean dish towel.

4 Spread a small amount of the tomato sauce in the base of a 3 quart ovenproof dish. Cover with a layer of lasagne and top with a layer of Béchamel Sauce. Continue layering in this way, ending with a layer of Béchamel Sauce that covers the pasta completely. Sprinkle with the cheese, if using.

5 Bake the lasagne in the oven at 400°F for 45 minutes–1 hour or until the lasagne is piping hot and well browned. Leave to stand for 15 minutes before serving.

SERVES 6

Vegetable Lasagne

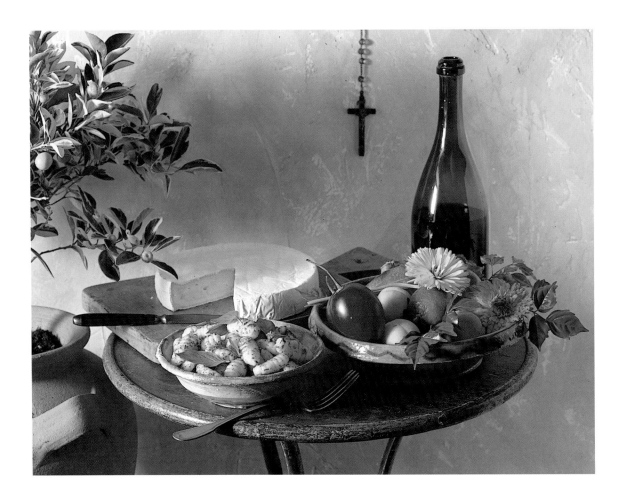

Potato Gnocchi

$\mathscr{P}$OTATO GNOCCHI

Gnocchi are little dumplings, made in this recipe from potatoes although there are other
versions made with semolina, spinach, and ricotta cheese. The Italians always eat gnocchi as a
first course, sometimes simply sprinkled with melted butter and grated Parmesan cheese, at
other times coated in a rich and pungent tomato sauce. The type of gnocchi and the way in
which they are served is purely regional; these potato gnocchi are fairly typical of the regions
of northern Italy. In Lombardy and Veneto, chopped fresh sage would be added to the melted
butter and cheese, whereas in Liguria they like to serve their gnocchi with pesto sauce.

2 lb all-purpose potatoes	**To serve**
salt	1 quantity Pesto (see page 193) or Tomato Sauce (see
4 tbsp vegetable margarine or butter	page 190)
1 free-range egg, beaten	freshly grated Parmesan cheese
2–2½ cups all-purpose flour	

1 Cook the potatoes in their skins in boiling salted water for about 20 minutes or until tender. Drain well, cool slightly, and peel.
2 While the potatoes are still warm, push them through a strainer into a large bowl. Add 1 tsp salt, the margarine or butter, egg, and half the flour. Mix well to bind together.
3 Turn the mixture out on to a floured surface and knead gently, gradually adding more flour, until the dough is soft, smooth and slightly sticky.
4 With floured hands, roll the dough into 1 inch thick ropes. Cut the ropes into ¾ inch pieces.
5 Press a finger into each piece of dough to flatten, then draw your finger towards you to curl the sides of the gnocchi. Alternatively,

make a decorative shape by using the same rolling technique, but roll each dumpling over the ends of the prongs of a fork. Spread the dumplings out on a floured dish towel.
6 Bring a large pan of salted water to the boil and reduce to barely simmering. Drop in a few gnocchi at a time and cook gently for 2–3 minutes or until they float to the surface.
7 With a slotted spoon, remove the gnocchi from the pan, then place them in a greased serving dish. Cover and keep warm while cooking the remaining gnocchi.
8 When all the gnocchi are cooked, toss them in the chosen sauce. Serve immediately, sprinkled with Parmesan.
SERVES 4 AS AN APPETIZER OR LIGHT MEAL

*R*ICOTTA GNOCCHI

Gnocchi made with ricotta cheese are light and easy to make. Taleggio is a semi-soft Italian cheese; use Gouda or Edam instead if you can't find it.

For the gnocchi	For the sauce
⅔ cup ricotta cheese	4 tbsp vegetable margarine or butter
2 tbsp vegetable margarine or softened butter	1 garlic clove, skinned and crushed
1 level tbsp all-purpose flour	2 level tbsp all-purpose flour
1 free-range egg	2½ cups milk
freshly grated nutmeg	½ lb taleggio, coarsely grated
salt and pepper	salt and pepper

1 Beat together all the gnocchi ingredients until smooth, adding nutmeg, salt, and pepper to taste. Cover and chill for 30 minutes.
2 Meanwhile, make the sauce. Melt the margarine or butter with the garlic and stir in the flour. Cook, stirring, for 1–2 minutes, then gradually add the milk. Bring slowly to the boil, stirring occasionally, then reduce the heat, and simmer for 3–4 minutes or until thickened. Remove from the heat and beat in the taleggio. Season with salt and pepper. Cover with damp parchment paper.
3 Bring a large pan of salted water to the boil

and reduce to barely simmering. Drop in teaspoonfuls of the gnocchi mixture and cook for 4–5 minutes or until they float to the surface. Lift out with a slotted spoon and transfer to one large, or four individual, buttered flameproof dishes. Coat with the sauce.
4 Bake in the oven at 400°F for 25–30 minutes (15–20 minutes for individual dishes). Brown under a hot broiler if necessary, then serve immediately.
SERVES 4 AS AN APPETIZER OR LIGHT MEAL

$\mathscr{S}$ PINACH GNOCCHI

If serving this as an appetizer, serve a light main course and dessert to follow.

2 lb washed fresh spinach or 1 lb frozen spinach	¼ level tsp freshly grated nutmeg
1 cup curd cheese	1¼ cups freshly grated Parmesan cheese
2 free-range eggs, beaten	salt and pepper
2 cups all-purpose flour	8 tbsp vegetable margarine or butter

1 Place the spinach in a saucepan without any water, cover, and cook gently for 5–10 minutes or until tender, or thawed if using frozen spinach. Drain very well and chop finely.
2 Mix together the curd cheese, eggs, flour, spinach, nutmeg, and half the Parmesan. Season with salt and pepper.
3 With floured hands, form the mixture into cork-sized croquettes, or balls the size of large marbles. Chill in the refrigerator for at least 1 hour.
4 Bring a large pan of salted water to the boil and reduce to barely simmering. Drop in a few gnocchi at a time and cook for 8–10 minutes or until they float to the surface.
5 With a slotted spoon, remove the gnocchi from the pan, then place them in a greased serving dish. Cover and keep warm while cooking the remaining gnocchi.
6 Melt the margarine or butter in a small saucepan and pour it over the gnocchi. Sprinkle with the remaining cheese and serve immediately.
SERVES 4 AS AN APPETIZER OR LIGHT MEAL

$\mathscr{P}$ ASTA GRATIN

To make this a vegan dish, omit the cheese and make the Béchamel Sauce with soy milk.

3 oz Gruyère cheese, grated	½ lb dried conchiglie or farfalle
¼ level tsp freshly grated nutmeg	1 quantity Tomato Sauce (see page 190)
1 quantity hot Béchamel Sauce (see page 189)	¼ cup freshly grated Parmesan cheese
salt and pepper	3 level tbsp dried breadcrumbs

1 Add the Gruyère cheese and nutmeg to the Béchamel Sauce, season with salt and pepper, and stir until the cheese has melted.
2 Cook the pasta in boiling salted water for about 10 minutes or until *al dente* (tender but still firm to the bite).
3 Drain the pasta and mix with the Tomato Sauce. Spread half this mixture in the bottom of a buttered ovenproof dish and pour over half the Béchamel Sauce. Repeat the layers, then sprinkle evenly with the Parmesan and breadcrumbs.
4 Bake in the oven at 375°F for 20 minutes, then brown under a hot broiler for 5 minutes. Serve immediately.
SERVES 3–4

—TEN—

RICE, GRAINS, AND NOODLES

Rice is the staple food for about half of the world's population. Infinitely versatile, it is easy to cook, convenient and relatively low in calories.

Cooking rice isn't difficult, providing you use a large enough pan (as when cooking pasta) and plenty of fast boiling salted water. As soon as the water boils, sprinkle the rice into the pan and keep the heat high until the water returns to the boil. Stir with a fork to loosen any grains that have sunk to the bottom of the pan, then lower the heat, and simmer (quite vigorously) for a minimum of 10 minutes or until the rice is tender. Providing you have sufficient water, and a large enough pan, the rice will not stick. There are so many varieties of rice on the market today that it's impossible to give an exact cooking time. Test the rice as it cooks.

While the rice is cooking, bring another pan of water to the boil. As soon as the rice is cooked, drain it through a strainer and rinse it with boiling water. Stir the grains with a fork and tip into a heated serving dish.

Brown rice is the whole grain with only the tough outer husk removed. Because the bran is retained, the rice has a chewy texture and nutty flavor. It is less refined than white rice so it takes longer to cook. It can be used in any recipes which call for long-grain rice, but if the dish is cooked by the absorption method, you should allow extra liquid. Basmati and Arborio rice are distinctive varieties.

Grains, such as barley, bulgar wheat, corn, cracked wheat, and millet, are the edible seeds of different grasses. They are high in vitamins and can be used whole, cracked or flaked. Bulgar wheat is a useful ingredient to keep in the storecupboard. It requires a mere 30 minutes' soaking in boiling water before it is ready as an accompaniment to stews or casseroles, or for flavoring with herbs, garlic and vegetables to make a quick nutritious salad (see page 48). Corn grain is ground into cornmeal for making polenta (see page 142), cornbread (see page 154), tortillas, and muffins.

Like pasta, noodles are now available in all shapes and sizes. Oriental noodles are most widely available dried and compressed into square packages. Allow about 3–4 oz per person.

FRAGRANT COCONUT RICE

Lemon grass lends a unique flavor and smell to anything it's cooked with. If you cannot find any in stores (but it really is worth looking for), add the finely grated rind of one lemon instead. This is not comparable, but adds a delicious flavor of its own. Galangal is a root that looks very similar to ginger. If you're lucky enough to find it fresh in an oriental grocery, use it in place of dried in this recipe.

1 oz creamed coconut, chopped	*1 cinnamon stick*
1 level tsp salt	*1 piece of lemon grass, split*
½ level tsp freshly grated nutmeg	*1 bay leaf*
freshly ground black pepper	*2 slices of dried or fresh galangal*
2 cloves	*2 cups basmati rice*

1 Put all the ingredients, except the rice, in a heavy-based saucepan with 2½ cups water. Bring slowly to the boil. Add the rice, stir with a fork, then cover, and simmer gently for 20 minutes or until the water has been absorbed and the rice is tender.

2 Leave to stand for 2 minutes before serving.
SERVES 4–6

USHROOM RISOTTO

To make a proper risotto, you will need to buy Arborio rice, a special variety from the Arborio region of Italy. It has the ability to absorb a large quantity of liquid during cooking without turning mushy. The perfect risotto is light and creamy, but not stodgy. Butter is traditionally added in copious quantities. It lends the best flavor, but vegetable margarine or olive oil can be used instead.

about 1½ quarts Mushroom, Brown Onion, or Vegetable stock (see pages 41–42)	½ lb mushrooms, wiped and sliced
8 tbsp butter or vegetable margarine	1¼ lb Arborio (risotto) rice
1 medium onion, skinned and very finely chopped	⅔ cup freshly grated Parmesan cheese
1 garlic clove, skinned and crushed	salt and pepper
¼ oz packet dried porcini (cepe) mushrooms, soaked in 1¼ cups warm water for 30 minutes	

1 Put the stock in a large saucepan and bring to the boil. Reduce the heat and keep at barely simmering point.

2 Meanwhile, melt half of the butter or margarine in a large heavy-based saucepan. Add the onion and garlic, and cook for about 5 minutes or until soft. Do not let them burn.

3 Drain the soaked dried mushrooms, reserving the soaking liquid. Chop any large mushrooms. Add to the onion and garlic with the fresh mushrooms and cook for 3–4 minutes, stirring all the time. Add the rice and cook for 1 minute.

4 Slowly pour the mushroom soaking liquid into the pan (being careful to leave any grit from the mushrooms in the bowl). Add about one-third of the stock. Cook gently, stirring occasionally, until the stock has been absorbed. Continue cooking and adding more stock, using a ladle, as soon as each addition has been absorbed, stirring frequently. You may not need all the stock, but continue cooking for about 20 minutes or until the rice is soft. When ready, add three-quarters of the Parmesan cheese, with the remaining butter or margarine, and season with salt and pepper. Serve sprinkled with the remaining Parmesan.
SERVES 6 AS AN APPETIZER OR 4 AS A MAIN COURSE

VARIATIONS
Pea and Saffron Risotto Omit the mushrooms. Shell 1½ lb fresh peas. Soak a large pinch of saffron strands in a little of the warm stock for about 10 minutes. Add to the onions in step 3 with ⅔ cup dry white wine and the peas. Continue as above. (Alternatively, use ¾ lb frozen petits pois and add them about 5 minutes before the end of the cooking time.)

Asparagus Risotto Cook as Pea and Saffron Risotto, but substitute ½ lb asparagus tips for the peas. Steam until just tender (see page 53 for a foolproof method) and stir into the risotto about 5 minutes before the end of the cooking time.

Almond and Zucchini Risotto If making a vegan risotto, use vegetable margarine. Cook as Pea and Saffron Risotto but substitute 1 lb zucchini, trimmed and thinly sliced, for the peas. Add them about 5 minutes before the end of the cooking time with 3 tbsp ground almonds. Continue as above but omit the cheese. Serve the risotto sprinkled with toasted sliced almonds and sesame seeds.

$\mathscr{S}$ESAME PILAFF WITH FENNEL

If fennel is not available, use only 1 quart stock and stir in 2 level tbsp chopped fresh parsley or scallion tops just before serving. It's important to use one of the suggested varieties of rice as it soaks up the liquid, becoming plump and tender rather than mushy.

¼ cup sesame seeds	pinch of ground turmeric
6 oz fennel	1¼ cups Arborio or dessert rice
4 tbsp vegetable margarine or butter	about 6 cups vegetable stock
1 medium onion, skinned and finely chopped	salt and pepper
1 large sweet green pepper, cored, seeded, and chopped	

1 Toast the sesame seeds under a hot broiler until golden brown, then leave to cool. Trim and finely chop the fennel, reserving the feathery tops. Finely chop the tops and set aside.
2 Melt the margarine or butter in a saucepan and add the onion, sweet pepper, fennel, and turmeric. Fry for 2–3 minutes or until beginning to soften, stirring constantly. Stir in the rice and continue to cook, stirring, for 1 minute, then add the stock and toasted sesame seeds. Season with salt and pepper.
3 Bring to the boil, cover, and simmer very slowly for about 45 minutes or until all the liquid has been absorbed and the rice is tender. Taste and adjust the seasoning, if necessary, and stir in the fennel tops just before serving.

$\mathscr{V}$EGETABLE BIRYANI

Serve with Curry Sauce (see page 188), Raita (see page 54), and Nan-style Bread (see page 155).

2 cups basmati rice	½ level tsp chili powder
salt and pepper	3 medium carrots, trimmed, peeled, and thinly sliced
4 tbsp ghee or clarified butter	½ lb green beans, trimmed and halved
1 large onion, skinned and chopped	½ lb small cauliflower florets
1 inch piece of fresh ginger root, peeled and grated	1 level tsp garam masala
1–2 garlic cloves, skinned and crushed	juice of 1 lemon
1 level tsp ground coriander	hard-boiled egg slices and coriander (cilantro) sprigs, to garnish
2 level tsp ground cumin	
1 level tsp ground turmeric	

1 Put the rice in a strainer and rinse under cold running water until the water runs clear.
2 Put the rice in a saucepan with 2½ cups water and 1 level tsp salt. Bring to the boil, then reduce the heat, and simmer for 10 minutes or until only just tender.
3 Meanwhile, melt the ghee or butter in a large heavy-based saucepan, add the onion, ginger, and garlic and fry gently for 5 minutes or until soft but not colored. Add the coriander, cumin, turmeric, and chili powder and fry for 2 minutes more, stirring constantly

to prevent the spices catching and burning.
4 Remove the rice from the heat and drain.
Add 3¾ cups water to the onion and spice
mixture and season with salt and pepper. Stir
well and bring to the boil. Add the carrots
and beans and simmer for 15 minutes, then
add the cauliflower, and simmer for a further
10 minutes. Lastly, add the rice. Fold gently to
mix and simmer until reheated.

5 Stir the garam masala and lemon juice into
the biryani and simmer for a few minutes
more to reheat and allow the flavors to
develop. Taste and adjust the seasoning, if
necessary, then turn into a warmed serving
dish. Garnish with egg slices and coriander
and serve immediately.
SERVES 4

Vegetable Biryani

COCONUT, RICE, AND LENTIL SALAD

This rice salad can also be served hot. Serve with other salads as part of a salad-based meal, or as an accompaniment to vegetable stews or casseroles.

2 tbsp vegetable oil
1 medium onion, skinned and chopped
2 bay leaves
1 cinnamon stick
4 whole green cardamom pods, split
3 oz moong dal (de-husked split green lentils)

3 oz split red lentils
2 oz creamed coconut, chopped
½ cup long-grain rice
salt and pepper
3 level tbsp chopped fresh parsley
2 tbsp toasted sliced almonds or cashew nuts

1 Heat the oil in a large saucepan and add the onion, bay leaves, cinnamon, and cardamoms. Fry for about 10 minutes or until golden brown, stirring constantly.
2 Stir in the moong dal, red lentils, coconut, and rice. Add about 3¾ cups cold water and ½ level tsp salt. Bring to the boil, and boil gently for about 10 minutes or until the rice and lentils are just cooked but still retain some 'bite'.
3 Drain well and rinse under cold running water. Leave to drain. Stir, season with salt and pepper, then stir in the parsley and nuts.
SERVES 6–8

NOODLES WITH FRIED EGGS

Buckwheat noodles are also known as soba noodles. They are sold in many health food stores, some supermarkets and, of course, Japanese groceries. If unavailable, use thin egg noodles instead and follow the cooking instructions on the packet.

4–6 oz buckwheat noodles
salt
2 tbsp sesame oil
1 onion, skinned and sliced
1 large carrot, trimmed, peeled, and very thinly sliced
1 small garlic clove, skinned and crushed
about 3 large leaves Chinese cabbage or a handful of spinach, roughly chopped

3 tbsp light soy sauce
1 level tsp sugar
1 tbsp white wine vinegar
vegetable oil for frying
2 free-range eggs

1 Cook the noodles in boiling salted water until tender. Follow the packet instructions.
2 Meanwhile, heat the sesame oil in a large frying pan. Add the onion, carrot, and garlic and fry over a very high heat until tinged with brown and softened, stirring all the time. Add the Chinese cabbage or spinach and the soy sauce, sugar, and vinegar, reduce the heat, and simmer very gently while cooking the eggs.
3 Heat a little vegetable oil in a frying pan and fry the eggs. Meanwhile, drain the noodles and stir into the vegetable mixture, tossing everything together to mix.
4 Divide the noodles between two plates and top each portion with an egg. Serve.
SERVES 2

$\mathscr{S}$INGAPORE NOODLES

Broccoli, green beans, baby corn, water chestnuts, and daikon are also suitable.

½ lb thin round egg noodles
salt
4 tbsp vegetable oil
2 garlic cloves, skinned and crushed
1 medium onion, skinned and chopped
1 inch piece of fresh ginger root, peeled and chopped
1 fresh green chili, seeded and chopped
2 carrots, trimmed, peeled, and thinly sliced

a handful of mustard greens, pak choi, or 2 leaves
Chinese cabbage, shredded
¼ lb snow peas, trimmed
4 scallions, trimmed and chopped
1 level tsp curry powder
2 tbsp light soy sauce
2 tbsp hoisin sauce

1 Cook the noodles in boiling salted water following the instructions on the packet. Drain and toss in 1 tbsp of the oil.

2 Heat the remaining oil in a wok or very large frying pan. Add the garlic, onion, ginger, and chili and stir-fry for 2–3 minutes.

3 Add the vegetables and sprinkle with the curry powder. Stir-fry for 3–4 minutes or until the vegetables are softened but still crisp. Add the noodles with the soy and hoisin sauces and stir-fry for 1–2 minutes until hot.

SERVES 4

GG FRIED RICE

Vegans can omit the eggs and make plain Fried Rice. If serving this as a main meal rather than an accompaniment, add a few more vegetables and increase the nuts to 1 cup.

2½ cups long-grain rice	4 scallions, trimmed and chopped
salt	½ cup unsalted cashew nuts or peanuts (optional)
about 2 tbsp vegetable oil	2 free-range eggs, beaten
1 large onion, skinned and chopped	1 level tsp sugar
1 green chili, seeded and chopped	2 tbsp light soy sauce
2 large carrots, trimmed, peeled, and coarsely grated	Crisp Fried Onions (see page 115), to serve (optional)
1 sweet green pepper, cored, seeded, and finely chopped	

1 Cook the rice in boiling salted water for about 10 minutes or until just tender. Do not overcook it or the fried rice will be mushy. Drain the rice, rinse with boiling water, then spread out on a large plate or tray while cooking the vegetables.
2 Heat the oil in a wok or very large frying pan. Add the onion, chili, carrots, and green pepper and stir-fry for 3–4 minutes or until the vegetables are softened. Add the scallions

and nuts, if using, and fry for 1 minute. Pour in the egg in a thin stream, stirring all the time so that it breaks up into small pieces. When all of the egg has set, add the rice, sugar, and soy sauce, and continue cooking, stirring all the time, until the rice is heated through. Add a little extra oil if the rice starts to stick. Serve immediately, sprinkled with Crisp Fried Onions, if liked.
SERVES ABOUT 6

EGETABLE COUSCOUS

Couscous is produced by moistening grains of semolina and forming them into tiny pellets. It's a staple food in North African countries where it is served with a meat or vegetable stew. The couscous grains are steamed above the stew in a *couscousière* or steamer. Serve this vegetable couscous with Harissa Sauce (see page 184).

¼ lb chick-peas, soaked overnight in cold water	½ level tsp paprika
2 cups couscous (not pre-cooked)	5 cups vegetable stock
2 medium leeks, trimmed, thickly sliced, and thoroughly washed	2 level tbsp tomato paste
8 tbsp vegetable margarine or butter	chili sauce, to taste
1 medium carrot, trimmed, peeled, and thickly sliced	salt and pepper
1 medium parsnip, trimmed, peeled, and roughly chopped	1 medium sweet red pepper, cored, seeded, and diced
½ lb rutabaga, peeled and roughly chopped	1 medium sweet green pepper, cored, seeded, and diced
1 level tsp ground cumin	1 lb tomatoes, skinned and quartered
1 level tsp ground coriander	½ lb zucchini, trimmed and sliced
	1 small cauliflower, divided into florets
	chopped fresh parsley, to garnish

1 Drain the chick-peas and put in a large saucepan. Cover with fresh water, bring to the boil, and cook for 1 hour. Drain well.

2 Place the couscous in a bowl and pour over 1 scant cup warm water. Work the water into the couscous with your fingertips, using a 'rubbing-in' motion to ensure all the grains are separate. Leave to stand for 15 minutes, then repeat the process twice more, using a total of 2½ cups water.

3 Melt 4 tbsp margarine or butter in a large saucepan with a capacity of at least 4 quarts, over which a perforated steamer will fit snugly. Add the prepared vegetables and sprinkle over the spices. Fry gently until lightly browned, then add the chick-peas with the stock, tomato paste, and chili sauce. Season with salt and pepper and bring to the boil.

4 Line a steamer with a double thickness of cheesecloth and spoon in the couscous, seasoning well with salt and pepper. Place over the vegetables and cover the steamer tightly. Bring the vegetables to a fast boil, then lower the heat, and simmer gently for about 30 minutes.

5 Take the pan and steamer off the heat and spoon the couscous into a large bowl. Cut the remaining margarine or butter into small pieces and add to the couscous. Stir well until the butter has melted and every grain is separate. Season again, if necessary.

6 Add the remaining prepared vegetables to the pan and stir well. Add a little extra chili sauce, if liked. Return to the heat and bring slowly to the boil. Spoon the couscous back into the lined steamer and place over the pan. Cover the steamer tightly, lower the heat, and simmer for another 15 minutes.

7 Turn the couscous into a dish and fork through. Serve the vegetable mixture separately, sprinkled with parsley.
SERVES 6

$\mathcal{M}$USHROOM FRICASSEE WITH LEMON COUSCOUS

Flat mushrooms give a delicious flavor to the fricassee, but can make the sauce very dark – a half-and-half mixture of button and flat mushrooms is best.

⅔ cup couscous	2 level tsp all-purpose flour
grated rind and juice of 1 lemon	⅔ cup milk
salt and pepper	2 level tsp Dijon-style mustard
6 tbsp vegetable margarine or butter	¼ cup pine nuts
8–10 oz flat or button mushrooms, wiped and sliced	

1 Bring ⅔ cup water to the boil and pour over the couscous. Add the lemon rind, season with salt and pepper, and leave to soak for about 5 minutes, stirring occasionally.

2 Heat 4 tbsp of the margarine or butter in a frying pan, add the mushrooms, and fry quickly until just beginning to soften.

3 Stir in the flour and milk and bring to the boil. Cook for 1–2 minutes, adding a little more milk if it's too thick. Remove from the heat and stir in the mustard and 2 tsp lemon juice. Taste and adjust the seasoning.

4 Meanwhile, heat the remaining margarine or butter in a separate frying pan. Add the pine nuts and couscous and cook over a high heat, stirring occasionally, until piping hot. Season and serve with the mushrooms.
SERVES 2

$\mathcal{T}$OASTED POLENTA

Polenta, or ground corn, is a staple of northern Italian cooking. It's often eaten hot, like grits, but it can also be cooled, cut into squares and then fried or broiled as here. Different types require varying cooking times; always ensure the mixture is tender and the liquid well reduced. The polenta squares can be prepared the day before you wish to serve them. Serve as an accompaniment to casseroles, stews or Broiled Vegetable Salad (see page 50).

1 level tsp salt	1 garlic clove, skinned and crushed (optional)
1¼ cups polenta	freshly ground black pepper
2 tbsp vegetable margarine or butter	

1 Pour 5 cups cold water into a large saucepan and bring to the boil. Add the salt, then pour in the polenta in a very fine stream, stirring vigorously all the time with a wooden spoon. Simmer for about 15 minutes or until the polenta is very thick and no longer grainy. Stir to prevent it sticking.
2 Remove the pan from the heat and stir in the margarine or butter, garlic, if using, and black pepper.

3 Turn out on to a wooden board or a plate and spread to a thickness of about ½–¾ inch. Cool, cover and chill in the refrigerator for at least 1 hour. Cut into 2 inch squares.
4 When ready to serve, toast the polenta squares on both sides under a hot broiler for 7–10 minutes. Serve at once or cover loosely and keep warm.
SERVES ABOUT 6

$\mathcal{B}$ARLEY WITH SPINACH AND GINGER

Barley was one of the earliest grains to be cultivated but it is now seldom used. This simple dish makes the most of the humble grain. Serve it with rice and plain yogurt.

1 cup pot or pearl barley	salt and pepper
3 cups vegetable stock	1 tbsp vegetable oil
½ lb frozen chopped spinach	1 level tsp cumin seeds
1 garlic clove, skinned and crushed	
1 inch piece of fresh ginger root, peeled and chopped	

1 Wash the barley, then put it in a large saucepan with the stock. Bring to the boil, then reduce the heat, cover, and simmer for 35–40 minutes or until most of the stock has been absorbed and the barley is tender. Stir occasionally to prevent the barley sticking.
2 Add the frozen spinach and stir over a low heat for about 10 minutes or until the spinach

has thawed. Add the garlic and ginger, lower the heat, re-cover, and cook for a further 5–7 minutes, stirring occasionally. Season with salt and pepper, then spoon into a serving dish.
3 Heat the oil in a small saucepan, add the cumin and cook for about 1 minute, stirring. Pour over the barley and spinach, and serve.
SERVES 4

—Eleven—

$\mathcal{P}$izzas, $\mathcal{B}$reads, and $\mathcal{R}$olls

Pizza at its best is wholesome, nourishing, and simply delicious. Don't spoil it with doughs that are dry, burnt, or soggy, and toppings too sparse or too overpowering to enjoy. These pitfalls can be avoided if you follow our recipe for a soft yeasty dough, or the quicker, more biscuit-like, alternative. Then add the topping of your choice – from a simple tomato and cheese mixture to a more flamboyant sweet pepper and garlic creation.

Yeast gives pizzas, breads, and rolls their characteristic smell and texture. It is available in several forms. Fresh yeast, also known as compressed yeast, is sold in blocks. It is creamy, fawn in color, and has a faint winy smell. It should have a smooth, compact texture and crumble easily. The best results are obtained when the yeast is very fresh, but it can be stored, tightly wrapped to prevent it from drying out, in the refrigerator for up to a month. It can also be frozen for up to 3 months, but it is advisable to divide it into usable 1 oz portions. Thaw at room temperature for a couple of hours before using.

Dried yeast should be mixed with a lukewarm liquid and left in a warm place for 15–20 minutes to become frothy, before being mixed with flour. If the liquid is water, add a pinch of sugar. This isn't necessary if you're using milk, because milk already contains lactose, a form of sugar. If the yeast fails to froth after 15–20 minutes, it's no longer active. Unfortunately it cannot be resurrected, so throw it away and start again.

Fast-action dried yeast is a revolutionary new form of yeast which is mixed straight into the flour without any pre-blending. When used to make a plain dough, fast-action yeast has the added advantage of rising the dough in a much shorter time; the dough needs to be left to rise only once.

Bread freezes very well. Wrapped tightly, it will keep for several months. Refresh it in a hot oven before serving. Unbaked bread dough can also be frozen. The best time to freeze dough is when it has been shaped and is in the pan ready to rise. Just place the dough and pan in a good-sized, oiled plastic bag, squeeze out the air, leaving a space above the dough, and freeze it (preferably on fast freeze). Thaw, still wrapped, in a warm place and leave to rise until doubled in size.

We tried freezing and reheating the completed pizzas, but we didn't feel the results did justice to the original recipe, so only resort to this if you really need to.

PIZZA

This basic pizza dough can be rolled out to almost any size or shape you choose, but, as a rough guide, it will make one large rectangular pizza measuring about 15 × 12 inches, two 12 inch round pizzas, or four thin 8 inch round pizzas. Be guided by the size of your baking equipment – special round pizza pans are available but not essential. A very large, flat baking sheet, or even a large roasting pan, works just as well.

Packet bread mix also makes a good, quick base. You will need two 10 oz packets (or the equivalent) to make the same quantity. When making up the mix, substitute 2 tbsp olive oil for some of the liquid.

When it comes to toppings for pizza, it is difficult, and unnecessary, to suggest exact quantities since it depends on the size of the pizza(s) made and your personal taste. Whichever combinations you choose, be generous! In addition to the toppings, sprinkle thinly sliced garlic, fresh or dried herbs, such as oregano, marjoram, or basil, or capers, chopped chilies, olives, pine nuts, or raisins on to the pizza for extra flavor.

4 cups white or wholewheat bread flour	*olive oil*
1 level tsp fast-action dried yeast	*three 14 oz cans chopped tomatoes*
salt and pepper	

1 Put the flour, yeast and 1 level tsp salt in a bowl and mix together. Make a well in the center and add 1¼ cups lukewarm water with 2 tbsp olive oil. Beat thoroughly with your hand until the dough leaves the sides of the bowl clean. You may need to add more lukewarm water, particularly if using wholewheat flour.

2 Turn the dough on to a lightly floured surface and knead for about 10 minutes or until smooth and elastic. Roll out to the size and shape of your choice and place on a baking sheet(s). Spread with the tomatoes and add the topping(s) of your choice (see right). Season with salt and pepper and drizzle over a little olive oil. Leave in a warm place for 20–30 minutes or until the dough looks puffy around the edges.

3 Bake in the oven at 425°F for 20–30 minutes (depending on size) or until golden brown and bubbling. Serve hot.

TOPPINGS

Roasted Pepper Roast four large sweet peppers under a hot broiler until the skin is blackened. Leave to cool, then remove the skin and seeds, and cut the flesh into strips. Scatter over the pizza(s) before cooking.

Artichoke Slice some drained bottled or canned artichoke hearts, and add to the pizza(s) before cooking.

Mushroom Thinly slice some mushrooms. Fry in olive oil with a little garlic, then drain well. Scatter over the pizza(s) before cooking.

Cheese Most firm cheeses with good melting properties are suitable for topping pizzas. Mozzarella is traditional, but try Bel Paese, Fontina, Taleggio, Gruyère, or Parmesan.

Vegetable Almost any vegetable is good on a pizza; steamed fresh spinach (or well drained frozen leaf spinach); eggplant, zucchini, or baby onions, cut into chunks or sliced and sautéed in olive oil; fresh tomatoes, sliced.

$\mathcal{Q}$UICK PIZZA BASE

This makes the same quantity as the recipe above.

4 cups self-rising flour	*8 tbsp vegetable margarine or butter*
1 level tsp salt	*1¼ cups milk*

1 Sift the flour and salt into a bowl, then rub in the margarine or butter until the mixture resembles fine breadcrumbs. Add the milk and mix to a soft dough. Turn out on to a lightly floured surface and knead until smooth. Roll out the dough and use as above.

$\mathscr{P}$ANZEROTTI

These deep-fried stuffed pizzas are delicious served hot as a snack or appetizer, or served cold as part of a picnic or *al fresco* buffet. You will only need about ⅓ cup of Tomato Sauce for the filling. We suggest that you make up one quantity of the recipe on page 190 and freeze the remainder or serve it with the Panzerotti instead of Pesto.

1 quantity pizza dough (see page 144)	*salt and pepper*
Tomato Sauce (see page 190) or tomato paste	*vegetable oil for deep-frying*
about 6 oz Mozzarella or goats' cheese, roughly chopped	*Pesto (see page 193) or leftover Tomato Sauce, to serve*

1 Make the pizza dough following the instructions on page 145 and leave in a warm place to rise.
2 Turn the risen dough out on to a floured surface, knead lightly and divide into 16 equal pieces. Using a rolling pin, roll each piece to a rough circle measuring about 4 inches in diameter.
3 Spread about 1 tsp Tomato Sauce or paste on to each circle, leaving a border around the edge (don't be over-generous or it will leak out during cooking). Sprinkle the cheese over the tomato and season.

4 Brush the edges of the dough with water, then fold in half to enclose the filling. Press the edges firmly together, then crimp to seal in the filling. Make sure that you do this thoroughly to prevent the filling leaking out.
5 Heat the oil in a deep-fat fryer to 350°F or until a 1 inch cube of bread browns in the hot oil in 1 minute. Deep-fry the Panzerotti in batches for 2–3 minutes or until golden brown. Drain on paper towels, then serve hot, topped with Pesto or Tomato Sauce.
MAKES 16

$\mathscr{I}$RISH SODA BREAD

Round loaves of soda bread were traditionally baked on a hot griddle over an open fire, and had a lovely crisp crust. The bread is moist, close-textured and delicious.

4 cups wholewheat flour	*1 level tsp baking soda*
1 cup all-purpose white flour	*1 level tsp salt*
⅔ cup rolled oats	*about 3¾ cups buttermilk*

1 Put the flours, oats, baking soda, and salt in a large bowl and mix together. Add enough buttermilk to mix to a soft dough.
2 Knead very lightly, then shape into a large round, and place on a greased baking sheet. Cut a deep cross in the top. Bake in the oven

at 450°F for 15 minutes, then reduce the oven temperature to 400°F and bake for a further 20–25 minutes or until the loaf sounds hollow when tapped on the bottom. Eat while still warm.
MAKES 1 LARGE LOAF

BASIC BREAD AND ROLLS

Shape and flavor this basic bread dough as desired.

*½ oz fresh yeast, or ½ level tsp dried yeast, or one 7 g
   sachet fast-action dried yeast*

about 1¼ cups lukewarm milk

4 cups wholewheat or white bread flour

1 level tsp salt

1 free-range egg, beaten

poppy, caraway, fennel, or sesame seeds

1 Dissolve the fresh yeast in the milk. If using dried yeast, sprinkle it into the milk and leave in a warm place for 15 minutes or until frothy. If using fast-action dried yeast, this stage is not necessary.

2 Put the flour and salt in a bowl. Add the fast-action dried yeast, if using. Make a well in the center, then pour in the yeast liquid, or just the milk if using fast-action dried yeast. Beat well together until the dough leaves the sides of the bowl clean. If using wholewheat flour, you will need to add a little extra milk. Turn on to a lightly floured surface and knead for about 10 minutes or until smooth and elastic.

3 If using fresh or dried yeast, place the dough in an oiled bowl, cover with a clean dish towel, and leave in a warm place for about 1 hour or until doubled in size. Turn the dough on to a floured surface and knead lightly. (This first rising and second kneading stage is not necessary if fast-action yeast has been used.)

4 Shape the dough into the desired shape or divide into eight and shape into rolls. Cover with a clean dish towel, and leave in a warm place for about 30 minutes or until doubled in size.

5 Brush with beaten egg to glaze and sprinkle with seeds. Bake in the oven at 450°F for 10 minutes, then reduce the temperature to 400°F and bake the loaves for a further 20–25 minutes or rolls for a further 10 minutes. Cool on a wire rack.

VARIATIONS

Nut Bread Add ¾ cup roughly chopped shelled walnuts or toasted hazelnuts to the basic mixture (step 2).

Cheese Bread Add ¼ lb grated well flavored Cheddar cheese and 1 level tsp dried mustard powder to the basic mixture (step 2). Sprinkle with a little extra cheese 15 minutes before the end of the cooking time.

MAKES 1 LARGE LOAF OR 8 ROLLS

OLIVE SOURDOUGH BREAD

If you make bread regularly, a sourdough starter is a convenient way of leavening bread.
Providing it is replenished as it is used, it will keep indefinitely.
After making the olive sourdough bread, blend about ⅔ cup bread flour with about 150 ml
⅔ cup water to make a runny paste. Stir it into the remaining starter, re-cover as before,
and leave for at least 24 hours before using.
Providing it is nourished every 4 days with a paste made from at least ¼ cup bread flour
and water, the starter will always be ready to use. If you do not use it for a few days, store it
in the refrigerator.

For the sourdough starter	¼ cup wholewheat flour
½ oz fresh yeast, or 1½ level tsp dried yeast and a pinch of sugar	1 level tsp salt
	3 level tbsp chopped mixed fresh herbs
2 cups white bread flour	3 tbsp virgin olive oil
For the bread	2 cups mixed pitted black and green olives, roughly chopped
3½ cups strong white flour	
¼ cup rye flour	

1 To make the sourdough starter, blend the fresh yeast with ⅔ cup lukewarm water in a large bowl. If using dried yeast, sprinkle it on to ⅔ cup water, add the sugar, and leave in a warm place until frothy.

2 Mix in a further 1¼ cups lukewarm water and enough of the flour to form a thick, pourable mixture. Don't worry if it's not perfectly smooth; the yeast will break down any lumps. Tightly cover the bowl with a damp cloth and leave at warm room temperature for 3 days to ferment and develop the sourdough flavor. (Wring out the cloth in cold water if it dries out.)

3 To make the bread, put the flours, salt, and herbs in a bowl and mix together. Add scant 1 cup of the starter and the olive oil and 1 cup lukewarm water, or enough to make a soft dough.

4 On a lightly floured surface, knead the dough for about 10 minutes or until smooth and elastic. Put the dough in a large oiled bowl, cover with a clean dish towel, and leave in a warm place for about 1 hour or until doubled in size.

5 Knock back the dough on a lightly floured surface, then carefully knead in the olives. Shape into a long sausage, then curl it round to form a coil. Wrap one end of the dough over the other and pinch with your fingers to mould them together into a circle.

6 Transfer the dough to a greased baking sheet and cover loosely with a clean dish towel. Leave in a warm place for about 20 minutes or until doubled in size.

7 Remove the dish towel and, with a sharp pair of scissors, snip around the top of the loaf to make a zig-zag pattern. Brush with water and bake in the oven at 450°F for 15 minutes. Reduce the temperature to 375°F and bake for a further 20–25 minutes or until the loaf sounds hollow when tapped on the base. Cool on a wire rack.

MAKES 1 LARGE LOAF

POTTED HERB BREAD

Small terracotta flowerpots are available from garden stores. Soak them overnight in cold water, then dry thoroughly before using. Alternatively, shape the dough into six neat rounds and place on a baking sheet. Leave to rise and bake as directed.

vegetable shortening, melted, for greasing

½ oz fresh yeast, or 1½ level tsp dried yeast and
    1 level tsp sugar, or one 7 g sachet fast-action dried
    yeast

4 cups white or wholewheat bread flour

1½ level tsp salt

4 tbsp vegetable margarine or butter

⅔ cup finely chopped fresh herbs, such as basil, parsley,
    thyme, or marjoram

1 Brush six 3½ inch diameter terracotta flowerpots with melted shortening. Blend the fresh yeast with 1¼ cups lukewarm water. If using dried yeast, sprinkle it into the water with the sugar and leave in a warm place for 15 minutes or until frothy. If using fast-action dried yeast, this stage is not necessary.

2 In a large bowl, mix together the flour and salt. Add the fast-action dried yeast, if using. Rub in the margarine and stir in the herbs.

3 Make a well in the center of the flour mixture and pour in the yeast liquid, or 1¼ cups lukewarm water if using fast-action dried yeast. Mix well (adding a little extra water if using wholewheat flour) and turn on to a floured surface. Knead for 10 minutes or until smooth.

4 If using fresh or dried yeast, put the dough in a large oiled bowl and cover with a clean dish towel. Leave to stand in a warm place until doubled in size. Knead the dough again for 2–3 minutes. (If fast-action dried yeast has been used, this first rising and second kneading stage is not necessary.)

5 Cut the dough into six pieces. Shape the pieces into elongated balls and drop them into the prepared pots. Leave in a warm place until the dough rises to the tops of the pots.

6 Brush the loaves with salt water and bake in the oven at 400°F for 10 minutes. Reduce the temperature to 350°F and bake for a further 20 minutes. Turn the loaves out of the pots and return them to the oven for 5 minutes to crisp the outsides, then cool slightly on a wire rack. Serve warm.

MAKES 6

SESAME AND CUMIN BREAD STICKS

These crisp, slightly spicy bread sticks are perfect for serving with hummus or your favorite dip.

½ oz fresh yeast, or 1½ level tsp dried yeast and
    1 level tsp sugar, or one 7 g sachet fast-action dried
    yeast

4 cups white bread flour

1½ level tsp salt

1 level tsp ground cumin

4 tbsp vegetable margarine or butter

2 tbsp sesame oil

2 tbsp vegetable oil

1 free-range egg, beaten

3 level tbsp sesame seeds

2 level tbsp cumin seeds

1 Blend the fresh yeast with scant 1 cup lukewarm water. If using dried yeast, sprinkle it into the water with the sugar and leave in a warm place for 15 minutes or until frothy. If using fast-action dried yeast, this stage is not necessary.

2 Put the flour, salt, and ground cumin in a large bowl. Add the fast-action dried yeast, if using. Put the margarine or butter and oils in a small saucepan and heat gently until the butter has melted. Make a well in the center of the dry ingredients and pour in the fat with the yeast liquid or scant 1 cup lukewarm water if using fast-action dried yeast. Mix to make a dough, adding a little extra water if necessary. Turn the dough out on to a floured surface and knead for 10 minutes or until smooth and elastic.

3 If using fresh or dried yeast, put the dough in an oiled bowl, cover with a clean dish towel and leave in a warm place for 1 hour or until doubled in size. Knead the dough for 2–3 minutes. (If fast-action dried yeast has been used, this first rising and second kneading is not necessary.)

4 Divide the dough into 32 pieces. Roll each piece into a sausage shape about 8 inches long and place on greased baking sheets.

5 Brush the dough sticks with beaten egg and sprinkle with the sesame and cumin seeds. Bake in the oven at 400°F for 15–20 minutes or until golden brown. Turn off the oven and leave the bread sticks to cool in the oven. When cold they should be crisp. Store in an airtight container.

MAKES ABOUT 32

$\mathcal{T}$OMATO HERB FOCACCIA

Sun-dried tomatoes lend a delicious flavor and a distinctive color to this Italian bread.

2 oz sun-dried tomatoes in olive oil, drained and chopped	*1 level tbsp chopped fresh thyme or rosemary*
4 cups white bread flour	*3 tbsp olive oil*
½ level tsp salt	*1 free-range egg*
4 tbsp vegetable margarine or butter	*coarse salt (optional)*
one 7 g sachet fast-action dried yeast	*chopped fresh thyme or rosemary, to serve*

1 Put the tomatoes in a bowl and pour over scant 1 cup boiling water. Leave to soak for 15 minutes.

2 Put the flour and salt in a bowl and rub in the margarine or butter. Stir in the yeast.

3 Drain the tomatoes, reserving the liquid, and stir into the flour with the herbs.

4 Beat together the reserved liquid, the olive oil, and egg. Make a well in the center of the flour mixture, pour in the egg mixture, and mix to a dough.

5 Turn the dough on to a floured surface and knead for 5 minutes or until smooth.

6 Put the dough on a greased baking sheet and press into a square measuring at least 10 inches across. Cover with a clean dish towel and leave in a warm place for about 30 minutes or until doubled in size. Brush with salt water. Slash the top with a sharp knife, or make indentations with a wooden spoon, and sprinkle with salt, if using.

7 Bake in the oven at 425°F for 15–20 minutes or until golden brown. Sprinkle with chopped fresh thyme or rosemary before serving.

MAKES 1 LOAF

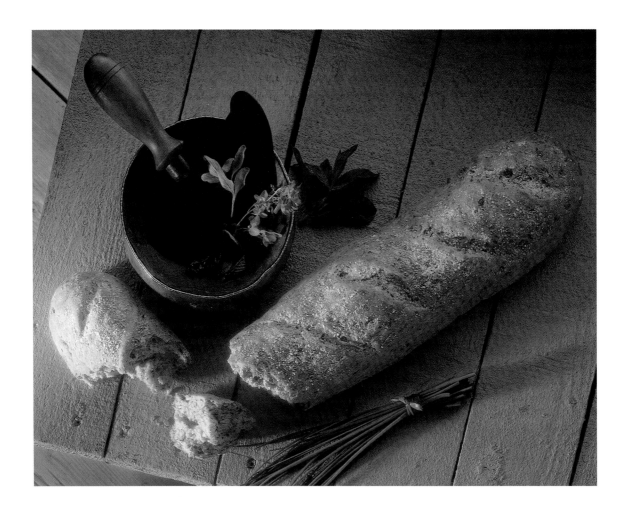

$\mathcal{H}$ERBED WHOLE-GRAIN BREAD

This is one recipe in which dried herbs are no substitute for fresh.

½ oz fresh yeast, or 1½ level tsp dried yeast and a pinch of sugar, or one 7 g sachet fast-action dried yeast	*2 level tbsp chopped mixed fresh herbs, such as mint, thyme, marjoram, rosemary, and chives*
3¾ cups whole-grain flour	*1 garlic clove, skinned and crushed (optional)*
1 level tsp salt	*2 tsp honey*
2 level tbsp chopped fresh parsley	*fine oatmeal for sprinkling*

1 Blend the fresh yeast with 1¼ cups warm water. If using dried yeast, sprinkle it into 1¼ cups warm water with the sugar and leave in a warm place for 15 minutes or until frothy.
2 Put the flour, salt, and herbs in a bowl and mix together. Add the fast-action dried yeast, if using. Make a well in the center. Stir the garlic, if using, and the honey into the yeast liquid (or 1¼ cups warm water if using fast-action dried yeast), then pour into the center of the dry ingredients. Beat together until the

dough leaves the sides of the bowl clean. Turn the dough on to a lightly floured surface and knead well for about 10 minutes.
3 If using fresh or dried yeast, put the dough in a clean bowl. Cover with a clean dish towel and leave in a warm place for about 1 hour or until doubled in size. Turn the dough on to a floured surface and knead lightly. (If fast-action dried yeast has been used, this first rising and second kneading stage is not necessary.)

4 Shape the dough into a sausage shape about 16 inches long and place on a greased baking sheet. Cut several slashes on the top of the loaf. Cover and leave in a warm place for 30 minutes or until doubled in size.
5 Brush with a little milk and sprinkle with oatmeal. Bake in the oven at 450°F for 10 minutes, then reduce the oven temperature to 400°F, and bake for a further 15–20 minutes or until the loaf sounds hollow when tapped on the base. Leave to cool on a wire rack.
MAKES 1 LOAF

CHEESE AND HERB BISCUITS

Biscuits are quick to throw together at a moment's notice if you run short of bread. Serve them as an accompaniment to salads and soups, or for lunch, split and filled with salad, cheese, or hummus. They really are best served fresh and warm from the oven.

2 cups self-rising flour	3 tbsp vegetable margarine or butter
pinch of salt	¼ lb mature Cheddar cheese, finely grated
1 level tsp mustard powder	about ⅔ cup milk
1 level tsp baking powder	

1 Grease a baking sheet. Sift the flour, salt mustard powder, and baking powder together into a bowl. Rub in the margarine or butter until the mixture resembles fine breadcrumbs. Stir in half the cheese and enough milk to give a fairly soft, light dough.
2 On a lightly floured surface, roll out to about ¾ inch thick, and cut into rounds with a 2 inch cookie cutter. Put on the baking sheet, brush the tops with milk, and sprinkle with the remaining cheese.
3 Bake in the oven at 425°F for about 10 minutes. Cool on a wire rack.
MAKES ABOUT 12

VARIATIONS
Olive and Herb Biscuits Omit the cheese and mustard. Finely chop ¼ cup pitted black or green olives, or a mixture, and stir into the rubbed-in ingredients with 2 level tbsp chopped mixed fresh herbs. Push half of an olive into the top of each biscuit and sprinkle with a few herbs before baking.
Tomato and Garlic Biscuits Omit the cheese and mustard. Finely chop 1 oz sun-dried tomatoes and stir into the rubbed-in ingredients. Add ½ a small garlic clove, skinned and crushed, to the milk. Sprinkle the biscuits with a few herbs or a little grated Parmesan cheese before baking.
Nut Biscuits Omit the mustard. The cheese may be omitted or left in as preferred. Add ½ cup chopped mixed nuts to the rubbed-in ingredients. Sprinkle the biscuits with sesame or poppy seeds before baking.
Plain Biscuits To make plain biscuits, for serving with jam and cream, follow the basic recipe but omit the herbs, cheese, and mustard (you should add salt to sweet biscuits).
Sweet Fruit Biscuits Add ⅓ cup dried mixed fruit to the plain biscuit mixture above.

POTATO BISCUITS

Potato biscuits should be made from floury potatoes, which will mash well without lumps.

---

1 lb floury all-purpose potatoes, peeled

salt

2 tbsp vegetable margarine or butter

about 1 cup all-purpose flour

---

1 Cook the potatoes in boiling salted water for about 20 minutes or until tender. Drain and mash until smooth. Add 1 level tsp salt and the margarine or butter, then work in enough flour to make a stiff dough.

2 Turn on to a floured surface, knead lightly, and roll out until ¼ inch thick. Cut into about twelve 2½ inch rounds.

3 Cook on a greased griddle or in a heavy-based frying pan for 4–5 minutes on each side or until golden brown. Serve hot with butter, or as an accompaniment to stews, casseroles, omelets, and poached or fried eggs.

MAKES ABOUT 12

CORNBREAD

½ oz fresh yeast, or 1½ level tsp dried yeast, or one 7 g sachet fast-action dried yeast

about 1⅔ cups lukewarm milk

3 cups cornmeal

4 cups white bread flour

½ cup packed light brown sugar

2 level tsp salt

4 tbsp vegetable margarine or butter

cornmeal for sprinkling

---

1 Blend the fresh yeast with the milk. If using dried yeast, sprinkle it into the milk, and leave in a warm place for 15 minutes or until frothy. If using fast-action dried yeast, this stage is not necessary.

2 Put the cornmeal, flour, sugar, and salt in a bowl. Add the fast-action dried yeast, if using. Rub in the margarine or butter. Make a well in the center, then pour in the yeast liquid (or 1⅔ cups lukewarm milk if using fast-action dried yeast) to make a soft dough, adding a little more milk if necessary. Knead on a floured surface for 10 minutes or until smooth and elastic.

3 If using fresh or dried yeast, put the dough in an oiled bowl, cover with a clean dish towel, and leave to rise in a warm place for about 1 hour or until doubled in size. Turn the dough on to a floured surface and knead for 5 minutes. (If fast-action dried yeast has been used, this first rising and second kneading stage is not necessary.)

4 Divide the dough into two, shape each piece into a 6 inch round, and place on two greased baking sheets. Cover and leave in a warm place until doubled in size.

5 Using a sharp knife, mark the top of each loaf in squares. Brush with water, then sprinkle generously with cornmeal. Bake in the oven at 450°F for 15 minutes, then reduce the temperature to 375°F for 15 minutes or until well risen and the loaves sound hollow if tapped on the bottom. Cool on a wire rack.

MAKES 2 LOAVES

Nan-style Bread

This flat, tear-drop shaped Indian bread is traditionally baked on the side of a tandoor oven. This version is not entirely authentic but it does produce a soft, puffy nan-style bread that's perfect for mopping up curries and Indian foods.

½ oz fresh yeast, or 1½ level tsp dried yeast, or one 7 g sachet fast-action dried yeast	2 level tsp sugar
scant 1 cup lukewarm milk	1 free-range egg, beaten
4 cups all-purpose flour	2 tbsp vegetable oil
1 level tsp baking powder	¼ cup plain yogurt
1 level tsp salt	vegetable ghee or melted butter, for brushing

1 Blend the fresh yeast and ⅔ cup of the milk together. If using dried yeast, sprinkle it into ⅔ cup of the milk and leave in a warm place for 15 minutes or until frothy. If using fast-action dried yeast, this stage is not necessary.
2 Sift the flour, baking powder, and salt into a large bowl. Add the fast-action dried yeast, if using. Make a well in the center and stir in the sugar, egg, oil, and yogurt.
3 Add the yeast liquid, or scant 1 cup lukewarm milk if using fast-action dried yeast, and mix to a soft dough, adding more milk if necessary. Turn the dough on to a lightly floured surface and knead for 10 minutes or until smooth and elastic.
4 Put the dough in a bowl, cover with a clean cloth, and leave to rise in a warm place for about 1 hour or until doubled in size.
5 Knead the dough on a lightly floured surface for 2–3 minutes, then divide into six equal pieces. Roll out each piece and shape into a large tear-drop about 10 inches long.
6 Place one nan on a baking sheet and put under a preheated hot broiler. Cook for 1½–2 minutes on each side or until golden brown

and puffy. Brush the cooked nan with melted ghee or butter. Cook the remaining nan in the same way. Serve warm.

VARIATION
Peshawari Nan (Nan with Golden Raisins and Almonds) Follow the recipe above to the beginning of step 5. To make the filling, mix together ⅔ cup golden raisins, 1¼ cup ground almonds, ¼ cup vegetable ghee or butter, and 3 tbsp chopped fresh coriander. Knead the dough on a lightly floured surface and divide into six equal pieces. Roll each piece into a round about 6 inches in diameter. Spoon the filling into the center of each nan and fold over the dough to enclose the filling completely. Press the edges well together to seal. Cook for 1½ minutes on one side, turn over, brush with plenty of melted ghee or butter and sprinkle with a few flaked almonds. Cook for 1½–2 minutes or until golden brown and puffy. Serve warm, sprinkled with chopped fresh coriander.
MAKES 6

AJOWAN PARATHAS

Parathas are surprisingly easy to make once you've mastered the procedure. Ajowan is a spice with a strong thyme-like flavor. Use cumin instead if you can't find it in Indian stores.

3 cups wholewheat flour	¾ level tsp chili powder
1 level tbsp ajowan seeds	vegetable ghee, butter, or vegetable margarine, melted, for
1 level tsp salt	brushing

1 Put the flour, ajowan seeds, salt, and chili powder in a bowl and mix well together. Add about 1¼ cups cold water and bind to a soft pliable dough – it may be slightly sticky.
2 Turn the dough on to a lightly floured surface and knead with floured hands for 6–8 minutes or until smooth and elastic. Cover the dough with a clean damp cloth and leave to rest for about 15 minutes.
3 Divide the dough into 12 pieces. Take a piece of dough and shape it into a smooth ball. Roll it out on a lightly floured surface into a round about 6 inches across.
4 Brush a little ghee, butter, or margarine over the paratha, then roll it into a long sausage shape. Hold the rolled paratha upright and place one end in the center of your hand. Wind the rest of the roll carefully around the center point to form a small fat disc.

5 Press the disc lightly together and roll out on a floured surface to a round about 6 inches in diameter. Cover with a clean damp cloth and roll out the remaining dough to make 12 parathas altogether.
6 Heat a heavy frying pan or griddle. Place one paratha in the pan and cook over a low heat until small bubbles appear on the surface. Turn the paratha over and brush the top with melted ghee, butter, or margarine. Cook for about 30 seconds or until golden brown.
7 Turn the paratha again and brush with more fat. Press down the edges of the paratha with a spatula to ensure even cooking, and cook the other side until golden brown.
8 Brush with more fat and serve at once or wrap in foil and keep warm while cooking the remainder.
MAKES 12

— T WELVE —

COOKING FOR ONE

If you live on your own or often eat alone, or if there is just one vegetarian in the family, this chapter will be useful. Here are delicious recipes, scaled down to make just enough for one.

Don't be shy about buying in small quantities. Family units are becoming progressively smaller than they have traditionally been, and suppliers are prepared to market their goods accordingly. Avoid supermarkets where everything is pre-packaged and geared to buying in quantity; instead opt for markets and stores where you can pick out exactly what and how much you want. Try to be organized and plan your shopping and meals for the week.

When buying fresh fruit and vegetables, it is particularly important to choose sound, good quality produce. If you're cooking meals for one it is likely that you will want to store them whole or in part for several days. Obviously, fruit and vegetables in peak condition will keep for much longer than those that are bruised or shrivelled. To prolong storage, keep them in the refrigerator. With fruit, watch out for pieces that are ripening more quickly than the others in the bag. Remove the ripe fruit immediately and

cook or eat it since it will encourage the others to deteriorate. Use this natural process to your advantage if you want something to ripen quickly (particularly avocados) by putting the under-ripe fruit in a sealed paper bag with a fully ripe fruit.

As well as the recipes in this chapter, other recipes throughout the book make suitable meals for one, particularly omelets, soups, baked potatoes, and pasta. It's sensible to make soups in larger quantities and to freeze them in individual portions. Similarly, beans and lentils can be soaked, cooked, and frozen or stored in the refrigerator for future use. If you cook too much pasta or rice by mistake, toss it with a well-flavored dressing and a few vegetables or beans to serve as a salad later in the week. It's worth noting that cooked boiled rice freezes well (as long as it's not overcooked) and it reheats in minutes in the microwave.

Apart from the desserts in this chapter, baked apples or poached pears (cooked in the oven or the microwave) are obvious puddings for one. Raspberry Rose Ice Cream (see page 219) or Coconut Ice Cream (see page 217) are also worth making as they can be stored in the freezer for up to 3 months and used as required.

$\mathscr{S}$OUFFLÉED CAULIFLOWER

This makes a generous meal for one served with steamed or boiled green vegetables. Use fromage blanc labelled "8 per cent fat" (rather than 1 per cent) for the best result.

1 cup cauliflower florets	1 level tsp Dijon-style mustard
salt and pepper	1 free-range egg, separated
⅓ cup fromage blanc	2 oz Cheddar cheese, grated

1 Cook the cauliflower florets in boiling salted water for about 5 minutes or until tender but still slightly crisp. Drain well. Grease a small, shallow ovenproof dish and put the cauliflower in the bottom.
2 Put the fromage blanc and mustard in a bowl and stir in the egg and half the cheese. Season.

3 Put the egg white in a separate bowl and whisk until stiff. Fold carefully into the cheese mixture and spoon over the cauliflower. Sprinkle with the remaining cheese and bake in the oven at 375°F for about 25 minutes or until risen and golden.
SERVES 1

☞NOW PEA AND MUSHROOM MAYONNAISE

This is a really simple, light, and healthy lunch dish. If you're not in a hurry to eat it, the dressing is improved if left to stand for 30 minutes to allow the flavors to develop.

⅔ cup snow peas	*1 level tbsp chopped fresh parsley*
salt and pepper	*1 level tbsp chopped chives*
2 tbsp mayonnaise	*2 oz button mushrooms, wiped and sliced*
1 tbsp plain yogurt	

1 Trim the snow peas and cut into diamond-shaped pieces. Blanch in boiling salted water for 1 minute, then drain, and refresh under cold running water.
2 Beat together the mayonnaise, yogurt,

parsley, and half the chives. Season.
3 Arrange the snow peas and mushrooms on a plate and top with the mayonnaise mixture. Sprinkle with the remaining chives.
SERVES 1

Snow pea and Mushroom Mayonnaise

MIXED VEGETABLE AND EGG DINNER

Make a similar dish with leftover Ratatouille (see page 96). Serve with lots of crusty bread or toast smeared with Dijon-style mustard, to mop up the juices.

1 tbsp olive oil	a pinch of dried rosemary
1 large zucchini, trimmed and sliced	2 tomatoes, chopped
½ small sweet green pepper, cored, seeded, and roughly chopped	salt and pepper
1 small onion, skinned and sliced	1 free-range egg
½ small garlic clove, skinned and crushed	1 oz Cheddar or Gruyère cheese, grated

1 Heat the oil in a small saucepan. Add the zucchini, pepper, and onion and cook for about 5 minutes or until beginning to soften and brown, stirring occasionally.
2 Stir in the garlic, rosemary, and tomatoes. Season with salt and pepper and simmer, uncovered, for 3–5 minutes or until the vegetables are tender and the liquid has been well reduced. Transfer the mixture to an individual flameproof dish.
3 Make a slight hollow in the vegetable mixture and break the egg carefully into it. Season the egg with salt and plenty of pepper. Sprinkle with the cheese.
4 Cook under a preheated broiler for 8–10 minutes (depending on how well done you like your eggs). Eat straight away!
SERVES 1

PASTA WITH SAUTÉED MUSHROOMS

This dish is everything that a weekday dinner for one should be – it's quick to make, requires little effort, yet it's delicious. Have ready a glass of robust Italian red wine and perhaps a green salad (if you have the time or the inclination to make it) to complete the feast.

4–6 oz dried pasta	1 garlic clove, skinned and crushed
salt and pepper	a large knob of butter
2 tbsp olive oil	a few chopped fresh herbs (optional)
6 oz mushrooms (medium-sized open-cap or oyster mushrooms are best), wiped and thickly sliced	a few spoonfuls of heavy cream (optional)
	freshly grated Parmesan cheese, to serve

1 Cook the pasta in boiling salted water according to the packet instructions or until *al dente* (tender but still firm to the bite).
2 Meanwhile, heat the oil in a frying pan and fry the mushrooms over a high heat for 2–3 minutes or until slightly browned. Lower the heat, add the garlic, and continue cooking the mushrooms until the pasta is cooked.
3 When the pasta is cooked, drain and return it to the saucepan with the butter and plenty of black pepper.
4 Season the mushrooms with salt and pepper and add the herbs and cream, if using. Tip the pasta on to a plate, top with the mushrooms, and serve immediately with freshly grated Parmesan cheese.
SERVES 1

FRENCH BREAD PIZZA

Try spreading the toasted bread with a little Pesto (see page 193), or whole-grain mustard, or rubbing it with a cut clove of garlic, for extra flavor.

6 oz ripe tomatoes, chopped	*½ small baguette*
4 black olives, pitted	*olive oil for brushing*
2 oz Mozzarella or Bel Paese cheese, grated	*dried oregano or marjoram*
freshly ground black pepper	

1 In a bowl, combine the tomatoes, olives, and half of the cheese. Season with pepper.
2 Trim the end off the baguette and split the loaf in half lengthways. Toast both pieces on each side, then brush the cut sides with a little olive oil.

3 Spoon on the tomato mixture, then top with the remaining grated cheese. Sprinkle with the herbs and cook under a hot broiler for 2 minutes or until the cheese melts. Serve immediately.
SERVES 1

MARINATED TOFU KEBABS

Pressed tofu is firmer for broiling, and because it contains less liquid, it will absorb more marinade, and therefore more flavor. You will only need 3 oz tofu (weighed before pressing) to make enough for one meal, but it is worth pressing and marinating the whole ½ lb packet for use in other recipes. Follow this basic idea to vary as you like – chunks of zucchini, baby corn, eggplant, and small onions all work well. Peanut sauce (see page 24) is a good accompaniment, as is Harissa Sauce (see page 184) or Curry Sauce (see page 188).

3 oz firm tofu	*1 tbsp vegetable oil*
1 garlic clove, skinned and crushed	*1 small sweet green pepper, cored, seeded, and cut into*
1 inch piece of fresh ginger root, peeled and grated	* chunks*
2 tbsp soy sauce	*a few cherry tomatoes*
2 tbsp dry sherry	*a few small mushrooms*

1 To press the tofu, put it on a plate or board, cover with a second plate or board, and weight this down (cans of tomatoes or beans are useful for this). Leave for 1 hour, draining off the liquid as necessary.
2 Cut the tofu into bite-sized chunks. Mix together the garlic, ginger, soy sauce, sherry, and vegetable oil. Add the tofu, sweet pepper, tomatoes, and mushrooms and stir so that

everything is coated in the marinade. Cover and leave in the refrigerator to marinate for at least 1 hour or overnight.
3 Thread all the ingredients on to two bamboo kebab skewers. Broil under a hot broiler for 5–8 minutes or until the vegetables are cooked, turning frequently and brushing with the marinade.
SERVES 1

CATALAN SWEET RED PEPPERS

If you prefer to eat this hot, keep the sweet pepper in the oven until the filling is ready. Rinse the rice with boiling, not cold, water, pile it into the warm pepper, pour over the dressing, and serve immediately.

1 sweet red pepper	*a few mixed black and green pitted olives, chopped*
olive oil	*2 tsp capers*
¼ cup mixed long-grain and wild rice	*2 tsp white wine vinegar*
salt and pepper	*½ small garlic clove, skinned and crushed*
2 tomatoes	*lettuce, to serve*
2 scallions, trimmed and chopped	

1 Rinse and dry the pepper, then put it on a baking sheet, and brush lightly with oil. Bake in the oven at 425°F for 15–20 minutes or until just tender. Cool, halve, and remove the core and seeds. (The skin can also be removed, if wished, but the pepper will not hold its shape so well.) Pat dry with paper towels.

2 Meanwhile, cook the rice in boiling salted water according to the packet instructions or until tender. Drain and rinse under cold running water, then drain well again. Quarter the tomatoes, discard the seeds, and roughly chop the flesh. Mix into the rice with the scallions, olives, and capers.

3 Whisk together 2 tbsp olive oil, the vinegar and garlic, and season with salt and pepper. Stir into the rice mixture.

4 Pile the rice into the pepper halves and arrange on a serving plate. Cover and chill for 30 minutes before serving on a bed of lettuce. SERVES 1

$\mathscr{E}$GG AND SPINACH CROÛTE

If you keep a bag of chopped spinach spheres in your freezer, add one or two to the hot sauce and simmer until thawed – much quicker and easier than cooking spinach from scratch.

1 inch thick slice of bread, toasted	⅔ cup milk
½ garlic clove, skinned	freshly grated nutmeg
1 cup packed fresh spinach, trimmed and washed	salt and pepper
1 tbsp vegetable margarine or butter	a few drops of vinegar
1 level tbsp all-purpose flour	1 free-range egg

1 With a 3 inch cookie cutter, stamp out one round from the slice of toast, rub with the garlic clove, and set aside.
2 Cook the spinach with only the water that clings to the leaves for 3–4 minutes or until wilted. Drain well and chop finely.
3 Melt the margarine or butter in a small saucepan, add the flour, and cook gently, stirring, for 1–2 minutes. Remove from the heat and gradually blend in the milk. Bring to the boil, stirring constantly, then simmer for 3 minutes. Stir in the spinach and season with nutmeg, salt, and pepper.

4 Meanwhile, half fill a frying pan with water and a few drops of vinegar, and bring to the boil. Break the egg into a cup, then slide it into the simmering water. Cook gently for 3–4 minutes or until lightly set, then lift out of the water with a slotted spoon. (Alternatively, use an egg poacher if you have one).
5 Top the toasted croûte with the poached egg and spoon over the spinach sauce. Serve immediately.
SERVES 1

$\mathscr{I}$NDIVIDUAL BREAD AND BUTTER PUDDING

If you prefer a very crisp top, brown the cooked pudding under a hot broiler for about 2 minutes. This makes a generous serving for one.

1 large slice of bread, crusts removed	1 level tbsp sugar
vegetable margarine or butter	1 small free-range egg
⅓ cup raisins	⅔ cup milk

1 Thickly spread the bread with margarine or butter and cut into fingers or small squares. Put half into a greased 2 cup ovenproof dish and sprinkle with all the fruit and half the sugar. Top with the remaining bread, buttered side up, and sprinkle with the remaining sugar.

2 Beat the egg with the milk and strain over the bread. Leave to stand for 30 minutes, so that the bread absorbs some of the liquid.
3 Bake the pudding in the oven at 325°F for 35–45 minutes or until set and the top is crisp and golden.
SERVES 1

CINNAMON BANANA

Serve with chilled cream or vanilla ice cream. Alternatively, if you prefer the combination of sweet and tart flavors, serve with plain yogurt or fromage blanc.

1 tbsp vegetable margarine or butter	*¼ level tsp ground cinnamon*
1 tbsp soft brown sugar	*1 banana*
2 tbsp orange juice	*a few pitted prunes, halved*
2 tbsp sherry	

1 Melt the margarine or butter in a heavy-based frying pan. Add the remaining ingredients, except the banana and prunes, and heat gently, stirring, until the sugar has dissolved.
2 Peel the banana, then cut in half lengthways. Place in the pan with the prunes and cook over a gentle heat for 5–10 minutes or until hot but still retaining its shape. Baste the banana frequently with the sauce and turn the pieces over once during cooking. Serve immediately.
SERVES 1

PLUM CROÛTE

This recipe works equally well with firm nectarines or peaches. Omit the cinnamon and flavor the sugar with a little grated orange rind and a pinch of ground mixed spice instead.

1 large slice of white bread	*1 tbsp brown demerara sugar*
1 tbsp vegetable margarine or butter, melted	*¼ level tsp ground cinnamon*
2 ripe plums	

1 Cut the crusts off the slice of bread and discard. Brush both sides of the bread with the melted margarine or butter, making sure the bread is coated right to the edges.
2 Place the bread in an individual popover pan, pressing it down well, but leaving the four corners protruding over the edge.
3 Bake the croûte in the oven at 400°F for 15–20 minutes or until crisp and golden brown.

4 Meanwhile, halve and pit the plums, then place in a pan with the sugar and cinnamon. Sprinkle in 1–2 tsp water, then cook gently for about 5 minutes or until the plums are tender and juicy but still retaining their shape.
5 When the croûte is cooked, transfer to a serving plate. Spoon the plums in the center and serve immediately.
SERVES 1

—THIRTEEN—

Young Eats

From around the age of two, children can eat much the same as the rest of the family (although most dislike highly spiced, very garlicky food). Nevertheless, they should be encouraged to eat and become familiar with a wide variety of foods. By all means, cook them meals to eat with the family using recipes from throughout the book, but in this chapter you will find a selection of recipes written specifically with young vegetarians in mind. Because all but the most steadfast children are influenced by their peer group, we've included vegetarian sausages and burgers to be enjoyed while non-vegetarian friends eat meaty versions. Soup makes a warming, nutritious meal for youngsters, too; most of the recipes in Chapter Two are suitable. Purée very chunky soups, to make them more manageable for children.

A very high fiber diet is unsuitable for young children because it is so bulky. Young children have small appetites and they fill up on these foods quickly before eating sufficient quantity to get the nutrients they need. For the same reason, do not give young children uncooked bran. Similarly, 1 and 2 per cent low-fat milk and low-fat foods should be avoided until around the age of two. They don't contain the high concentration of calories young children need and they contain less of the vitamins A and D than their full-fat counterparts. So, when making cheese- and milk-based sauces, use full-fat milk. Vegan children should be given fortified soy milk.

Aim to present most meals with a selection of vegetables (if fresh are unavailable, frozen are almost as good), cucumber slices, halved cherry tomatoes, or carrot sticks.

*B*EANY PIES

You need a very small can of beans for these pies; if you can only buy a large can, transfer the remaining beans to a clean container, cover, and keep in the refrigerator. Follow this procedure with all opened cans – once exposed to the air, any acids in the food react with the metal lining of the can and contaminate it.

8 thin slices of wholewheat bread cut from a small loaf	*5 oz can baked beans in tomato sauce*
3 tbsp vegetable margarine or butter, melted	*1 oz Cheddar cheese, grated*

1 Using a large round cookie cutter, cut four circles from half of the bread slices, just large enough to line four 4 inch shallow muffin pans. Brush some of the margarine or butter over both sides of the bread.
2 Line four muffin pans with the bread, pressing down well. Divide the baked beans between the bread-lined muffin pans.
3 Cut four circles from the remaining bread,

just large enough to cover the prepared pies. Brush both sides with the remaining margarine or butter and place on top of the pies, pressing firmly around the edges to seal.
4 Sprinkle with the cheese and bake at 400°F for 20–25 minutes or until golden brown and crisp. Remove from the pans, leave to cool slightly, then serve.
MAKES 4

HEESEY SAUSAGES

For adult-sized sausages, shape the mixture into 8 instead of 16.

2 cups fresh breadcrumbs	salt and pepper
¼ lb Cheddar cheese, grated	1 free-range egg
1 small leek, trimmed, washed, and very finely chopped	about 2 tbsp milk
1 level tbsp very finely chopped fresh parsley	all-purpose flour for coating
a large pinch of mustard powder	vegetable oil for frying or broiling

1 In a large bowl, mix together the breadcrumbs, cheese, leek, parsley, and mustard, and season with salt and pepper. Add the egg and mix thoroughly, then add enough milk to bind the mixture together.
2 Divide the mixture into 16 and shape into small sausages.
3 If shallow frying, roll the sausages in the flour to coat. Heat a little oil in a frying pan, add the sausages and fry for about 5 minutes or until golden brown. To broil, lightly brush the sausages with oil and cook under a hot broiler for 3–4 minutes or until golden brown, turning occasionally. Serve hot immediately, or leave to cool, and serve cold.
MAKES 16

URGERS

Shape this mixture into burgers that are a manageable size for your children. Older children will probably prefer larger burgers which can be served in buns with lettuce and ketchup, while younger children will prefer smaller burgers with peas or beans and oven fries. The ingredients include Worcestershire sauce; check the labels in the supermarket for a brand that does not contain anchovies.

½ lb packet original tofu	1 tbsp Worcestershire sauce
¼ lb carrots, trimmed, peeled, and finely grated	2 tsp yeast extract
1¼ cups fresh breadcrumbs	1 free-range egg
1 small onion, skinned and finely chopped	salt and pepper
1 level tsp mixed dried herbs	vegetable oil for frying

1 Put the tofu in a bowl and mash with a potato masher. Add the carrots, breadcrumbs, onion, herbs, Worcestershire sauce, yeast extract, and egg. Season with salt and pepper and mix well.
2 Divide the mixture into eight or less, and shape each into a round flat cake.
3 Heat some oil in a large frying pan and cook the burgers for 4–5 minutes on each side or until golden brown and cooked through. To broil, lightly brush the burgers with oil and cook under a hot broiler for about 4 minutes each side or until golden brown. Drain on paper towels. Serve hot.
MAKES ABOUT 8

MINI QUICHES

These freeze well so it's worth making a batch for quick lunches or teatime meals. To freeze, cool, then pack in a rigid container, interleaved with parchment paper. Freeze for up to 3 months. Reheat from frozen at 350°F for 10–15 minutes or until warmed through.

1 quantity Shortcrust Pastry (see page 69)	*about ¼ cup corn kernels*
2 free-range eggs, medium	*2 small tomatoes, chopped*
1 cup milk	*1 oz Cheddar cheese, finely grated*
2 scallions, trimmed and sliced	*¼ cup frozen petits pois, thawed*

1 Thoroughly grease two 12-hole muffin pans. Roll out the pastry on a floured surface and cut out twenty-four 2¾ inch rounds with a fluted cutter. Press a round of pastry into each hole in the muffin pan.
2 Beat the eggs with the milk in a bowl. Put a few scallion slices and a few corn kernels in eight of the pastry cases. Divide the tomato

and cheese between a further eight cases. Divide the petits pois amongst the remaining cases.
3 Carefully pour the custard into the pastry cases and bake in the oven at 400°F for 35 minutes or until the filling is just set and the pastry lightly browned. Serve warm or cold.
MAKES 24

POTATO NESTS

Much of a potato's goodness is in the skin, which serves here as an edible container. If you have a microwave oven, save time by cooking the pricked potatoes on HIGH for 12–15 minutes (depending on their size). Turn them over halfway through cooking. The final cooking in the oven makes them crisp.

4 small baking potatoes, each weighing about 7 oz, scrubbed	*1 tomato, finely chopped*
2–3 tbsp plain yogurt, mayonnaise, or fromage blanc	*3 tbsp corn kernels*
salt and pepper	*3 oz hard cheese, finely grated*

1 Prick each potato several times with a fork. Bake in the oven at 400°F for about 1½ hours or until tender.
2 Cut a thin slice horizontally from the top of each potato, then carefully scoop most of the potato into a bowl, leaving shells about ¼ inch thick.
3 Mix the scooped-out potato with the yogurt, mayonnaise, or fromage blanc. Season

with salt and pepper and mix in the tomato, corn and half the cheese. Spoon back into the potato shells and place in a shallow ovenproof dish.
4 Sprinkle the filling with the remaining cheese and return to the oven for about 20 minutes or until melted and lightly browned.
MAKES 4

$\mathcal{V}$EGETABLE POPOVERS

This works well with most vegetables. It is also a good way of using up leftovers. You will need a popover or shallow muffin pan with four 4 inch compartments. Serve with Tomato Sauce (see page 190) or chutney.

6 oz prepared mixed vegetables, such as carrots, zucchini, green beans, and broccoli	½ cup all-purpose flour
	a pinch of salt
4 cherry tomatoes	1 free-range egg
white vegetable shortening	¾ cup full-fat milk and water mixed

1 Depending on the ages of the children you are cooking for, cut the vegetables into small or large chunks. Steam or boil the vegetables until just tender. Prick the tomatoes with a fork.

2 Put a knob of shortening into each compartment of a four-hole popover pan. Put the pan in the oven at 425°F for about 5 minutes to heat the oil.

3 Meanwhile, sift the flour and salt into a bowl and make a well in the center. Break the egg into the well, then add half the liquid.

Gradually mix the flour into the liquid to make a smooth, thick paste, then gradually work in the remaining liquid. Beat until smooth. If necessary, remove any lumps with a balloon whisk.

4 Divide the vegetables between the compartments in the muffin pan and pour over the batter. Bake on the top shelf in the oven for 30–35 minutes or until well risen and golden brown. Serve with Tomato Sauce (see page 190) or chutney.

SERVES 4

$\mathscr{M}$ACARONI CHEESE

This makes a fairly large amount (in children's terms), but it is a good idea to make a lot and freeze the extra in portion sizes ready for reheating in the microwave. Serve with halved cherry tomatoes, or steamed or boiled carrots, peas, beans, or zucchini.

½ lb elbow macaroni or small pasta shapes	a pinch of freshly grated nutmeg or ½ level tsp prepared mustard (optional)
5 tbsp vegetable margarine or butter	
5 tbsp all-purpose flour	½ lb mature Cheddar cheese, grated
3½ cups full-fat milk	3 level tbsp fresh wholewheat breadcrumbs
salt and pepper	

1 Cook the macaroni in boiling salted water for about 10 minutes or until just tender. Drain well.

2 Meanwhile, melt the margarine or butter in a saucepan, stir in the flour, and cook gently for 1 minute. Remove the pan from the heat and gradually stir in the milk. Bring to the boil and continue to cook, stirring, until the sauce thickens, then remove from the heat, season with salt and pepper, and add the nutmeg or mustard, if using, most of the cheese and the macaroni.

3 Pour into an ovenproof dish and sprinkle with the remaining cheese and the breadcrumbs.

4 Brown under a hot broiler or place on a baking sheet and bake in the oven at 400°F for 25–30 minutes or until golden and bubbling.

VARIATION

Cauliflower Cheese Omit the macaroni. Trim 1 large cauliflower and cut into very small florets (you will need about 1¾ lb florets). Cook the florets in fast boiling salted water for about 10 minutes or until just tender, then drain. If making cauliflower cheese for very young children, chop the florets into tiny pieces. Place in an ovenproof dish. Make the sauce and pour over the cauliflower. Sprinkle with the remaining cheese and breadcrumbs and brown under a hot broiler or bake in the oven as for Macaroni Cheese.

SERVES ABOUT 4 ADULTS OR 8 CHILDREN

$\mathscr{L}$ENTIL POTATO PIES

Put the cooked mixture straight into individual foil (or china if you plan to reheat it in the microwave) containers ready for freezing.

½ cup split red lentils	salt and pepper
1 onion, skinned and halved	1 lb all-purpose potatoes, cooked
1 large carrot, trimmed, peeled, and coarsely grated	about 3 tbsp milk or a large knob of vegetable margarine
½ level tsp yeast extract	vegetable oil for brushing
½ lb mixed vegetables, such as corn, green beans, zucchini, and parsnips, prepared and finely diced (if necessary)	

1 Put the lentils, onion, carrot, yeast extract, mixed vegetables, and 1¼ cups water in a saucepan. Bring to the boil, cover and simmer gently for 20–25 minutes or until the lentils are very soft and mushy and all of the water has been absorbed, adding a little extra water if necessary. Season with salt and pepper and discard the onion halves. Divide the mixture between four or six individual ovenproof dishes.

2 Mash the potatoes with the milk or margarine or a little water to make it very soft. Spoon the potato on top of the lentil mixture, covering it completely. Brush with a little vegetable oil. Stand the pies on a baking sheet and bake in the oven at 425°F for 15–20 minutes or until golden brown. Alternatively, brown the pies under a hot broiler (better for younger children who prefer their food lukewarm).
MAKES 4–6 PIES

$\mathscr{C}$HOCOLATE MUESLI BARS

For young children, cut into small squares and save as an occasional treat. The chocolate and syrup mixture could be melted in the microwave. It will take about 3–4 minutes on LOW. Stir occasionally to prevent it burning.

2 tbsp vegetable margarine or butter	3 oz plain chocolate, broken into pieces
1 tbsp light corn syrup	2 cups no-added-sugar muesli

1 Grease a 7 inch square pan. Heat the margarine or butter, syrup, and chocolate in a heavy-based saucepan until the butter and chocolate have melted. Stir in the muesli and mix thoroughly together.

2 Spoon the mixture into the pan and level the surface. Chill in the refrigerator until set, then cut into 14 bars.
MAKES 14

$\mathcal{O}$ ATY BARS

These oaty bars are ideal as a lunch-box filler or a mid-morning snack for younger children.
If you have a microwave oven, melt the margarine, milk, and honey on HIGH for
1–2 minutes.

6 tbsp vegetable margarine	*½ level tsp baking soda*
2 tbsp milk	*½ level tsp light brown sugar*
1 tbsp honey	*1 cup rolled oats*
¼ cup wholewheat flour	*⅔ cup dried apricots, chopped*

1 Grease two baking sheets. In a small saucepan, melt the margarine with the milk and honey.
2 Put the flour, baking soda, sugar, oats, and apricots in a bowl. Mix together, then make a well in the center. Pour in the melted mixture and mix well.
3 Divide the mixture into 8 pieces and shape each into a bar about 2½ inches long. Place on the baking sheets and bake in the oven at 400°F for 10–15 minutes or until golden brown. Leave to cool on the baking sheets for 2–3 minutes, then transfer to a wire rack to cool completely.
MAKES 8

$\mathcal{O}$ RANGE MOLD

A very simple soft-set mold made using agar-agar. Serve with a selection of fresh fruit, such as strawberries, tangerines, raspberries, or mango.

1¼ cups orange juice	*1 level tbsp sugar*
1 level tbsp agar-agar	

1 Mix the orange juice with 1¼ cups water and pour half into a small saucepan with the agar-agar. Bring to the boil, reduce the heat, and simmer for 5 minutes or until dissolved, stirring all the time. Add the remaining juice, stir in the sugar, remove from the heat, and leave to cool slightly.
2 Pour the orange mixture into four wetted individual molds or dishes, then leave in the refrigerator for 1–2 hours or until set. Turn out on to a serving plate just before serving.
SERVES 4

-FOURTEEN-

$\mathcal{V}$EGETABLE SIDE DISHES

An interesting side dish can transform the dullest of meals into something special. If you've no time to make a spectacular main course but need a vegetable to serve with something, perhaps from the chilled cabinet, or a store-bought prepared vegetable, tofu or nut burger, or a baked potato, then look no further. Here are vegetable dishes with a twist. Most are quick to cook, but all are full of flavor and character.

Serve Roast Potatoes and Garlic (see page 180) and perhaps Creamed Celery Root and Apple (see page 178) with a nut roast or one of the pies in Chapter Five. Sag Aloo (see page 179) and Okra with Onion and Chili (below) complement most curry dishes. If your time or energy won't even stretch to one of these accompaniments, steam or boil root vegetables and toss with Pesto (see page 193) or a little herb or lemon butter, or stir-fry

Chinese cabbage leaves, snow peas, pak choi, or spring greens with a little sesame oil and garlic or ginger. Alternatively, toss a mixture of cooked vegetables in one of the dressings in Chapter Fifteen.

Remember, if you cook vegetables in water, the water soluble vitamins will leach out into the cooking water. So, always use the minimum possible (don't fill the pan right to the top – a couple of inches of water should be enough) and reserve all cooking water for adding to stocks and soups.

If you've got a microwave, it's excellent for cooking small quantities of vegetables in the minimum of water. Ensure that the vegetables are trimmed to an even size and cook them in a large shallow dish in preference to a deep bowl. Time carefully, because unlike when cooked conventionally, you can't see them and they are easily overcooked.

OKRA WITH ONION AND CHILI

Okra are long, thin, tapering vegetables which are used extensively in Indian as well as Southern cooking. When trimming the ends in step 1, take care not to cut the flesh or a sticky substance will be released during cooking.

1 lb fresh okra	*2 small fresh green chilies*
3 tbsp vegetable oil	*2 level tsp ground cumin*
1 medium onion, skinned and finely sliced	*salt and pepper*

1 Wash the okra and trim off the stalk ends. Dry well on paper towels.
2 Heat the oil in a large, heavy-based frying pan or wok, add the onion, and fry over a moderate heat, stirring constantly, for about 5 minutes or until turning golden.
3 Meanwhile, trim the ends off the green chilies and cut the flesh into fine rings with a sharp knife. Remove as many seeds as you like, according to how hot the dish is to be.

4 Add the okra, chilies, and cumin to the pan. Season with salt and pepper and continue cooking over a moderate heat for 10–15 minutes, stirring constantly. The okra should be cooked but still quite crisp and the onions a deeper brown. Taste and adjust the seasoning, if necessary, then turn into a warmed serving dish.
SERVES 4

$\mathcal{S}$AUTÉED ARTICHOKES WITH ORANGE

Jerusalem artichokes, or sunchokes, are knobbly little roots looking rather like ginger root. They have a soft, sweet, almost earthy flavor. They're quite delicious, but should only be eaten in moderate quantities as they have a well-founded reputation for causing flatulence!

2 lb Jerusalem artichokes	*2 tbsp vegetable oil*
salt and pepper	*2 tbsp vegetable margarine or butter*
lemon juice	*chopped fresh parsley (optional)*
1 orange	

1 Scrub the artichokes. If possible, leave them whole; if not, cut them into large chunks about the size of golf balls.

2 Put the artichokes in a saucepan and cover with salted water acidulated with lemon juice. Bring to the boil, then reduce the heat, cover, and simmer for 8–10 minutes or until the artichokes are barely tender. Finely grate the orange zest and section the flesh.

3 Drain the artichokes and refresh under cold running water. Peel off the skins and divide the flesh into good-sized chunks.

4 Heat the oil and margarine or butter in a frying pan and add the artichokes with the orange zest. Fry over a moderate heat, turning frequently, until golden brown.

5 Stir in the orange sections and parsley, if wished. Taste and adjust the seasoning, if necessary, before serving.

SERVES 4

Sautéed Artichokes with Orange

*E*GGPLANT with MUSTARD SEEDS and YOGURT

Broiling whole eggplant until the skins char gives the flesh a wonderful smoky flavor. If you are making this dish in the summertime, the flavor will be even more accentuated if the eggplant are charred over a grill. Serve as a cooling accompaniment to very spicy dishes or as a main meal with pilau rice.

3 medium eggplant, about 2 lb total weight	¼ cup chopped fresh coriander (cilantro)
¼ cup vegetable oil	1 level tsp salt
2 level tbsp black mustard seeds, ground	1¼ cups plain yogurt
½ level tsp chili powder	

1 Put the eggplant under a preheated broiler for about 15 minutes, turning occasionally. The skins should be black and charred and the flesh soft.
2 Leave the eggplant until just cool enough to handle, then peel the skins off and discard. Chop the flesh roughly.
3 Heat the oil in a heavy-based frying pan, add the ground mustard seeds, chopped eggplant flesh, and the chili powder. Stir over a moderate heat for about 5 minutes or until thoroughly hot, then add the coriander.
4 Beat the salt into the yogurt, then stir into the eggplant until evenly blended. Turn into a warmed serving dish and serve immediately.
SERVES 4–6

*S*UMMER CARROTS in SPICED DRESSING

Fresh coriander could be substituted for the chives.

1 lb young carrots, trimmed and scrubbed	1 tsp honey
4 tbsp vegetable margarine or butter	2 level tbsp roughly chopped chives
⅓ cup sliced almonds	1 tsp lemon juice
1 level tsp ground cumin	salt and pepper
2 level tsp ground coriander	

1 Steam the carrots or cook in boiling salted water for 4–5 minutes or until just tender. Drain well.
2 Melt the margarine or butter in a large frying pan and stir in the almonds and spices. Cook, stirring, for 1–2 minutes or until the almonds are golden brown. Toss in the carrots, honey, chives, and lemon juice. Stir over a high heat until well mixed, then season with salt and pepper and serve.
SERVES 4

Summer Carrots in Spiced Dressing left, Potted Herb Bread (page 150)

CREAMED CELERY ROOT AND APPLE

Serve this delicate purée with mild-flavored main courses – it won't cope well with spicy casseroles.

2 lb celery root	*2 level tsp creamed horseradish relish*
salt and pepper	*2 tbsp light cream*
lemon juice	*chopped fresh parsley*
¼ lb tart apples	

1 Peel the celery root, thinly slice, and immediately drop into cold salted water acidulated with lemon juice. Bring to the boil, cover, and simmer for 25–30 minutes or until tender.
2 Peel, quarter, core, and slice the apples. Add to the pan and simmer for 3–4 minutes longer or until the apple is tender. Drain well.

3 Mash the celery root and apple, then return to the pan with the horseradish. Season with salt and pepper and reheat, stirring all the time, until all excess moisture has been driven off.
4 Stir in the cream with plenty of chopped parsley, reheat gently, then taste and adjust the seasoning, if necessary, before serving.
SERVES 4

PARSNIP AND GINGER GRATIN

This is perfect for mopping up the juices from bean casseroles and stews.

2 lb parsnips, trimmed, peeled, and thinly sliced	*2 free-range eggs*
salt and pepper	*2 tbsp vegetable margarine or butter*
½ oz piece of fresh ginger root, peeled and finely chopped	*finely grated rind and juice of ½ lemon*
¼ cup light cream	*sliced almonds*

1 Cook the parsnips in boiling salted water for about 15 minutes or until tender. Drain the parsnips, then mash them.
2 Stir the ginger into the parsnip purée with the cream, eggs, margarine or butter, the lemon rind, and 1 tbsp lemon juice. Beat well to mix and season.

3 Turn into a lightly greased 1 quart shallow ovenproof dish. Sprinkle the surface lightly with almonds.
4 Bake at 400°F for 20–25 minutes or until golden brown and lightly set.
Serve immediately.
SERVES 4

$\mathscr{S}$AG ALOO

Ghee is a type of clarified butter originally made in India but now produced elsewhere. It has a better flavor than ordinary clarified butter and is particularly useful for frying at high temperatures. Commercially produced vegetarian ghee, made from hydrogenated vegetable oil, is now available in some Indian stores.

2 lb fresh spinach, or 1 lb frozen leaf spinach, thawed and drained	1 level tsp black mustard seeds
¼ cup vegetable ghee or oil	½ level tsp ground turmeric
1 medium onion, skinned and thinly sliced	¼ level tsp chili powder
2 garlic cloves, skinned and crushed	¼ level tsp ground ginger
2 level tsp ground coriander	salt
	1 lb all-purpose potatoes, peeled and thickly sliced

1 If using fresh spinach, wash well, put in a large saucepan without any water and cook over a very gentle heat for about 15 minutes. If using frozen spinach, cook over a gentle heat for 5 minutes. Drain well and cool.
2 With your hands, squeeze out all the moisture from the spinach. Chop finely.
3 Melt the ghee or oil in a heavy-based saucepan or flameproof casserole, add the onion, garlic, spices, and salt to taste and fry gently for about 5 minutes or until the onion begins to brown, stirring frequently.
4 Add the potatoes and stir gently to mix with the onion and spices. Pour in ⅔ cup water and bring to the boil, then lower the heat and simmer, uncovered, for 10 minutes. Stir occasionally and add a few more spoonfuls of water if necessary.
5 Fold the spinach gently into the potato mixture. Simmer for a further 5–10 minutes or until the potatoes are just tender. Serve hot.
SERVES 4–6

$\mathscr{H}$ERB-GLAZED TOMATOES

This dish also cooks well in the microwave. Cover the prepared tomatoes with a plate or a lid and cook on HIGH for 5–7 minutes or until tender, rearranging halfway through cooking.

4 beefsteak tomatoes, about 1¼ lb total weight	1 tsp lemon juice
2 tbsp vegetable margarine or butter	1½ tbsp shredded fresh basil
salt and pepper	basil sprigs, to garnish
3 tbsp heavy cream	

1 Cut the tomatoes in half and trim away the cores. Melt the margarine or butter in a large frying pan and gently fry the tomatoes for 1 minute on each side. Arrange the tomatoes in a greased, shallow ovenproof dish and season.
2 Add the cream, lemon juice, and half the basil to the juices in the frying pan, mix well and drizzle over the tomatoes. Sprinkle with more pepper.
3 Bake in the oven at 375°F for about 8 minutes. Sprinkle with the remaining basil and cook for a further 2–3 minutes. Serve hot, garnished with basil.
SERVES 8

ROAST POTATOES AND GARLIC

Once roasted, garlic is deliciously mild and creamy. Encourage your guests to slip the cloves from their skins and mash them into their gravy or sauce.

4 lb potatoes, peeled	2 whole heads of garlic
salt and pepper	chopped fresh parsley, to garnish
olive oil	

1 Cut the potatoes into large even-sized pieces, put them in a saucepan of cold salted water, and bring to the boil. Boil for 2 minutes, then drain thoroughly.
2 Heat the oil in a roasting pan in the oven. Add the potatoes and baste with the oil until all sides are coated. Separate the garlic into cloves, and remove the loose papery skins, leaving the inner skins attached. Scatter the garlic over the potatoes. Cook in the oven at 350°F for about 45 minutes, turning occasionally.
3 Increase the oven temperature to 425°F and continue cooking the potatoes for a further 20–25 minutes or until crisp and golden brown. Season with salt and pepper and sprinkle with parsley.
SERVES 8

FRIED MASALA POTATOES

These highly spiced potatoes are rather high in calories – but worth every tasty mouthful! Serve as an accompaniment to a simple (preferably low-calorie) main course.

2 lb new potatoes	4 garlic cloves, skinned
vegetable ghee or oil for deep-frying	2 medium onions, skinned and chopped
2 level tsp cumin seeds	3 tbsp vegetable ghee or oil
1 level tbsp coriander seeds	1 level tsp chili powder
1½ level tsp garam masala	½ level tsp ground turmeric
1 inch piece of fresh ginger root, peeled and roughly chopped	1 level tsp salt
	1¼ cups plain yogurt

1 Wash the potatoes and scrub clean if necessary. Cut into 1 inch pieces. Pat dry with paper towels.
2 Heat the oil in a deep-fat fryer to 350°F and deep-fry the potatoes in batches for 10 minutes or until golden brown. Remove from the oil and drain on paper towels.
3 Place the cumin and coriander seeds in a blender or food processor with the garam masala, ginger, garlic, and onions. Process until smooth, adding a little water if necessary.
4 Heat the ghee or oil in a heavy-based frying pan, add the masala paste and fry gently for about 5 minutes. Add the chili, turmeric, and salt and fry for a further 1 minute.
5 Pour in the yogurt, then add the potatoes. Stir well and cook for another 5 minutes or until completely heated through. Serve piping hot.
SERVES 4–6

-Fifteen-

Sauces and Dressings

Successful sauce making is easy provided a few basic rules are adhered to. Choose a good heavy-based pan to reduce the risk of burning. If the roux does burn, there's no remedy – you'll have to throw it away and start again. A burnt roux makes a bitter sauce (with unappetizing black bits in it). Don't despair if the sauce is lumpy – vigorous mixing with a large balloon whisk will usually do the trick, or as a last resort, push it through a strainer. Most sauces can be prepared ahead of time and refrigerated. To prevent a skin forming, lay a piece of damp parchment paper on the surface of the sauce. Reheat gently, whisking in more liquid if the sauce has become too thick.

Smooth sauces freeze very well. Freeze in usable quantities as large blocks of sauce take quite a while to thaw. It's preferable to reheat in a double boiler to prevent scorching, or in a large bowl in the microwave. Sauces containing pieces of tomato, mushroom, and so on, don't freeze so well as they're difficult to whisk when reheating.

The foundation of most good dressings is the oil. Virgin oils are those obtained from a first, cold pressing. These unrefined oils have the strongest flavor and are therefore the most expensive. Good virgin olive oil is essential for well flavored vinaigrette dressings. Rich and mellow walnut, hazelnut, and almond oils lend their own characteristic flavors. They're too strong to be used alone, so blend with a blander oil such as sunflower or groundnut. Sesame oil adds interesting oriental tones to salads, but avoid very dark-colored brands; they are overpowering and cloying.

Oils gradually lose their flavor and become rancid, particularly nut oils, so store them in a cool, dark place and adhere to the use-by date.

Vinegars now come in all sorts of flavors as well. As a change from the familiar wine vinegars, try cider, sherry, or raspberry vinegar or varieties flavored with herbs, spices, or garlic. Balsamic vinegar is wonderfully dark with a sweet-sour flavor. Its fine, distinctive flavor turns the humblest salad into something special. Use it in moderation because it is very strong. Both oils and vinegars can be flavored at home with herbs, spices, garlic, or soft fruits such as raspberries, strawberries, or blackcurrants.

Use this collection of sauces and dressings to embellish the recipes in this book or your own favorite dishes.

WHITE SAUCE 1

This is one of the basic sauces which has infinite possible variations. The quantities given here make a pouring sauce suitable for serving as an accompaniment to pies, nut roasts, vegetables, and pulses. To make a thicker sauce for binding ingredients to fill pancakes, pies, etc, increase the amounts of flour and shortening to ¼ cup.

1 tbsp vegetable margarine or butter	1¼ cups milk
1 tbsp all-purpose flour	salt and pepper

1 Melt the margarine or butter in a saucepan, stir in the flour and cook gently for 1 minute, stirring.
2 Remove the pan from the heat and gradually stir in the milk. Bring to the boil slowly and continue cooking, stirring all the time, until the sauce comes to the boil and thickens.
3 Simmer very gently for a further 2–3 minutes. Season with salt and pepper.
MAKES 1¼ CUPS

QUICK METHOD

Put the fat, flour, milk, salt, and pepper in a saucepan. Heat, whisking continuously, until the sauce thickens and is cooked.

BLENDER OR FOOD PROCESSOR METHOD

Put the fat, flour, milk, salt, and pepper in the machine and blend until smooth. Pour into a saucepan and bring to the boil, stirring, until the sauce thickens.

MICROWAVE METHOD

Put all the ingredients in a large bowl and cook on HIGH for 4–5 minutes, or until thickened, whisking every minute.

VARIATIONS

Add the following to the hot sauce with the seasoning:

Cheese Sauce 2 oz grated mature Cheddar cheese and a large pinch of mustard powder.
Parsley or Herb Sauce Add about 2 tbsp chopped fresh parsley or herbs of your choice.
Blue Cheese Sauce Add 2 oz crumbled Stilton, or other hard blue cheese, and 2 tsp lemon juice.
Mushroom Sauce Add 1 cup lightly cooked sliced mushrooms.
Onion Sauce Add 1 medium onion, chopped and cooked.
Egg Sauce Add 1 hard-boiled free-range egg, finely chopped.
Sweet Sauce Add 1–2 level tbsp sugar.

WHITE SAUCE 2

This white sauce is thickened with cornstarch and contains less fat than White Sauce 1. Use it when you want a lower-calorie sauce. Using 2 per cent low-fat milk or a mixture of milk and stock reduces the calorie content even more. Any of the variations for White Sauce 1 can be used with this as a base.

5 level tsp cornstarch	*a knob of vegetable margarine or butter*
1¼ cups milk	*salt and pepper*

1 Put the cornstarch in a bowl and blend with ⅓ cup milk to a smooth paste. Heat the remaining milk with the margarine or butter until boiling, then pour on to the blended mixture, stirring all the time to prevent lumps forming.
2 Return the mixture to the saucepan, bring to the boil slowly, and continue to cook, stirring all the time, until the sauce comes to the boil and thickens.
3 Simmer gently for a further 2-3 minutes, to make a white, glossy sauce. Season with salt and pepper.
MAKES 1¼ CUPS

HARISSA SAUCE

This is a fiery hot sauce, usually served with couscous and rice and bean dishes. It cooks well in the microwave. Simply put everything in a bowl, cover, and cook on HIGH for 8–10 minutes or until the sweet pepper is really soft. Add the water, re-cover, and cook for 3–4 minutes or until the water is boiling. Complete as below.

1 tbsp vegetable oil
1 large sweet red pepper, cored, seeded, and finely chopped
2 red chilies (or more to taste), seeded and chopped
2 garlic cloves, skinned and crushed

1 level tbsp ground coriander
1 level tsp ground caraway
2 level tbsp tomato paste
salt and pepper

1 Heat the oil in a large heavy-based saucepan. Add all the ingredients, except salt and pepper, and cook over a medium heat for about 5 minutes or until the pepper has softened.
2 Add 1¼ cups water and bring to the boil.

Reduce the heat, cover, and simmer gently for about 10 minutes or until the pepper is really soft. Purée in a blender or food processor until smooth. Season to taste with salt and pepper. Serve hot or cold.
MAKES ABOUT 1¼ CUPS

SOUR CREAM AND HORSERADISH SAUCE

The strength of commercially prepared horseradish sauce or relish varies considerably. Some are labelled 'hot' and give a considerable 'kick' to the sauce; others are very mild. Add your chosen brand a little at a time to get the desired effect. Serve with beets, carrots, mushrooms, baked onions, and, of course, nut roasts.

3 tbsp vegetable margarine or butter
3 level tbsp all-purpose flour
1¼ cups vegetable stock

1½ cups sour cream
about 3 level tbsp horseradish sauce
salt and pepper

1 Melt the margarine or butter in a heavy-based saucepan, add the flour, and cook for 2 minutes, stirring all the time.
2 Remove from the heat and gradually add the stock, stirring briskly. Bring to the boil and stir until thick. Simmer for 5 minutes.

3 Add the sour cream and mix in well.
4 Stir in the horseradish sauce to taste and season with salt and pepper. Reheat gently without boiling.
MAKES ABOUT 2½ CUPS

GARLIC CHEESE AND WALNUT SAUCE

Serve this with stuffed baked onions, or sweet peppers, steamed broccoli, or Brussels sprouts, or as a topping for baked potatoes.

3 tbsp vegetable margarine or butter	5 oz full-fat soft cheese with garlic and herbs
8 level tsp all-purpose flour	¼ cup walnuts, chopped
1¼ cups milk	salt and pepper

1 Melt the margarine or butter in a heavy-based saucepan, add the flour, and cook for 2 minutes, stirring all the time.
2 Remove from the heat and gradually add the milk, beating between each addition.
3 Cook until thickened, stirring all the time, then simmer for about 5 minutes.
4 Off the heat, beat in the cheese a little at a time, making sure it melts. Stir in the chopped walnuts. Season with salt and pepper. Reheat but do not boil.
MAKES ABOUT 1¼ CUPS

VINAIGRETTE DRESSING

Make up a large batch of dressing and store in the refrigerator ready for use when required. Increase or decrease the proportion of oil to vinegar within the suggested range, according to how sharp you like your dressing. The flavor can be varied with any of the suggestions shown below.

¼–1 cup olive oil	2 level tsp Dijon-style mustard
3 tbsp white wine, red wine, garlic, or herb vinegar	salt and pepper
½ level tsp sugar or honey	

Whisk together all the ingredients until thoroughly combined. Season with salt and pepper.

VARIATIONS
Herb Whisk into the dressing 2 level tbsp finely chopped, fresh mixed herbs, such as parsley, thyme, marjoram, chives, sage, etc.
Mustard and Parsley Stir in 1 level tbsp whole-grain mustard and 2 level tbsp finely chopped fresh parsley
Sweet and Spiced Add 1 level tsp mango chutney, 1 level tsp mild curry paste and ½ level tsp ground turmeric.
Roquefort Place the dressing in a blender or food processor. Add 1 oz Roquefort cheese and 2 tbsp light cream. Blend until smooth.
Garlic Crush 1–2 garlic cloves into the dressing.
MAKES ABOUT 1 CUP

$\mathcal{T}$ARRAGON AND TOMATO VINAIGRETTE

Use very ripe, bright red tomatoes for the best flavor.

2 tbsp red wine vinegar	1 level tbsp chopped onion (preferably red)
¼ cup olive oil	a few drops of Tabasco
1 tbsp mustard oil	salt and pepper
1 level tsp tomato paste	¼ cup skinned, seeded, and chopped tomatoes
1 level tbsp each chopped fresh tarragon and parsley	a pinch of sugar (optional)

1 Whisk together the vinegar, oils, tomato paste, herbs, onion, and Tabasco. Season with salt and pepper.

2 Stir in the tomatoes and add sugar if wished. Taste and adjust the seasoning, if necessary.

MAKES ABOUT ⅔ CUP

$\mathcal{R}$ICH GARLIC DRESSING

Balsamic vinegar produces a dark, sweet-sour dressing, ideal with strong-flavored foods.

¼ cup balsamic vinegar	2 garlic cloves, skinned and crushed
⅔ cup olive oil	salt and pepper
½ level tsp sugar	

1 Whisk together the vinegar, oil, sugar, and garlic until thoroughly combined.

2 Season with salt and pepper.

MAKES ABOUT 1 CUP

$\mathcal{H}$ERB PURÉE

This aromatic purée is ideal for stirring into steamed vegetables, pasta, rice, or noodles.

1½ cups fresh mixed herb leaves, such as basil, thyme, or marjoram	⅔ cup olive oil
	¼ cup freshly grated Parmesan cheese

Roughly chop the herbs in a food processor. Slowly pour in the oil and blend into a thick purée. Blend in the cheese. Transfer to a jar and store in the refrigerator. The purée will keep for 2–3 weeks.

SERVES 4

A selection of sauces and dressings

CURRY SAUCE

This is a fairly simple curry sauce to serve with hard-boiled eggs, cooked vegetables, and pulses. This basic recipe can, of course, be embellished by the addition of chilies, ginger, a few cardamoms, or chopped fresh coriander (cilantro).

2 tbsp vegetable oil	1 level tsp ground cumin
1 large onion, skinned and chopped	⅓ cup split red lentils
1 garlic clove, skinned and crushed	3¾ cups vegetable stock
2 level tsp ground coriander	salt and pepper
2 level tsp ground turmeric	⅔ cup plain yogurt
1 level tsp fenugreek seeds	

1 Heat the oil in a heavy-based saucepan. Add the onion and garlic and fry for 5 minutes or until softened. Add the spices and fry for 2 minutes, stirring.
2 Add the lentils and stock, bring to the boil,

then reduce the heat, cover, and simmer for 30 minutes or until the lentils are very soft. Season with salt and pepper. Stir in the yogurt and reheat gently before serving.
MAKES ABOUT 2½ CUPS

LEEK SAUCE

Serve with steamed, boiled, or roast vegetables.

4 tbsp vegetable margarine or butter	⅔ cup light cream
1 lb leeks, trimmed, thoroughly washed, and finely chopped	salt and pepper
¼ cup vegetable stock	2 level tsp green peppercorns in brine, drained and chopped
4 tsp lemon juice	

1 Melt the margarine or butter in a saucepan and fry the leeks for 1–2 minutes. Cover with a tight-fitting lid and cook over a low heat for about 5 minutes or until very soft, stirring occasionally. Add the stock and simmer gently, covered, for a further 10 minutes. Leave the stock mixture to cool slightly.

2 In a blender or food processor, purée the leeks and stock with the lemon juice. Strain the resulting mixture back into the rinsed-out saucepan. Stir in the cream, seasoning, and peppercorns. Reheat gently without boiling for 1–2 minutes before serving.
MAKES ABOUT 2½ CUPS

*B*ÉCHAMEL SAUCE

Flavored milk gives a delicate aroma to this white sauce. There is a long and short method. The long method is strictly for the purist; this simplified version makes a splendid sauce in half the time. It's delicious served plain or with the addition of mildly flavored ingredients such as egg or mushroom.

1¼ cups milk	*1 blade of mace*
1 slice of onion	*1 tbsp vegetable margarine or butter*
1 bay leaf	*scant 1 tbsp all-purpose flour*
6 peppercorns	*salt and pepper*

1 Pour the milk into a saucepan. Add the onion, bay leaf, peppercorns, and mace and bring to scalding point. Remove from the heat, cover, and leave to infuse for 10–30 minutes. Strain.

2 Melt the margarine or butter in a saucepan. Remove from the heat and stir in the flour until evenly blended. Gradually pour on the warm milk, stirring well. Season lightly with salt and pepper.

3 Bring to the boil, stirring constantly, and simmer for 2–3 minutes.

MAKES ABOUT 1¼ CUPS

*H*OLLANDAISE SAUCE

Hollandaise should always be served warm. Bear in mind that it curdles easily: if this happens, simply add an ice cube, whisk well, and the sauce should come back together again. It's traditionally served with steamed asparagus as an appetizer, but it makes an excellent accompaniment to most vegetables.

3 tbsp white wine vinegar	*6–8 tbsp butter, at room temperature*
6 peppercorns	*2 free-range egg yolks*
1 small bay leaf	*salt*
1 blade of mace	

1 Place the vinegar, peppercorns, bay leaf and mace in a small saucepan. Bring to the boil and boil rapidly until reduced to only 2 tsp. Set aside.

2 Soften the butter slightly. In a small heatproof bowl, cream the egg yolks with a small piece of butter and a pinch of salt. Strain the herb and vinegar mixture into the bowl.

3 Place the bowl in a double boiler over a gentle heat until the mixture becomes thick, stirring constantly.

4 Gradually add the remainder of the butter in small pieces, stirring constantly. When 6 tbsp of the butter has been added, season the sauce lightly with salt. If still too sharp, add a little more butter. The sauce should be lightly piquant. Serve lukewarm.

SERVES 4

$\mathcal{T}$OMATO SAUCE

This makes a deliciously rich, well flavored sauce for serving with pasta, vegetable bakes, or roasts. To make a spicy sauce, add 1–2 chopped fresh chilies and a little chopped fresh coriander. Add other flavorings, such as garlic, bay leaves, thyme, or rosemary, to make a sauce to complement whatever it's being served with.

2 tbsp olive oil	a large pinch of dried oregano
1 small onion, skinned and finely chopped	1¼ cups dry red wine or vegetable stock
2 level tbsp tomato paste	a large pinch of sugar
1 level tsp mild paprika	salt and pepper
two 14 oz cans chopped tomatoes	

1 Heat the oil in a heavy-based saucepan, add the onion, and fry for 5–10 minutes or until very soft. Add the tomato paste and paprika and fry for 2–3 minutes. Add the tomatoes, oregano, red wine or stock, and sugar.

2 Season the sauce with salt and pepper, then bring to the boil and simmer for about 20 minutes or until the sauce is slightly reduced.
MAKES ABOUT 2½ CUPS

$\mathcal{G}$RAVY

It's not that difficult to make a delicious vegetarian gravy, providing you use a good, well flavored stock (Brown Onion or Mushroom, pages 41 and 42, both work well) or use a mixture of red wine and stock. Add a dash or two of gravy browning or yeast extract to get a dark brown colour, if necessary.

1 tbsp vegetable oil	2 level tbsp all-purpose flour
1 large onion, skinned and chopped	2½ cups stock or stock and red wine
¼ lb mushrooms, wiped and chopped	a sprig of fresh thyme
1 garlic clove, skinned and crushed (optional)	salt and pepper

1 Heat the oil in a heavy-based saucepan. Add the onion, mushrooms, and garlic, if using. Fry over a high heat for about 10 minutes or until the onions start to turn golden brown. Stir all the time so that they brown evenly rather than burn.
2 Add the flour and cook over a low heat for about 5 minutes or until the flour starts to brown, stirring all the time. Take the pan off

the heat and leave to cool for 1–2 minutes.
3 Gradually blend in the stock (or stock and wine), return to the heat, and bring to the boil. Add the thyme, season with salt and pepper, lower the heat, cover, and simmer for 20 minutes. Strain into a clean saucepan. Taste and adjust the seasoning, if necessary, just before serving.
MAKES ABOUT 1¾ CUPS

MAYONNAISE

The ingredients for Mayonnaise should be at room temperature. Never use eggs straight from the refrigerator or cold larder as this may result in curdling. (See below for rescue remedies.)

1 free-range egg yolk	¼ level tsp pepper
½ level tsp mustard powder or 1 level tsp Dijon-style mustard	½ level tsp sugar
	1 tbsp white wine vinegar or lemon juice
½ level tsp salt	about ⅔ cup vegetable oil

Put the egg yolk into a bowl with the mustard, salt, pepper, sugar, and 1 tsp of the vinegar or lemon juice. Mix thoroughly, then add the oil, drop by drop, whisking constantly, until the sauce is thick and smooth. If it becomes too thick, add a little more of the vinegar or lemon juice. When all the oil has been added, add the remaining vinegar or lemon juice gradually and mix thoroughly.
MAKES ABOUT ⅔ CUP

Making Mayonnaise in a blender or food processor Most blenders and food processors need at least a two-egg quantity in order to ensure that the blades are covered. Put the yolks, salt and pepper, and half the vinegar or lemon juice into the blender jar or food processor bowl and blend well. If your machine has a variable speed control, run it at a slow speed. Add the oil gradually, while the machine is running. Add the remaining vinegar and season.

Rescue remedies If the Mayonnaise separates, save it by beating the curdled mixture into a fresh base. This base can be any one of the following: 1 tsp hot water; 1 tsp vinegar or lemon juice; 1 level tsp Dijon-style mustard or ½ level tsp mustard powder; or an egg yolk. Add the curdled mixture to the base, beating hard. When the mixture is smooth, continue adding the oil as above. (If you use an extra egg yolk you may find that you need to add a little extra oil.)

Storing Mayonnaise Home-made Mayonnaise does not keep as long as store-bought varieties because it lacks their added emulsifiers, stabilizers, and preservatives. However, Mayonnaise should keep for 3–4 days in a screw-top glass jar in the refrigerator. Allow to come to room temperature before stirring or the Mayonnaise may curdle.

TOFU MAYONNAISE
To make Tofu Mayonnaise, a vegan alternative to egg-based Mayonnaise, follow the blender or food processor method above. Omit the egg and replace with a 10½ oz packet of silken tofu. Reduce the oil to 6 tbsp.
MAKES ABOUT 1¼ CUPS

VARIATIONS
Curried Tofu Mayonnaise Flavor with 1 tsp hot curry paste.
Garlic and Herb Tofu Mayonnaise Flavor with 1 garlic clove, skinned and crushed and 2 level tbsp chopped mixed fresh herbs.

*F*LAVORED MAYONNAISE

Add one of the following flavorings to ⅔ cup home-made or store-bought mayonnaise.

Curry Cream Sauce Sauté 2 level tsp chopped onion and 1 crushed garlic clove in 1 tbsp oil for 2–3 minutes. Stir in 2 level tsp curry powder and 1 level tsp tomato paste. Add 6 tbsp water, 1 slice of lemon, and 2 level tsp apricot jam. Simmer for 5–7 minutes. Strain the mixture and leave to cool. When cold, whisk into the mayonnaise. Taste and adjust the seasoning, if necessary.

Watercress and Lemon Beat 4 level tbsp finely chopped watercress and the finely grated zest of 2 lemons into the mayonnaise. Taste and adjust the seasoning, if necessary.

Thousand Island Stir in 2 level tbsp finely chopped green olives, 2 level tsp each finely chopped parsley and onion, 2 level tsp tomato paste, 2 level tbsp finely chopped sweet green pepper, and 1 chopped hard-boiled egg. Taste and adjust the seasoning, if necessary.

Blue Cheese and Toasted Walnut Beat ¼ lb crumbled Danish Blue cheese, ⅓ cup sour cream, ½ quantity Vinaigrette Dressing (see page 185), 1 skinned and crushed garlic clove, ¼ cup toasted chopped walnuts, and 1 level tbsp chopped fresh parsley into the mayonnaise. Taste and adjust the seasoning, if necessary.

Aïoli (Garlic Mayonnaise) See the recipe on page 22 for Fried Zucchini with Rosemary Aïoli.

*Y*OGURT AND TAHINI CREAM

Use to dress coleslaw, or serve with hard-boiled eggs, warm potatoes, or vegetable crudités.

6 tbsp plain yogurt	*¼ cup thin tahini (see page 14)*
3–4 tsp white wine vinegar	*salt and pepper*
6 tbsp olive oil	

1 Whisk together the yogurt and vinegar. Slowly stir in the olive oil until thoroughly combined.

2 Beat in the tahini and then season with salt and pepper.
MAKES ABOUT 1 CUP

*P*ESTO

This is the classic Genoese pasta sauce. It uses copious quantities of fresh basil – dried will not do. Use it to flavor soups, dressings, and pizzas as well as pasta.

1½ cups fresh basil leaves	*salt and pepper*
2 garlic cloves, skinned	*½ cup olive oil*
2 tbsp pine nuts	*⅔ cup freshly grated Parmesan cheese*

Put the basil, garlic, pine nuts, salt, pepper, and olive oil in a blender or food processor and blend at high speed until very creamy. Transfer the mixture to a bowl, fold in the cheese and mix thoroughly. Store for up to 2 weeks in a screw-top jar in the refrigerator.

MAKES 2½ CUPS; ENOUGH FOR 4–6 SERVINGS OF PASTA

*H*AZELNUT AND CORIANDER PESTO

This makes a vibrant green pesto with a pungent smell and a strong flavor. Serve it separately for guests to mix to taste with their individual plates of steaming pasta, dilute it with fromage blanc or yogurt and toss with cooked vegetables and pulses, or use in small amounts to flavor vinaigrette dressings for hot or cold salads.

¾ cup hazelnuts	*finely grated rind and juice of ½ lemon*
1 large bunch of coriander (cilantro)	*about ⅔ cup olive oil*
2–3 garlic cloves, skinned and crushed	*salt and pepper*

1 Toast the hazelnuts under a hot broiler. Tip them on to a clean dish towel and rub off the loose skins. Toast again under the broiler until golden brown on all sides. Leave to cool, then tip into a blender or food processor.
2 Trim the stalks from the coriander and discard. Put the leaves into the blender with the hazelnuts. Add the garlic and the lemon rind and juice. Process until finely chopped, then, with the machine still running, gradually add the oil in a thin, steady stream until you have a fairly thick sauce-like consistency.
3 Season with black pepper and a little salt. Turn into a bowl or a jar, cover tightly, and use as required. Store in the refrigerator for 1–2 weeks.

MAKES ABOUT 1¼ CUPS; ENOUGH FOR 4–6 SERVINGS OF PASTA

*F*RESH PEAR DRESSING

To produce a smooth dressing, choose very ripe pears. Serve with Spinach Ricotta Terrine (see page 18), salads, and fried dishes.

¼ lb ripe, juicy pears	a few drops of red wine vinegar
⅔ cup walnut oil	salt and pepper
⅔ cup olive oil	

Peel, halve, and core the pears. Roughly chop and put in a blender or food processor. Add the oils and vinegar, and season with salt and pepper. Purée until smooth, then taste, and adjust the seasoning, if necessary. Whisk the dressing again just before serving.
MAKES ABOUT 1¼ CUPS

*B*RANDY AND CELERY SAUCE

If you're nervous about setting the brandy alight (see step 5), make the sauce with heavy cream, instead of light, add the brandy to the sauce, and boil for 1–2 minutes. Don't try to boil a sauce containing light cream – it will curdle. The higher fat content of heavy cream means it can be boiled without risk of curdling, but it will also increase the calorie content!
Serve with Wild Mushroom Strudel (see page 78), nut roasts, and vegetable burgers.

2 tbsp vegetable margarine or butter	1 level tbsp chopped fresh dill or 1 level tsp dried dill weed
4 celery sticks, trimmed and finely chopped	salt and pepper
1 level tbsp rice flour or all-purpose flour	⅓ cup light cream
1¼ cups vegetable stock	1–2 tbsp brandy

1 Heat the margarine or butter in a saucepan, add the celery, and cook gently until almost tender.
2 Stir in the flour and cook for 1 minute. Remove from the heat, gradually blend in the stock, and bring to the boil, stirring all the time. Mix in the dill, season with salt and pepper, and simmer for about 5 minutes. Cool slightly.
3 Purée the sauce in a food processor, then strain into a clean saucepan.
4 Whisk the cream into the sauce and heat gently without boiling, stirring occasionally. Taste and adjust the seasoning, if necessary.
5 Gently heat the brandy until warm, but not boiling. Remove from the heat, set alight and stir into the sauce to taste.
MAKES ABOUT 1¼ CUPS

—Sixteen—

Cakes and Quickbreads

Vegans and non-egg eating vegetarians can have a hard time finding suitable recipes for cakes and quickbreads. Here, we have devised a delicious selection of recipes, many without eggs, milk, or dairy produce. In fact the Eggless Chocolate Cake (see page 197) is so moist, rich, and delicious that no one will realize that it's egg-free.

Flours vary enormously – look for a finely ground wholewheat flour for cakes, cookies, and quickbreads; the coarser types tend to give a much crumblier texture. Wholewheat flour absorbs more liquid than white flour, so when substituting one for the other use slightly more liquid. Cakes made solely with wholewheat flour are denser and heavier – a mixture of half white and half wholewheat gives a lighter result.

Most of these recipes will keep well for several days, and in some cases for up to 2 weeks if wrapped in parchment paper and foil and then put into an airtight container. Alternatively, they can be frozen. We recommend that you thaw them, still wrapped, overnight, but if time does not allow, unwrap until thawed, then immediately overwrap again.

Many of the recipes contain dried fruits and nuts. Some manufacturers treat dried fruit with sulphur dioxide gas to prevent it becoming too dark in color. Choose unsulphured brands if you're interested in reducing your consumption of chemical additives. Buy dried fruit in small quantities and store it in an airtight container.

Nuts contain a high proportion of oil so they tend to become rancid rather quickly. Buy them in small quantities from a store with a fast turnover, and keep them in the refrigerator or a cool dark place.

FRUIT AND NUT BARS

If you have a microwave, cook the apples and fruit juice on HIGH, covered, for about 5–6 minutes.

1 lb sweet apples, peeled, cored, and chopped	¾ cup self-rising wholewheat flour
5 tbsp unsweetened fruit juice	⅓ cup shredded coconut
½ lb mixed dried fruit, such as dried apricots, dates, raisins, chopped if necessary	¼ cup pumpkin seeds
1 cup chopped mixed nuts	2 tbsp vegetable oil
⅔ cup rolled oats	2 tbsp pear and apple butter or apricot conserve

1 Put the apples and fruit juice in a heavy-based saucepan, cover and cook gently for 10–15 minutes or until the apple is very soft, shaking the pan occasionally (don't remove the lid). Beat thoroughly to make a smooth purée.
2 Add all the remaining ingredients except the butter or conserve, and beat well together. Oil an 8 inch square pan and line the base with parchment paper. Oil the paper. Spoon the mixture into the pan and bake in the oven at 350°F for about 40 minutes or until firm to the touch.
3 Turn out on to a wire rack. Brush with the butter or conserve while still warm and mark into 12 bars. Leave to cool, then cut through into bars.
MAKES 12

*E*GGLESS CHOCOLATE CAKE

No one will ever guess that there's anything unusual about this cake! It's really moist, chocolaty, and irresistible. It also keeps very well, wrapped in foil or in an airtight container.

1 cup creamed coconut	*a large pinch of salt*
9 tbsp cocoa	*1 cup packed light brown sugar*
3½ cups self-rising flour	*½ cup plus 6 tbsp sunflower oil*
1 level tsp baking powder	*confectioners' sugar for dusting (optional)*

1 Oil and line a 2 quart loaf pan.
2 Pour 2¾ cups boiling water over the coconut and stir until it dissolves. Cool.
3 Sift the cocoa, flour, baking powder, and salt into a bowl and mix together with the sugar. Make a well in the center, then pour in the coconut mixture and the oil. Using a wooden spoon, beat the ingredients together thoroughly to make a smooth, batter.
4 Pour into the prepared pan and bake in the oven at 350°F for 1¼ hours or until well risen and just firm to the touch. Leave to cool in the pan for 10 minutes, then turn out and leave to cool completely. Dust with confectioners' sugar before serving, if liked.
MAKES ABOUT 12 THICK SLICES

*C*ARROT CAKE

Root vegetables were often used to lend sweetness to 18th-century cakes and desserts. Beets, parsnips, and carrots were all common ingredients, but of these, only carrot is still favored today. It makes a very pleasant, moist cake, without any hint of carrot in the taste.

1 cup vegetable margarine or butter	*1 level tsp baking powder*
1 cup packed light brown sugar	*⅔ cup ground almonds*
4 free-range eggs, separated	*1¼ cups walnut pieces, chopped*
finely grated zest of ½ orange	*¼ lb young carrots, trimmed, peeled, and grated*
4 tsp lemon juice	*½ lb cream cheese*
1½ cups self-rising flour	*2 tsp honey*

1 Grease and line a deep 8 inch round cake pan.
2 Cream the margarine or butter and sugar together in a bowl until pale and fluffy. Beat in the egg yolks, then stir in the orange zest and 3 tsp of the lemon juice.
3 Sift in the flour and baking powder, then stir in the almonds and 1 cup walnuts.
4 Whisk the egg whites until stiff, then fold into the cake mixture with the carrots. Pour into the pan and hollow the centre slightly.
5 Bake at 350°F for 1½ –2 hours or until a skewer inserted in the center comes out clean. Cover the top with foil after 1 hour if it starts to brown.
6 Leave to cool slightly, then turn out on to a wire rack, and remove the lining paper. Cool.
7 To make the topping, beat together the cheese, honey, and remaining lemon juice and spread over the top of the cake. Sprinkle the topping with the remaining walnuts.
MAKES 8–10 SLICES

*H*AZELNUT AND CHOCOLATE OAT SQUARES

Jumbo oats are available from health food stores. They give these cookies a crunchy texture.

½ cup hazelnuts	*1 tbsp light corn syrup*
1 cup packed light brown sugar	*2 cups jumbo oats*
8 tbsp vegetable margarine or butter	*¼ cup milk chocolate morsels*

1 Lightly grease a shallow, rectangular baking pan measuring 11 × 7 inches along the top. Roughly chop the hazelnuts.
2 Melt together the sugar, margarine or butter, and syrup. Stir in the hazelnuts and oats. Allow to cool slightly, then stir in the chocolate morsels.

3 Spoon into the pan and bake at 350°F for about 30 minutes or until golden and firm.
4 Cool in the pan for a few minutes before cutting into squares. Turn out on to a wire rack to cool completely.
MAKES ABOUT 12

*L*EMON AND COCONUT CAKE

If you prefer to use wholewheat flour, add an extra ½ level tsp baking powder and a little extra lemon juice to the creamed mixture.

8 tbsp softened butter or vegetable margarine	*1 level tsp baking powder*
½ cup plus 6 tbsp sugar	*2 free-range egg whites*
2 free-range eggs	*⅓ cup shredded coconut*
2 lemons	*confectioners' sugar, to dust*
1 cup self-rising flour	

1 Grease and base-line a shallow, rectangular baking pan measuring 11 × 7 inches along the top.
2 Beat together the butter or margarine, ½ cup of the sugar, two eggs, grated zest of one lemon, flour, and baking powder.
3 Add about 1 tbsp lemon juice or enough to form a soft dropping consistency. Spoon into the pan.
4 Whisk the egg whites until stiff but not dry. Fold in the remaining sugar, grated zest of one lemon, and the coconut. Spoon roughly over the mixture. Bake at 350°F for about 30 minutes or until golden.

5 Cool in the pan for a few minutes before turning out on to a wire rack to cool. Dust the cake squares lightly with confectioners' sugar.
MAKES 12 FINGERS

VARIATION
Coffee and Walnut Omit the lemon zest and juice in the cake mixture and beat in 1 level tsp instant coffee, dissolved in 1 tbsp hot water. For the topping, use light brown sugar instead of white sugar and chopped walnuts instead of coconut.

$\mathcal{O}$RANGE AND POPPY SEED CAKE

The finished loaf could be decorated with a little white icing made by blending sifted confectioners' sugar with enough orange juice to give a smooth coating consistency.

1 cup vegetable margarine or butter	*1 level tsp baking powder*
¾ cup sugar	*a pinch of salt*
3 free-range eggs	*finely grated zest and juice of 2 oranges*
3 cups self-rising wholewheat flour	*¼ cup poppy seeds*

1 Grease and line a 1½ quart loaf pan. Put all the ingredients except the poppy seeds in a blender or food processor and process until smooth and well mixed. Fold in the poppy seeds.

2 Spoon the mixture into the prepared pan. Bake at 350°F for 50 minutes–1 hour or until well risen and firm to the touch. Turn out and cool on a wire rack.

MAKES ABOUT 12 SLICES

$\mathscr{S}$PICED APPLE CAKE

This deliciously moist cake is equally good served with cream and eaten warm as a dessert.
It is best consumed within 2 days of being made.

8 tbsp vegetable margarine or butter
¾ cup packed dark brown sugar
2 free-range eggs, beaten
2 cups wholewheat flour
1 level tsp ground mixed spice
1 level tsp ground cinnamon
2 level tsp baking powder
1 lb tart apples, peeled, cored, and chopped
3–4 tbsp milk
1 tbsp honey
1 level tbsp sugar

1 Grease and line a deep 7 inch round cake pan with parchment paper.

2 Cream the margarine or butter and sugar together until pale and fluffy. Add the eggs, a little at a time, beating well after each addition. Add the flour, spices, and baking powder and mix well. Fold in the apples and milk to make a soft dropping consistency.

3 Turn the mixture into the prepared pan and bake at 325°F for 1½ hours or until well risen and firm to the touch. Turn out on to a wire rack to cool.

4 When the cake is cold, brush with the honey and sprinkle with the sugar.

MAKES ABOUT 10 SLICES

$\mathscr{P}$EANUT AND RAISIN COOKIES

Leave the chopped ingredients in chunks so the cookies retain some bite and texture.

8 tbsp softened butter or vegetable margarine
⅔ cup sugar
1 free-range egg
1¼ cups all-purpose flour
½ level tsp baking powder
½ level tsp salt
1½ cups crunchy peanut butter
1 cup raisins

1 Grease two baking sheets.

2 Beat together all the ingredients except the raisins, until well blended. Stir in the raisins.

3 Spoon large teaspoonfuls of the mixture on to the baking sheets, leaving room to spread. Bake at 375°F for about 15 minutes, or until golden brown around the edges. Cool slightly before lifting on to a wire rack to cool completely.

MAKES ABOUT 30

VARIATIONS

Chocolate Nut Omit the peanut butter and raisins and add 1 tsp vanilla extract. Stir in 1 cup chocolate morsels and ¾ cup roughly chopped walnuts.

Coconut and Cherry Omit the peanut butter and raisins, reduce the sugar to ⅓ cup and stir in ⅓ cup shredded coconut, and 1 cup rinsed, roughly chopped glacé cherries.

Oat and Cinnamon Omit the peanut butter and raisins and add 1 tsp vanilla extract. Stir in 1 level tsp ground cinnamon and 1 cup rolled oats.

$\mathcal{M}$ALTED FRUIT QUICKBREAD

Fruit loaves keep well and the flavor actually improves if they are kept for a day or two before eating. Malt is the raw material from which beer and malt whisky are made and it's this that makes this sticky cake particularly more-ish. Serve thinly sliced and spread with butter.

2 cups self-rising flour	2 tbsp light corn syrup
a pinch of salt	3 tbsp malt extract
2 tbsp dark brown sugar	⅔ cup milk
1 cup mixed dried fruit	

1 Grease a 1 quart loaf pan and line the base and sides with parchment paper.
2 Put the flour, salt, sugar, and fruit in a bowl and mix together. Make a well in the center.
3 Put the syrup, malt extract, and milk in a saucepan and heat gently until melted. Pour into the well in the center of the dry ingredients, then beat thoroughly together.

Add a little extra milk, if necessary.
4 Turn the mixture into the prepared pan and bake at 325°F for about 1–1¼ hours. Turn out and leave to cool on a wire rack. When completely cold, wrap in parchment paper and foil and store for 1 day before eating.
MAKES 10 SLICES

$\mathcal{M}$ARBLED CHOCOLATE QUICKBREAD

It's much easier to melt the chocolate in a microwave, if you own one. It will take about 2–3 minutes on LOW. Stir occasionally.

1 cup butter or vegetable margarine	few drops orange flower water (optional)
1 cup sugar	3 oz plain chocolate
3 free-range eggs, beaten	1 level tbsp cocoa
1 cup self-rising flour	1 cup self-rising wholewheat flour
finely grated zest of 1 large orange	1 tbsp milk
2 tbsp orange juice	

1 Grease a 1 quart loaf pan and line the base and sides with parchment paper.
2 Cream the fat and sugar together until pale and fluffy, then gradually beat in the eggs, beating well after each addition.
3 Transfer half of the mixture to another bowl and beat in the white flour, orange zest, juice, and orange flower water, if using.
4 Break the chocolate into pieces, put into a small bowl, and place over a pan of simmering water. Stir until the chocolate melts. Stir into

the remaining cake mixture with the cocoa wholewheat flour, and milk.
5 Put alternate spoonfuls of the two mixtures into the prepared pan. Use a knife to swirl through the mixture to make a marbled effect, then level the surface.
6 Bake at 350°F for 1¼–1½ hours, until well risen and firm to the touch. Turn out on a wire rack to cool.
MAKES ABOUT 14 SLICES

MIXED FRUIT QUICKBREAD

This foolproof quickbread is really moist and well flavored. The only catch is that you need to remember to soak the fruit overnight, and it is best if wrapped and stored for 1–2 days before slicing.

1⅓ cups raisins	1 free-range egg, beaten
⅔ cup golden raisins	2 cups wholewheat flour
¾ cup packed brown sugar	1½ level tsp baking powder
1¼ cups strained cold tea (without milk)	½ level tsp ground mixed spice

1 Grease and base-line a 2 lb loaf pan. Put the dried fruit and sugar in a large bowl. Pour over the tea, stir well to mix and leave to soak overnight.
2 The next day, add the egg, flour, baking powder, and mixed spice to the fruit and tea mixture. Beat thoroughly with a wooden spoon until all the ingredients are evenly combined. Spoon into the prepared pan and level the surface.
3 Bake in the oven at 350°F for about 1¼ hours or until the cake is well risen and a skewer inserted in the center comes out clean.
4 Turn the cake out of the pan and leave on a wire rack until completely cold. Wrap in parchment paper and foil and store in an airtight container for 1–2 days before slicing.
MAKES ABOUT 14 SLICES

BANANA BREAD

Use very ripe bananas for the best flavor. A few chopped nuts or a handful of sultanas or currants can also be added, if liked.

8 tbsp vegetable margarine or butter	¾ cup wholewheat flour
½ cup sugar	finely grated zest of ½ lemon
2 free-range eggs, beaten	2 large ripe bananas
1 cup self-rising flour	

1 Grease a 1½ quart loaf pan and line the base with parchment paper.
2 Cream together the butter and sugar until pale and fluffy. Gradually beat in the eggs. Sift in the flours, adding any bran left in the strainer. Mash the lemon zest with the bananas and fold into the mixture with the flour.
3 Spoon into the prepared pan and level the surface. Bake in the oven at 325°F for 1–1¼ hours or until firm to the touch. Leave to cool in the tin for 5 minutes, then turn out and cool on a wire rack.
MAKES ABOUT 14 SLICES

PRICOT PASTRIES

These more-ish pastries look remarkably professional yet they're really quick and easy to make using ready rolled squares of puff pastry (you'll find them in the freezer cabinet in supermarkets). Serve the pastries fresh from the oven for breakfast or with morning coffee.

1 lb can apricot halves in syrup

3 ready-rolled puff pastry sheets, each measuring about 8 inches square

8 oz packet white almond paste or marzipan

beaten free-range egg, to glaze (optional)

a few sliced almonds

1 Empty the can of apricots into a strainer placed over a small saucepan. Let them drain for a couple of minutes to catch all the syrup. Remove the apricots from the pan and set aside. Bring the syrup to the boil and boil for 2–3 minutes until it is reduced and thickened slightly. Remove from the heat and cool.

2 Trim the edges of the pastry squares and cut each one in half lengthways to make a total of six rectangles. Cut the almond paste lengthways into six equal slices. Using your fingers or a rolling pin, slightly flatten each slice so that it is slightly smaller than a piece of pastry. Place each piece of marzipan on a piece of pastry.

3 Arrange the pastries on a baking sheet. Brush with egg glaze, if using, then top each with two apricot halves, cut side down. Sprinkle with a few sliced almonds. Bake in the oven at 425°F for 15–20 minutes or until golden brown. As soon as they come out of the oven, brush with the syrup to glaze.

MAKES 6

Apricot Pastries

ASPBERRY AND APPLE CAKE

A stunning, moist cake, packed with apples and raspberries. It works equally well with
frozen raspberries if they're added to the creamed mixture while frozen.

2 cups self-rising flour	2 free-range eggs, beaten
a large pinch of salt	3 tbsp milk
¾ cup vegetable margarine or butter	½ lb firm but ripe raspberries, or frozen raspberries
⅔ cup ground almonds	⅔ cup sliced almonds
1 cup sugar	confectioners' sugar, for dusting
½ lb sweet apples, peeled, cored, and chopped	

1 Grease and base-line an 8 inch springform
cake pan.
2 Sift the flour and salt into a large bowl.
Rub in the shortening until the mixture
resembles fine breadcrumbs. Stir in the
almonds, sugar, and apples, using a wooden
spoon. Beat in the eggs and milk, then
carefully fold in half of the raspberries.
3 Spoon the mixture carefully into the pan

and level the surface. Sprinkle over the
remaining raspberries and the almonds. Bake
in the oven at 350°F for about 1–1¼ hours or
until well risen, golden brown and firm to the
touch in the center. Dust with confectioners'
sugar and serve warm or cold, on its own or
with yogurt, cream, or crème fraîche.
MAKES 8–10 SLICES

RUNE AND PEAR TORTE SLICE

Prunes are used extensively in the cooking of southwest France and appear in a variety of
cakes and tortes. The French might not approve of ready-made filo pastry, but it does make
a delicious torte. If time and motivation allow, you could make your own strudel pastry
instead!

1½ cups pitted prunes	4–6 tbsp butter, melted
1¼ cups warm tea (without milk)	4 large sheets filo pastry – about 11 × 19 inches each
3 tbsp lemon juice	3 level tbsp quince or apricot preserve
1 lb ripe dessert pears	½ cup walnut pieces
⅓ cup fresh white breadcrumbs	confectioners' sugar to dust

1 Very roughly chop the prunes. Place in a
medium bowl with the tea and 2 tbsp lemon
juice. Cover and leave to soak overnight.
2 The next day, strain the soaking liquor into
a saucepan. Peel, quarter, core, and roughly
chop the pears. Stir into the prunes with the
breadcrumbs and 1 tbsp lemon juice.

3 Place one sheet of pastry on the work
surface, brush with melted butter. Continue
to layer up the pastry, buttering each layer.
4 Spoon the filling in a strip along one long
edge of the pastry, leaving 2 inches clear at
each end. Fold the ends up over the filling,
buttering the underside of each flap; then roll

up the pastry to enclose the prune mixture. Lift carefully onto a baking sheet and brush all over with butter.

5 Bake at 400°F for about 30 minutes or until well browned. Cool for about 20 minutes.

6 Meanwhile, place the quince preserve in the saucepan with the soaking liquor. Bubble down until a syrupy glaze remains, then strain. Broil walnuts until lightly browned.

7 Brush a little glaze over the torte and sprinkle over the nuts. Carefully brush with remaining glaze. Dust with confectioners' sugar. Serve warm, with crème fraîche or yogurt.

SERVES 8

Prune and Pear Torte Slice

CHOCOLATE NUT MUFFINS

These are particularly good served warm, fresh from the oven. If using wholewheat flour, you will need to add a little extra milk. The muffins freeze well; when thawed, warm through for 5 minutes in a hot oven.

¼ lb dark chocolate	1 cup milk
1 cup Brazil nuts, roughly chopped	¼ cup sunflower oil
2 cups self-rising flour	1 tsp vanilla extract
1 level tsp baking powder	1 free-range egg
¼ cup packed dark brown sugar	

1 Grease 12 deep muffin or bun pans. Place a paper case in each.
2 Break up the chocolate into a bowl and melt over a pan of simmering water. Remove the chocolate from the heat and beat in the nuts and all the remaining ingredients.
3 Spoon the mixture into the paper cases and bake at 425°F for 15–20 minutes. Cool in the pans.

VARIATION
Banana and Honey Omit the chocolate and Brazil nuts. Use 2½ cups self-rising wholewheat flour instead of white flour. Beat together all the remaining ingredients with 8 oz mashed banana, 2 tbsp honey, the grated zest of one lemon, and an extra ½ level tsp baking powder.

SPICED CITRUS MINCEMEAT

We're always asked for a vegetarian mincemeat recipe – so here it is!

⅔ cup each dried apricots, raisins, and sliced almonds	6 whole green cardamom pods
2 cups golden raisins	finely grated zest and juice of 1 orange
½ lb carrots, peeled and grated	finely grated zest and juice of 1 lemon
6 oz shredded vegetarian suet	finely grated zest and juice of 1 lime
½ cup packed dark brown sugar	3 tbsp Grand Marnier
1½ level tsp ground cinnamon	⅔ cup medium sherry
½ level tsp grated nutmeg	

1 Snip the apricots into small pieces and place in a bowl with the roughly chopped raisins, almonds, and golden raisins. Stir in the carrot with the suet, sugar, and ground spices.
2 Split the cardamoms and remove the seeds. Crush the seeds, using a mortar and pestle or in a strong bowl with the end of a rolling pin. Add to the fruit with the orange, lemon and lime zest and 6 tbsp strained juices.

3 Pour in the Grand Marnier and sherry and stir well to mix. Leave to stand for about 1 hour, then pack tightly into sterile jars. Cover with a round of wax paper, and secure with an elastic band. Store in a cool place for at least 2 weeks to mature before using to make mince pies and tarts with sweet Shortcrust Pastry (page 69).
MAKES ABOUT 2½ LB

— Seventeen —

Desserts

Given the option, most people can manage something sweet at the end of a meal, whether it is something simple, like a piece of fruit or a bowl of yogurt flavored with honey or fruit purée, or something outrageously sweet and rich. Here you will find a range to suit all occasions, palates, and waistlines!

If you want something really wholesome, poach a mixture of dried fruits, such as apricots, prunes, pears, and apples, in fruit juice, spices, and a splash of port or sherry, or stuff apples with mincemeat (see page 206) or marzipan, prick the skins, and cook in the oven or microwave until soft.

If the dessert is to follow a light, perhaps low-protein, main course, consider serving a protein-packed cheesecake, home-made real dairy ice cream or Fudge Nut Tranche (see page 211). To accompany the desserts, try our non-dairy Almond "Cream" or home-made yogurt (see page 216), or sweet White Sauce (see page 182), or make your own custard with custard powder if you must, but the real thing is far superior (and incidentally, provides yet more protein). Put 1¼ cups milk and a vanilla bean in a small heavy-based (preferably non-stick) saucepan. Bring slowly to the boil, then remove from the heat and leave to infuse for at least 10 minutes. Pour the milk on to 2 beaten eggs with 1 tbsp sugar. Strain back into the pan and cook very gently, stirring all the time until the custard just coats the back of a spoon. Do not boil. Remove the vanilla bean before serving. If you're worried about overcooking the custard, cook it in a double boiler or in a large bowl placed over a pan of simmering water. Made this way it will take much longer to thicken.

FRESH FIG TART

This quick, easy 'crunch dough' is a revelation to anyone who's nervous of pastry making. The edges of this tart aren't even trimmed – they're simply folded over the filling.

¾ cup unsalted butter, diced	2 tbsp lemon juice
2½ cups all-purpose flour	2 level tbsp brown sugar
½ level tsp salt	1 free-range egg yolk
1 level tsp sugar plus extra for sprinkling	2 tsp milk
8 small ripe figs	honey
1¼ lb sweet apples	

1 Stir the butter into the flour with the salt and sugar. Stir in ½ cup cold water and bind to a rough dough. Do not overmix. Wrap in parchment paper and chill for about 10 minutes. Meanwhile, slice the figs. Peel, quarter, core, and slice the apples. Mix with the lemon juice and brown sugar.
2 Thinly roll out the pastry on a lightly floured surface to a round about 14 inches in diameter and place in a 9 inch loose-bottomed tart pan. Press the dough over the base and into the sides, but do not trim away the edges.
3 Spoon the apple mixture into the pan and arrange the figs on top. Fold the excess pastry up and over the figs, glaze with the egg yolk beaten with the milk, and sprinkle generously with sugar.
4 Bake at 400°F for about 20 minutes or until well browned. Cool slightly, then brush with a little honey.
SERVES 8

UMMER PUDDING

You do not have to wait until summer to enjoy summer pudding; it can be made very successfully with frozen fruits.

6 oz red currants, stalks removed	*½ lb raspberries, hulled*
¾ lb black currants, stalks removed	*½ lb loganberries, hulled*
½–¾ cup sugar	*12 thick slices of white bread, about 2 days old, crusts removed*
thinly pared zest of 1 large orange	

1 Place the currants, sugar, and orange zest in a large saucepan. Cover and cook gently until the juices flow and the sugar has dissolved. Add the raspberries and loganberries, and continue cooking for about 5 minutes until they are softened. Leave to cool.
2 Cut a round from one of the slices of bread, large enough to fit in the base of a 1½ quart bowl. Place the round in the bowl, then line the sides of the bowl with slightly overlapping slices of bread, reserving the rest for the center and top.
3 Remove the orange zest from the fruit.

Spoon half of the fruit and juice into the lined bowl, then place a layer of bread on top. Add the remaining fruit and juice, then cover completely with the remaining bread.
4 Put a small, flat plate on the top of the bowl. Stand it on a plate to catch any juices that overflow. Place some heavy weights on top of the plate. Chill overnight.
5 To serve, gently loosen the pudding from the sides of the bowl with a spatula, then turn out on to a flat plate. Serve with cream, yogurt, fromage blanc or ice cream.
SERVES 8

RUIT CRISP

Everybody has their favorite recipe for crisps. Purists use a simple mixture of flour, sugar, and butter. We prefer a nutty mixture of oats, spices, and chopped nuts. For the fruit, a mixture of either apples or pears, with a soft fruit such as raspberries, black currants, or blackberries was favored by our tasters.

8 tbsp butter or vegetable margarine	*¼ cup light brown or white sugar*
1½ cups all-purpose flour	*1 level tsp ground cinnamon*
⅔ cup rolled oats	*1 level tsp ground mixed spice*
¼ cup sunflower seeds	*2 lb prepared mixed fruit*
½ cup chopped mixed nuts	

1 Rub the shortening into the flour. Mix in all the remaining ingredients, except the fruit.
2 Put the fruit into a large, deep baking dish. Spoon the crisp mixture over the top and press down lightly, particularly around the

edge of the dish, to seal the fruit in. Bake in the oven at 350°F for about 45 minutes or until the crisp is golden brown and the fruit is just bubbling through.
SERVES 6

RHUBARB AND ORANGE CRUMB CAKE

A light orange-flavored sponge, topped with rhubarb and a crunchy crumb topping. Add a few chopped nuts, sunflower seeds, or shredded coconut to the topping or use other poached or canned fruit, as the fancy takes you.

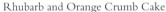

¾ cup vegetable margarine or butter	two 1¼ lb cans rhubarb, well drained
½ cup sugar	1 cup all-purpose flour
1 cup self-rising flour	2 level tbsp granulated sugar
2 free-range eggs, beaten	½ level tsp ground cinnamon
finely grated zest of 1 orange	confectioners' sugar

1 Grease a 9 inch springform cake pan and line the base with parchment paper. To make the cake, beat 8 tbsp of the shortening, the sugar, self-rising flour, eggs, and orange zest together until smooth and well mixed. Spoon into the pan.
2 Spoon the rhubarb over the cake mixture. To make the crumb mixture, rub the remaining fat into the all-purpose flour, then stir in the sugar and the cinnamon. Sprinkle the mixture over the rhubarb. Bake in the oven at 400°F for 45 minutes–1 hour or until firm to the touch and golden brown. Serve warm, dredged with confectioners' sugar.
SERVES 8

Rhubarb and Orange Crumb Cake

LEMON CARAMEL RICE

This variation on the children's favorite has a light, creamy texture with a delicious caramelized lemon topping. Low-fat milk works equally well.

butter or vegetable margarine	*grated zest of 2 lemons*
½ cup ground rice or semolina	*2 free-range eggs, separated*
2½ cups milk	*2 level tbsp lemon curd*
¼ cup sugar	*confectioners' sugar*

1 Lightly grease a 1½ quart soufflé dish.
2 Place the ground rice, milk, sugar, and lemon zest in a medium saucepan and simmer for about 10 minutes, stirring all the time until thickened.
3 Off the heat, beat in the egg yolks, and then cool slightly. Whisk the egg whites until stiff but not dry and gently fold into the rice mixture. Spoon into the prepared dish. Bake at 325°F for about 50 minutes–1 hour or until golden and firm.
4 Mix the lemon curd to a pouring consistency with 1 tbsp water. Drizzle over the cooked pudding. Sift a little confectioners' sugar over the whole surface and brown under a hot broiler until caramelized. Serve.
SERVES 4

FUDGE NUT TRANCHE

This tranche is wickedly rich but quite delicious too! Serve it after a light, healthy main course to ease the conscience and the waistline.

1 cup butter or vegetable margarine	*1 cup pecan nuts, toasted and chopped*
1½ cups all-purpose flour	*1 lemon*
2 tbsp sugar	*1 free-range egg, beaten*
⅓ cup packed light brown sugar	*1½ cups mixed whole nuts, such as Brazils,*
⅓ cup heavy cream	*walnuts, or hazelnuts*
1 cup skinned hazelnuts, toasted and chopped	*2 level tbsp warm apricot jelly, to glaze*

1 Rub half of the butter or margarine into the flour until the mixture resembles fine breadcrumbs. Stir in the sugar and bind to a dough with 2–3 tbsp water. Roll out and use to line a 13½ × 4½ inch loose-based fluted tranche pan or a 9 inch fluted tart pan. Bake blind at 400°F for 10–15 minutes or until golden and well dried out.
2 Meanwhile, warm the remaining shortening with the brown sugar and the cream until it has melted and the sugar has dissolved.
3 Cool slightly, then stir in the chopped nuts, finely grated lemon zest, 2 tbsp lemon juice, and the beaten egg. Mix well.
4 Pour into the tart case. Arrange the whole nuts over the top. Bake at 350°F for 25–30 minutes, or until lightly sct.
5 Brush the tart evenly with the warm apricot jelly; serve warm.
SERVES 8

ANADE

Using sweet apples and pears means that there's no need to add sugar to the filling of this tart, based on one of the specialities of the boulangeries of Provence.

¾ cup butter or vegetable margarine	1½ lb ripe pears
2 cups all-purpose flour	grated zest and juice of 1 large orange
a large pinch of ground cinnamon	beaten free-range egg and sugar, for glazing
1½ lb sweet apples	

1 Rub 8 tbsp butter or margarine into the flour and cinnamon until the mixture resembles breadcrumbs. Add about 6 tbsp chilled water, to bind to a soft paste.
2 Roll the dough out thinly and line a 9½ inch loose-bottomed fluted tart pan. Re-roll the excess pastry and cut into ½ inch wide strips. Cover and refrigerate until required. Bake the tart blind in the oven at 400°F for about 20 minutes.
3 Meanwhile, melt the remaining butter in a large non-stick frying pan. Stir in the peeled, cored and grated apples and pears, the orange zest, and 3 tbsp orange juice.
4 Cook over a high heat, stirring constantly, until all excess moisture has evaporated and the mixture is dry. Spoon into the tart.
5 Quickly lattice the pastry strips over the fruit mixture. Brush with beaten egg and dust with sugar. Bake at 400°F for about 20 minutes, or until golden.
SERVES 6–8

RANGE SEMOLINA SOUFFLÉS

These individual soufflés, baked in orange shells, are good served with thinly sliced oranges sprinkled with a little orange-flavored liqueur or orange flower water.

5 large juicy oranges	3 free-range eggs, separated
2 tbsp sugar	confectioners' sugar, for dusting
2 tbsp semolina	

1 Finely grate the zest and squeeze the juice from 2 of the oranges. You will need 1¼ cups juice. Make up with juice from one of the remaining oranges if necessary.
2 Halve the remaining oranges. Scoop out any loose flesh still attached to the skins and eat separately or use in another recipe. You need six clean orange halves. Cut a thin slice from each so that they stand flat.
3 Place the orange juice and zest, sugar, and semolina in a pan and simmer until thickened, stirring all the time.
4 Cool slightly, then stir in the egg yolks. Whisk the egg whites until stiff and fold into the mixture. Spoon into the reserved orange shells and stand on a baking sheet.
5 Bake in the oven at 400°F for 15–20 minutes or until risen and golden brown. Dust with confectioners' sugar and serve.
SERVES 6

PINEAPPLE TARTE TATIN

Ginger cream makes a delicious accompaniment to this dessert inspired by the classic Tarte Tatin. Simply stir together equal quantities of whipped cream and thick plain yogurt. Gently fold in a few pieces of finely chopped stem ginger and sugar to taste.

¼ cup superfine sugar	¼ cup heavy cream
¾ cup butter or vegetable margarine	2 lb fresh pineapple
2 free-range egg yolks	Kirsch (optional)
1 cup self-rising flour	fresh mint sprigs, to decorate
½ cup sugar	

1 In a medium bowl, beat together the superfine sugar and 4 tbsp of the butter or margarine until pale and light. Beat in the egg yolks then fold in the flour and knead lightly together to form a smooth dough. Wrap and chill for 30 minutes.

2 In a small saucepan, slowly heat the remaining butter or margarine with the sugar until both have melted. Bring to the boil, then simmer for 3–4 minutes, beating continuously until the mixture is smooth, dark, and fudge-like. (It will probably separate at this stage, but don't worry as it will come back together again.) Take off the heat, cool for 1 minute and stir in the cream, beating until smooth. If necessary, warm gently, stirring, until completely smooth. Spoon into a shallow 8½ inch round non-stick cake pan.

3 Peel, core, and thinly slice the pineapple. Arrange neatly in overlapping circles on the fudge mixture. Drizzle over 1 tbsp Kirsch if wished.

4 Roll out the prepared pastry to a 10 inch round. Place over the pineapple, tucking and pushing the edges down the side of the pan. Trim off any excess pastry. Stand the pan on a baking sheet.

5 Bake at 400°F for about 20 minutes or until the pastry is a deep golden brown. Run the blade of a knife around the edge of the pan to loosen the pastry. Leave to cool for 2–3 minutes, then invert on to a heatproof serving dish. Cook under a hot broiler for 2–3 minutes to caramelize the top.

SERVES 6

STICKY PEAR UPSIDE DOWN PUDDING

A hearty dessert that is quickly put together from storecupboard ingredients, yet is hard to resist. Ideal to serve at short notice.

¾ cup butter or vegetable margarine	½ level tsp grated nutmeg
1¼ cups packed light brown sugar	1 level tbsp ground cinnamon
two 14½ oz cans pear halves in natural juice	finely grated zest and juice of 1 large lemon
2 cups all-purpose flour	1 cup black molasses
1 level tsp baking soda	scant 1 cup milk
a pinch of salt	2 free-range eggs, beaten
2 level tsp ground ginger	

DESSERTS

1 To make the pear layer, warm half of the butter and 8 tbsp of the sugar together until the fat melts. Spoon into a 2½ quart shallow ovenproof dish. Drain the pears and arrange cut side down around the base of the dish.

2 To make the cake, mix the flour, remaining sugar, baking soda, salt, and spices together in a bowl. Add the lemon zest, then make a well in the center of the dry ingredients.

3 Warm the molasses and remaining butter together. When the fat has melted pour into the well with the milk and 3 tbsp lemon juice. Add the eggs and beat well.

4 Spoon the cake mixture over the pears. Stand the dish on an edged baking sheet.

5 Bake in the oven at 400°F for about 25 minutes. Reduce the oven temperature to 375°F and continue to cook for about a further 50 minutes, covering lightly if necessary. The pudding should be firm to the touch.

6 Leave the pudding to stand for about 5 minutes. Run a blunt-edged knife around the edge of the pudding. Invert on to an edged platter. Serve warm.

SERVES 6–8

CHRISTMAS PUDDING

Around November we are inundated with letters and telephone calls asking for our Christmas Pudding recipe. Here's our vegetarian version. Serve it with lashings of custard, cream, or brandy butter.

1¼ cups prunes, pitted and chopped	1½ cups fresh breadcrumbs
3 cups raisins	¼ lb shredded vegetarian suet
1½ cups golden raisins	½ cup packed dark brown sugar
2 tbsp blanched almonds, chopped	2 free-range eggs, beaten
finely grated zest and juice of 1 lemon	2 tbsp black molasses
1 cup all-purpose flour	⅔ cup dark beer
½ level tsp grated nutmeg	⅔ cup brandy, rum, or sherry
½ level tsp ground cinnamon	⅓ cup brandy, to flame
½ level tsp salt	

1 Grease a 2 quart heatproof bowl.

2 Place the dried fruits, nuts, lemon zest, and juice in a large bowl. Mix well.

3 In a separate bowl, sift the flour, nutmeg, cinnamon, and salt together. Add the breadcrumbs, suet, and sugar and mix.

4 Pour in the beaten egg, black molasses and beer, and beat well. Stir in the dried fruit until evenly incorporated. Cover and leave in a cool place for 24 hours.

5 The next day, add the brandy, stirring well. Pack the mixture into the bowl.

6 Cover with pleated parchment paper and

foil. Secure with string. Steam for 4–5 hours.

7 Remove the pudding from the pan and leave to cool completely for 1–2 hours. Unwrap the pudding, then rewrap in fresh parchment paper and foil.

8 Store in a cool, dry place for at least 1 month (or up to 1 year) before serving.

9 To serve, steam for 2–3 hours. Turn out on to a warmed serving dish.

10 To flame the pudding, warm the brandy gently in a small saucepan, pour over the pudding, and light carefully with a match.

SERVES 8

YOGURT

The consistency of the finished yogurt depends on the milk used. Rich, creamy full-fat milk or condensed milk give the thickest results. Low-fat milk makes a less creamy yogurt but one that is lower in calories. The addition of skimmed milk powder makes it even thicker. Goats', ewes' or soy milk can be used to make yogurt.

2½ cups milk of your choice (see above)	2 level tbsp skimmed milk powder (optional)
1 tbsp 'live' plain yogurt, beaten	

1 Bring the milk and skimmed milk powder, if using, to the boil in a large, heavy-based saucepan. Remove from the heat and leave to cool to 110°F on a thermometer. If using condensed milk it does not have to be boiled; just heated to the correct temperature.
2 Meanwhile, rinse a clean wide-necked vacuum flask or a 1 quart container (with a lid) with boiling water.
3 When the milk is the correct temperature, gradually blend it into the yogurt. Pour into the warmed vacuum flask or container. Replace the lid and leave in a warm place for 6–8 hours, undisturbed, until just set. (Once you've made it a few times you will get to know how long it takes.)
4 As soon as it is set, transfer to the refrigerator to chill. Once set, yogurt is best used within 4 days. Save some of the yogurt for making your next batch.

NOTES
If making vegan yogurt using soy milk, the first batch will not be totally vegan because of the yogurt – but use a spoonful of this to make a second batch and that will be.

If the yogurt does not set it could be because the milk was not brought up to boiling point, the milk was stale to start with, the starter yogurt was not mixed in properly, the starter was not "live", the temperature was not correct – too high when the starter was added or not warm enough when the yogurt was left. Too much starter makes sour, grainy yogurt.

To make thick yogurt, line a colander with a double thickness of cheesecloth, spoon in the yogurt, and leave to drain. Transfer to a clean bowl, cover, and refrigerate.
MAKES ABOUT 2½ CUPS

ALMOND "CREAM"

This makes a useful sauce to serve in place of dairy products like cream, ice cream, and fromage blanc. It's based on tofu. If you don't like tofu, don't be put off – you'll never know that it's there. Increase or decrease the quantity of water to achieve the desired consistency.

¼ lb tofu	2 level tbsp vanilla sugar, or to taste
1 cup very fresh ground almonds	ground cinnamon, to decorate

Put everything in a blender or food processor with 3 tbsp water and process until well blended. Add a few more tablespoons of water to achieve the desired consistency. Serve sprinkled with a little ground cinnamon.
SERVES 4

CREAMY CHEESECAKE

A simple, delicately flavored cheesecake baked in a pastry shell.

8 tbsp butter or margarine	*½ tsp vanilla extract*
2 cups all-purpose flour	*scant 1 cup heavy cream*
¼ cup plus 3 tbsp superfine sugar	*⅓ cup sour cream*
14 oz full-fat soft cheese	*confectioners' sugar, for dusting*
2 free-range eggs, separated	

1 Rub the butter into the flour with the 3 tbsp superfine sugar. Bind to a dough with about 4 tbsp water. Roll out on a lightly floured surface and use to line an 8½ inch deep, fluted loose-bottomed tart pan. Chill for 15 minutes, then bake blind at 400°F for 20–25 minutes or until pale golden brown and cooked through.
2 Beat together the soft cheese, egg yolks, and vanilla extract. Gradually beat in the creams.
3 Whisk the egg whites until they just hold their shape. Fold in half the remaining sugar and whisk until stiff. Whisk in the remaining sugar. Fold into the cheese mixture.
4 Spoon into the pastry case. Stand the pan on a baking sheet and bake at 425°F for 20 minutes. Reduce the oven temperature to 350°F for a further 35–40 minutes or until the cheesecake is golden brown and just set. Cool in the pan.
5 Serve warm dusted with confectioners' sugar.
SERVES 6

COCONUT ICE CREAM

We felt this was best made with canned coconut milk which is sold in Indian and Asian groceries. However, it works almost as well if made with creamed coconut or dried coconut milk (sold in sachets). If using creamed coconut, use four ½ lb packets each made up with 3¾ cups water. If using instant coconut milk powder, you will also need four 1½ oz packets, each made up with 1¼ cups water.

1¼ cups sugar	*four 1¼ cup cans coconut milk*
2½ cups water	

1 To make the syrup, place the sugar and water in a medium saucepan. Heat gently until the sugar dissolves, then boil gently for 10 minutes without stirring. Leave to cool.
2 Mix the cold syrup with the coconut milk and pour into a shallow freezer container. Cover and freeze on fast freeze for about 3 hours or until just frozen all over. The mixture will have a mushy consistency.
3 Spoon into a bowl and mash with a fork to break down the ice crystals. Work quickly so that the ice cream does not melt completely.
4 Return the mixture to the container and freeze for about 2 hours, or until mushy. Mash as step 4. Return to the freezer and freeze for about 3 hours or until firm.
5 Remove from the freezer and leave at room temperature for 20–30 minutes to soften before serving.
SERVES 8

ARINATED FRUITS

Store the fruits for at least 2 hours to give them lots of time to absorb the wine before serving.

2 lb fresh raspberries or a mixture of summer fruits, such as strawberries, blackberries, and currants

⅓ cup superfine caster sugar
about 1¼ cups red wine

1 Pick over the fruit, brushing off any dirt and discarding any damaged fruit. Halve the strawberries, if using.

2 Layer the fruit and sugar in a bowl. Pour over the wine so the fruit is covered.

3 Cover tightly and store in the refrigerator for up to 24 hours.

SERVES 6–8

ASPBERRY ROSE ICE CREAM

This makes a relatively low calorie, egg free ice cream based on custard.

1 level tbsp instant custard powder	*1 lb raspberries*
1 level tbsp superfine sugar	*1 tbsp rose water (optional)*
1¼ cups milk	*1¼ cups heavy cream*

1 Blend the custard powder and sugar to a paste with 1–2 tbsp milk.
2 Heat the remaining milk until boiling, then pour on to the blended mixture, stirring.
3 Return the mixture to the pan and bring to the boil, stirring continuously. Cook for 1–2 minutes after the mixture has thickened to make a smooth, glossy sauce. Leave to cool. Cover the surface of the custard with a piece of damp parchment paper.
4 While the custard is cooling, mash the raspberries then push through a nylon strainer to make a purée. Stir in the rosewater, if using.

5 Whisk the cream into the cold custard mixture, then stir in the raspberry purée. Pour into a shallow non-metalic, freezer container. Cover and freeze for about 3 hours.
6 Spoon into a bowl and mash with a fork to break down the ice crystals. Work quickly.
7 Return the mixture to the container and freeze again for about 2 hours until mushy.
8 Mash again as step 4, then return to the freezer for a further 3 hours or until firm.
9 Remove from the freezer and leave at room temperature for 20–30 minutes to soften.
SERVES 6

RAGRANT FRUIT SALAD

Exotic fresh lychees are available in some produce stores and markets. They lend a unique texture, flavor, and fragrance to this special fruit salad.

¼ cup superfine sugar	*1½ lb lychees*
grated zest and juice of 1 lemon	*3 ripe mangoes, peeled*
2 pieces of stem ginger (from a jar of ginger in syrup), finely chopped	*1 lb fresh or canned pineapple in natural juice*
¼ cup ginger wine	*4 ripe kiwi fruit, peeled*
	a few Cape gooseberries, to decorate (optional)

1 Put the sugar in a pan with ⅔ cup water and the lemon rind and juice. Heat gently until the sugar dissolves. Bring to the boil and simmer for 1 minute. Remove from the heat and stir in the chopped ginger and wine. Leave to cool.
2 Peel the lychees, cut in half, and remove the shiny pits. Cut the mango flesh away from the pits. Cut the flesh into cubes.
3 If using fresh pineapple, peel, slice, and

remove the tough center from each slice. Cut the pineapple slices into cubes. Thinly slice the kiwi fruit and halve the slices.
4 Mix together the fruit and syrup. Cover and refrigerate for several hours to allow the flavors to develop. If using Cape gooseberries, peel back each calyx to form a "flower". Clean the orange berries by wiping with a damp cloth. Arrange on top of the fruit.
SERVES 8

CARAMELIZED CLEMENTINES

We used whole clementines for this. Sections of larger citrus fruit could also be used.

1¼ cups sugar	vegetable oil
18 small clementines	4–6 tbsp superfine sugar

1 First prepare the caramel sauce. Put the sugar in a medium, heavy-based saucepan with ½ cup water. Heat gently until all the sugar dissolves, then bring the mixture to a rapid boil. Have ready ½ cup warm water. Bubble down the sugar mixture, gently shaking the pan occasionally, until it turns a rich dark caramel. Immediately take off the heat. Cover your hand – the mixture may splutter – and pour in the warm water in one fast stream. Stir until evenly mixed, returning to a low heat if necessary, until the mixture is smooth. Pour into a heatproof pitcher and leave to cool.

2 Peel the clementines, removing all pith but keeping them whole. Place in a bowl. Pour the syrup over the fruit and gently stir. Cover and chill until required.

3 Line a small baking sheet with foil and brush generously with oil. Sprinkle the superfine sugar evenly over the foil. Cook under a hot broiler until melted and golden. Don't take your eyes off it for a second as it can suddenly catch and burn! The sugar will have run into uneven pools of caramel. Remove from the broiler immediately and allow to cool slightly before peeling off the foil and breaking into pieces. Store in an airtight container.

4 To serve the fruit, transfer to a glass serving dish and scatter with the caramel pieces. (Add them just before serving or they will dissolve.)

SERVES 6–8

MULLED PEARS

Mulled Pears are best served cold but not chilled, with Almond "Cream" (see page 216).

8 small pears, firm but ripe	a few strips of orange zest
1¼ cups medium dry red wine	4 cloves
⅔ cup orange juice	1 mulled wine spice sachet
3 cinnamon sticks	¼ cup dark brown sugar, or to taste

1 Peel the pears, leaving the stalks attached. Put them in a heavy-based saucepan with the remaining ingredients, cover, and simmer very gently for 35–40 minutes or until tender. While the pears are cooking, baste them with the liquid from time to time, and move them about in the saucepan so that they all get evenly cooked and colored red. Some may cook quicker than others so test them.

2 Remove the cooked pears from the saucepan using a slotted spoon and arrange in a heatproof serving dish. Bring the cooking liquid to the boil and boil rapidly for 5–10 minutes or until reduced by half. Pour over the pears and leave to cool. Serve cold.

SERVES 4–6

Caramelized Clementines

INDEX

V indicates a vegan recipe.